The *END* of Your *OCD* Religious *Scrupulosity!*

The **Unrecognized** Truth
About God's *Astonishing* Love
Vanquishing OCD Religious Fears
– **Forever!**

I AM
Sure That,
When I Come
Unto You,
I *Shall* Come
In the **FULLNESS**
of the Blessing
of the Gospel
Of
Christ

(Romans 15:29)

Copyright © 2016
by Mack W. Ethridge

Published by **Authentic Life Publications**

All rights reserved. Printed in the United States of America. Permission granted to quote brief portions of this book provided due credit is afforded the author.

Cover design selected by Mack Ethridge

Library of Congress Cataloging-in-Publications Data, Ethridge, Mack W.

The End of Your OCD Religious Scrupulosity! –
The Unrecognized Truth About God's Astonishing Love Vanquishing OCD Religious Fears Forever!
– Complete edition
(*Drawn from* The Divine Plan Revealed!)

1st Complete Amazon Softback Edition
March 2016

Dedication

This inspired book is reverently and worshipfully dedicated to the Great Revelator of the Deeper Teachings of the Gospel, **Jesus Christ our Saviour!** (Rev. 1:1) – *And* the spiritual Guardian and Redeemer of the human race! (I John 4:14) May this book be used as a powerful instrument in God's hands to allow us to *truly* survey the length and the breadth, the height and **the depth, of Redeeming Love**, so dimly comprehended by most, but destined one day to be fully grasped–*by all!*

Introduction to This *Unique* OCD Religious Scrupulosity Volume

The Gospel Of Christ

– Its <u>Fullness</u>!

Introduction to Volume

This book is a wondrous disclosure of the *Fullness* of the Gospel of Christ (His **Mature** teachings), which neither Christendom, New Thought, nor New Age adherents (including metaphysicians and mystics), as a whole, are even aware of, much less understand. It is a 'laying out' of the Creator's Program kept hidden since 'the foundation of the world', even from Angelic Beings, save for a witnessing, *hopeful few*, who were given to suspect Its ***glorious-beyond-belief*** aspects, since the dawn of human history. These **Final** and **Profound** teachings of Christ are pre-

Introduction to Volume
– Con.

sented in the language of everyday God-cherished people, and is not intended to be an exhaustive treatise utilizing theological or technical scholarly terms. Nor does it attempt to address every opposing view or objection. It merely seeks to present **God-Truth** with accuracy, clarity, conviction, persuasion, and Heart-fortifying, God-glorifying literary expression. The Truth of the matter is that these teachings are destined to redeem not only the terrestrial globe and its inhabitants of *all* eras, but also the entirety of the Cosmos, *one day!* May you, dear OCD person, above all others, be **graced** to know this – *now!*

Contents of Volume

Book 1

What Heaven's Son Achieved!

– The Cosmic Reach *of* Jesus'
  Life, Death, and Resurrection!

Book 2

God's True Message Proclaim!

– The Universal Scope *of* Christ's
  Love, Wisdom, and Power!

Contents of Volume
– *Con.*

Book 3

Love's Supreme Act Unveiled!

– The Valiant Victory of Life's Heart Over the World!

Book 1

What Heaven's Son *Achieved!*

The **Cosmic** *Reach*
 Of **Jesus'** Life, Death, and Resurrection!

<u>All</u> Things
Possible
Have *Come* To Pass!
And <u>All</u> Disbelief
Is **Discarded**, At Last!
The
<u>All</u>-*Redeeming* Love
Has <u>WON!</u>
Every Soul Back
– To Life's
*Radiant
Son!*

Copyright © 2010
by Mack W. Ethridge

Published by **Authentic Life Publications**

All rights reserved. Printed in the United States of America. Permission granted to quote brief portions of this book provided due credit is afforded the author.

Cover design selected by Mack Ethridge

Library of Congress Cataloging-in-Publications Data, Ethridge, Mack W.

What Heaven's Son Achieved!
– Complete edition

1st Complete Amazon Softback Edition
August 2012

Dedication

This book is reverently dedicated with fondest of remembrance and eternal gratitude to my beloved father, Floyd L. R. Ethridge, who was my life teacher, guardian, devotee, and guide. Not to mention, my dearest friend. For it was through his unfailing and wholly selfless, demonstrated love for me, through the years, that I came to know the **Reality** of the Living, Risen Christ, and *His* astonishing Love, made manifest *through* him, to me! I AM grateful!

The *Greatest* Discovery!

This book is the result of one man's heartfelt and lifelong efforts to probe the heights and **depths** of God's Love. Men believe they comprehend what Divine Love actually IS – Its true nature and capabilities – yet they are mistaken. God's Love is *Beyond* **anything** the world, as a whole, has ever dreamed! So GREAT is this Love, It is *far more wonderful* that men have **dared** to imagine. The Gentle Galilean taught Mercy, Forgiveness, and Compassion, **above all**, and one day the outcome of His unswerving commitment to these Virtues will astonish – and redeem, *a world!*

Contents of Book

Part I
The Birth and Childhood of Jesus – Their *Unsuspected* Purpose

Part II
The Ministry and Teachings of Jesus – Their *Unrealized* Message

Part III
The Crucifixion and Resurrection – Their *Unrecognized* Significance

Part IV
The Hidden Nature and Unknown Meaning of Jesus – Their *Supreme* Reality

Part V
The Crusade of Jesus of Nazareth – Its *Ultimate* and *Undreamed-of* Outcome

Part I

The Birth and Childhood *of* Jesus!

Their <u>*Unsuspected*</u> Purpose!

Child *Of* Living Light **I AM**, Come To *Rescue* – The World *Of* Men!

Jesus the Christ

Part I – Introduction

Part I of this book is not only about the celebrated **Nativity event**, so revered and honored, loved and cherished, but also about _you_, and the precious children you love. What the entrance of Love into the world _really_ **portended** few people have grasped, as so few people have been taught its **deeper** meaning. Jesus' birth was the **foretelling**, the initial **outpicturing**, of _something_ so wonderful as to be thought a 'fairy tale', yet nothing _could be further_ from **the Truth!** Come with the author and learn of a Love that _transfixes_ us with Its wholly unsuspected **Depth** and _Far-Reaching_ Heavenly Design. It all began in a lowly stable, but where it ultimately ends – _will Astound you!_

Part I – Contents

Oh! Lord of the Universe
Oh! Star So Super Nova Bright
Oh, Lowly Manger, What did You Mean
What Love! From Yonder Hilltop Flows
A Garment Worn That Day
Cave at the Start, Cavern at the Close
Taking Delight in His Beautiful Kin
I Hear the Life-Freeing Laughter
To You, My Lord, My Heart Does Go
A Smile that Shone So Bright
Lord of Heaven and of the Earth
What a Wonderful, Wonderful Feeling
Become As A Little Trusting Child
Hear Sacred Truth, My Precious Friend
Like Begets Like, As Mother to Son
When Jesus Was Born, Love Was Too
The Miracle Is Bestowed
Silent Night, Holy Night
Farewell Message

**Oh! Lord of the Universe
Precious *Infant*-King!
Might of the Ages
To *<u>Thee</u>* – We Sing!**

In Bethlehem, dear friend, not so long ago, among the blessed animals, an infant-King was born. No royal **robe** covered His small frame, yet a ***<u>blanket</u>* of <u>Calm</u>** lay about His body. No emerald **scepter of authority** did His miniature hand hold, yet, a ***<u>commanding</u> <u>Presence</u>* of <u>Peace</u>** emanated from His person. No kingly **crown** of burnished, **gleaming gold** did adorn his tiny head, yet a ***<u>Love-Infused</u> <u>Manifestation</u>* of <u>Light</u>** shone in splendor round His brow. *Before,* a mere stable, **<u>now</u>**, the historic Miraculous scene of **the <u>Very</u> *Heart* of <u>Life</u> *Everlasting*** – <u>breaking through into our world</u>*!* The Divine Presence *embodied* in Its Fullness! This *perfect* Innocence, Purity, and Love for *all* men, this *All*-Redeeming Good, did ***<u>never</u>*** waver, ***<u>nor</u>*** di-minish <u>toward</u> others! Nor will It ever– *<u>toward you</u>!*

**Oh! Star *So* Super Nova Bright
Lead Me *To* The <u>*One*</u> True Light!
As Wise Men Sought the One <u>Most</u> Wise
Awaken My Heart – <u>*Open*</u> My Eyes!**

Can you, my awe-inspired friend, tell me what the Holy Light over the manger truly *was?* Some say it was a comet, others a stellar conjunction, others still, an angel. But, only the Light *of* Love can lead one to **the <u>Source</u>** that ***IS*** Love. The Light of Love is the 'crystal cord', the shimmering, dark-shattering **brilliance**, leading one <u>*back*</u> to Love **Itself**. That great orb of Celestial Light, known as 'the Star *in the East'*, and 'the Star *of Bethlehem'*, was <u>the Great Representation</u> of the Light *of* Love. It had its origins in Eternity – the very ***Eternity*** that dwells in <u>*your*</u> heart! The light of <u>this</u> fallen world can lead <u>no one</u> to Christ, but <u>the Light</u> *<u>of the Soul</u>*, **the Bethlehem Star**, *<u>always</u> <u>will</u>!* It was this 'star' that was given <u>ultra</u>-**magnified <u>visible</u> expression** 2,000 years ago, that leads us on still – *<u>on</u> <u>to</u> <u>Him</u>!*

**Oh, Lowly Manger, *What* Did You Mean
What Was Your Significance 'Unseen',
The Whole of Truth You Did Portray
Evident, Yet Veiled – <u>*To Men Today*</u>!**

'Away in a <u>manger</u>, no crib for His bed,' so begins a beloved carol. Many people believe a 'manger' to be the **stable** where the Lord was born. A dilapidated barn where cows and sheep were housed. <u>This is not the case</u>! The word 'manger' means a ***feeding trough*** for livestock – a narrow **grain** storage bin, or container, for animal feed or water. This served as the Lord's crib, or cradle. But, *why?* Jesus, from the beginning, was destined to be **Living nourishment** for mankind. Recall, the Lord plainly declared, 'I AM the Bread of Life' Bread made from **'whole' grain**! Mary *placed* Jesus in a manger, not because she had no rocking crib, but to convey the *profound* **symbolic meaning** of Jesus being the **true** fare, or food, of mankind! Upon which the **lowliest** of all men will one day feed, be nourished – <u>*and healed*</u>!

What **Love! From Yonder Hilltop Flows**
The *<u>Heart</u>*-Radiance of – The <u>Mercy</u> Rose!
Billowing Out, O'er Hill, Vale, and Sea
To All Souls, Lost, Forlorn – *<u>Unfree</u>!*

Born under cover of night, He was wrapped in swaddle, strips of cloth **bound** about His form. The night air was cold, and this air-tight 'garment' would conserve His precious body warmth. Yet, what was <u>*not*</u> contained was the streaming **glow** of Love from His Infant Person, which outshone even ***the <u>Mysterious Light</u>*** far above the straw-strewn stable. Here lay a Gentleness *beyond* gentleness! **A Purity *beyond* purity!** All privileged to be there sensed It. The shepherds, the wise men, even the stable creatures. Three decades later, under cold darkness cover, strips *again* would **bind** Him. But as before, they could <u>*not*</u> contain His Magnificent Love! This myrrh- and aloes-***<u>hardened</u>*** garment was found empty. The Rose of Bethlehem, this Rose of Compassionate, Tender **Mercy**, was Born – *<u>Anew</u>!*

A Garment Worn *That* Day
When *He* Into Jerusalem Rode,
The Soldiers Vied to Own, and Say
'How *Strange!* Oh, So Beautiful! – *A Robe!*

The Robe was woven **seamless** throughout, no home-spun here! We are told people **strove** to touch it, *even* the hem brushing the dusty roads of Galilee. Did it possess some secret power? No. However, it did exhibit a strong attraction to others. Likely, Jesus donned this ***particular*** garment on special occasions, one being His triumphant entry into 'Salem'. Apparently, something was **Regal** about it! Its fabric, texture, perhaps even color and embroidering. Though we are not given an exact description, we can surmise something of its origin! Recall, **the Magi gave gifts to an Infant-King**. *What might they have been wrapped in?* Kings give *like* gifts to Kings! Jesus was known as a *'Magician'* by some, the Wise Men, as *'Magi'*. Was there a connection? One **Joyous** Day – *we'll know!*

**Cave at the Start, *Cavern* at the Close
Seeking to Contain the Light from The Rose,
A '*Castle*' in the Middle of Life's Noonday
Where Resurrection's Glory – <u>*Held Sway*</u>!**

Though not generally known, He Who was **the Light of the World** was born not simply in a stable, but a stable-<u>*cave*</u>. A domestic animal enclosure adjoining a hollowed-out man-made or natural depression into the earth. Without oil lamps or torches, darkness prevailed. Here, the Bethlehem Rose began to emanate His yet subtle, but **Irrepressible Light**. Later, thirty years hence, another confining space, a '**cavern**', sought to extinguish forever the Light of the former Radiant Rose, *Who* had delivered so many from darkness. But, there was a third limiting, encircling enclosure – the <u>***synagogue***</u>*!* Here, Jesus, as was His custom, sought to illumine spiritual darkness there <u>contained</u>! In two arenas, darkness was scattered, *but,* on <u>***Resurrection***</u> Day, it was **obliterated**–*<u>evermore</u>!*

Taking *Delight* in His Beautiful Kin
He Was Known As the *Joy Child* of Bethlehem,
Beaming With Gaiety, Enjoyment, and Mirth
He Treasured His Parents, Who'd
– *<u>Given Him Birth</u>*!

Though we have no written record of the disposition and personality of Mary's and Joseph's first-born child, we can surmise what He was like based upon His **unique** family circumstances. We can imagine His beloved father, as a master artisan, fashioning *<u>novel</u>* toys to *delight* his son, and telling <u>captivating</u> stories with *enthusiasm* and animation. Mary, knowing of her son's divine origin and destiny, must have *poured* all the **Joy** of her heart into His, <u>singing</u> to Him continually, <u>devising</u> games to *surprise* and promote *<u>glee</u>*. Smiles and *laughter* were lavished upon Him. Influenced so by His Godly parents, He naturally became a *<u>Joy Bringer</u>*. Family friends and relatives would describe Him as a ***<u>Delightful</u>*** child, for how could He have been otherwise, with the finely chiseled word '**JOY!**' carved over the mantel piece – *<u>of their door</u>!*

**To You, My Lord, My Heart Does Go
Sitting Before the Doctors So, Somehow I'm
Drawn *Back* to Your Childhood Self When, You
Mesmerized the *Learn*-ed, and Leaders–*of Men*!**

What is it, dear heart, about the occasion of Jesus' solitary visit to the temple, when He was a mere youth, that so *captivates* and *intrigues* one who reverences His person? The present falls away, along with its cares and concerns, and one finds oneself transported back to the wholly unusual scene where Jesus has the Jewish doctors of the Law **enthralled** with His maturity, wisdom, and knowledge. *Never* had these erudite men seen or heard the likes of this Jesus of Nazareth! **Here** we witness Jesus listening *intently* to the doctors, and then asking questions *of* them. Questions that no boy of twelve did ever entertain, *yet this One did.* Perhaps it is because in this Springtime of His youth, we, too, are carried back to a time when we were *so* interested, *so* enquiring, *so* intensely alive to Life! Let us, too, recapture His ardor to be 'about [our] Father's business'. We **must**, now – *or later!*

**I Hear the Life-*Freeing* Laughter
Of THY Most Holy Child, So Fair,
And *<u>Know</u>* Within My Heart of Hearts
That True Faith – *<u>Is</u> <u>There</u>!***

The Glorious Galilean, though He were a mature Man, was referred to by one of the Apostles on several occasions as '**Thy** [God the Father's] **Holy <u>Child</u>** Jesus.' Perhaps the occasion of Jesus' admonition to 'become <u>like</u> a little child' brought this to mind. Or the fact that Jesus loved to play and spend time with little ones as time allowed. What is known, for certain, is that children ***<u>love</u>*** to laugh. A child who does <u>not</u> laugh is either ill or filled with fear. This is an indisputable identifying characteristic of children around the world. But, most importantly, their laughter is a statement of unassailable Faith in Life that 'All is Well'. You can be sure, then, ***<u>Jesus laughed!</u>*** He ever sought to assure others of this. And His laughter was signal to us that True Faith brings Smiles – *<u>and</u> <u>good</u> <u>Cheer</u>!*

**A <u>Smile</u> that Shone So Bright
On HIS Face *<u>Beyond</u>* Compare,
Shines *<u>Still</u>*, In Children of the Light
Shedding Beams of Joy – *<u>Everywhere!</u>***

Beloved friend, I sincerely hope you have had the good fortune to have known a **<u>bearer</u>** of God's Joy. A person, child or adult, who manifests ***<u>such</u>*** goodwill towards and delight in another that you can literally *<u>feel</u>* in your soul their Life-***Affirming*** energy! An unknown saint once said, speaking of just such a person, 'And from <u>*your*</u> eyes He beckons me, And from <u>*your*</u> heart His Love is shed, 'Til I lose sight of you, as you, <u>*And see the Living Christ – instead!*</u>' To which could be added, 'And from <u>*your*</u> **Smile**, He streams forth **His** *Joy*, Unveiled – in <u>*your*</u> face, so all might see. Reminding me – once more, again, of God's **Radiant**, *<u>Ever</u>*lasting, Love for me!' This radiant Love has been, and always will be, the ***Joy-Filled Presence*** of the Lord! May you, dear friend, lose sight of all else – <u>*but this!*</u>

**Lord of Heaven and of the Earth
Oh! Grant Me! The *Miracle* of <u>Rebirth</u>,
To <u>See</u> a Wondrous World With Eyes Anew
And <u>*Awaken*</u> to *Your* Love, All About Me – *<u>Too</u>!***

If it is true, beloved, that *'we live, and move, and have our being in God'* as Holy Scripture so readily assures us, then it must **<u>also</u>** be true that wonders, and miracles, and signs must be eluding our vision continually! What marvels must be within the *very* Being of God where we are said to dwell! <u>*Yet,*</u> how is it, then, that we seem to reside in the realm of the mundane and commonplace? The answer lies in the teaching of **'Rebirth'**! Most believe it is a one-time event. But, even as we are 'born' out of *<u>physical</u>* sleep every day, we must be *'<u>born</u>'* out of spiritual slumber, also. We must **ask** the Lord to **open our eyes** to <u>witness</u> the imperishable beauty all about us always! So, declare, at break of day, 'I enter into a new world today!' Then, ***look for*** divine evidences of care, provision, and protection–*<u>a newborn's own</u>!*

**What a Wonderful, *Wonderful* Feeling
And a Holy Blessing From Above,
To Be Given a Precious Angel
Evermore – _to_ _Love!_**

Most kind friend, few joys can surpass the **Joy** of having been graced with a child _all_ _your_ _own_. A precious gift of Love, making your heart and life _far more complete_ than you could have _ever_ imagined! A sense that your life is now as it was meant to be! A small bundle of 'divinity' placed in your charge to love and **_cherish_**, and be loved and **_cherished_** in return. Some special little one to sing a lullaby to at night, as voiced by an unknown poet, 'A tiny turned up nose, two cheeks just like a rose, so sweet from head to toes, that little child of mine. Two eyes that **_shine_** so **bright!** Two lips to kiss goodnight! To me you'll always be, that little child of mine!' What **Joy** is expressed in those few words! Reflect on these sentiments, and relive **Joy**, once again, as did the blessed mother of Jesus our Lord–_in_ _your_ _heart!_

**Become As A Little Trusting Child,
And Heaven's Entrance Is Surely Made,
Become as an Innocent Babe, and
Love's Intimacy–_Is Portrayed!_**

To gain entrance into the **highest** Realm of Love, you must, as Jesus said, become 'as a little child.' **But**, to reach the level of intimacy Love desires, you must become 'as a **new-*born*** babe'! You see, my friend, such an infant cries out in an untaught tongue, '*Ma Ma!* I love thee! I need thee! *Come* to me! Comfort me! You are ALL to me!' An infant, in a language of Heaven, declares, 'I desire **only** to be cradled in your sheltering arms, to fall asleep upon your sweet breast! To *feel* the beating of the Melodious Heart that started mine! To *feel* the tenderness of your Soul steal into my own!' Or, as Jesus cried, 'Abba, Father!' – a term of the closest, tenderest intimacy! Yearn for a relationship as ***This!*** Where a babe's cry is uttered, and the returning warmth of mother/father's love–*is received!*

**Hear Sacred Truth, My Precious Friend
Tho I Once Were a Child, A Child I <u>*Still*</u> AM,
Empowered to Humble, Disarm, and Transform
The Most Darkened Heart –** *to Brightest Morn!*

As an eternal being of Love, Jesus can manifest Himself in child form, and does so, *often*, to the minds and hearts of recalcitrant, thought-to-be incorrigible people. Where *no other* power or persuasion can reach, the Holy Innocence of the *seemingly* <u>helpless</u> child of Bethlehem can go! The ancient carols depicting this infant that echo down the years have more than on one occasion struck a 'lost' soul with such conviction, repentance, and remorse over their wicked deeds, as to effect a **sudden** and miraculous transformation! <u>*What is it*</u> about the Christ-Child Image that can steal into a heart and melt its unmalleable nature? – *This child with outstretched arms <u>mirrors</u> <u>the</u> <u>Ever-</u> <u>and</u> <u>All-Embracing</u> (All-Loving) <u>**Cross**</u> <u>of</u> <u>the</u> <u>Saviour</u>!* It is the **welcoming** of the way-ward by the God-ward! The Healing of Life-weariness – <u>*by Love's Might*</u>*!*

**Like Begets Like, As Mother to Son
Blessed O'er All Others, A Heart Like No One,
Intent and Motive of the Purest, Ever New
To Bring Forth an Infant –** *of Radiant Hue!*

The *Light of the World* was born of a woman of exceptionally uncommon love, purity, and holiness! Having esteemed all others better than herself, God esteemed *her* as worthy of bearing and nurturing His Only-Begotten Son! Enfolded by her reverence and love, Jesus received nourishment for His Soul through this daughter of Light. Her Light served as a platform for His **Incomparable Light** to shine forth – *full*-orbed and *full*-spectrum. Theirs was a unique relationship, wherein His heart was mystically tied to hers, that all-vital feminine influence that would forever leave its mark upon His Soul! Beloved, the Sacred resides within *relationship*, within *interaction* of human beings, not person alone. Mary served as the Heart-Anchor for Jesus in human terms, hallowing the mother/child/human family relationship – *forever!*

**When Jesus Was Born, Love Was Too
Inseparable as Leaves and Morning Dew,
The *Branch* of David, This *<u>Shoot</u>* of Life
Immortally *Tender*, Toward – *All In Strife!***

Holy writ says, 'And He [Jesus] shall <u>grow</u> <u>up</u> before Him [God] as a *tender* plant.' Even as an infant, His countenance was especially tender (delicate). His person was tender (so gentle). His manner was tender (total *harmlessness*). This is because, from birth on, Jesus knew <u>*no*</u> internal conflict. There being <u>*no*</u> discord to contend with in his psyche and soul, He was *free* to focus <u>all</u> His energies and attention upon Love-impoverished humanity. Intuitively attuned to His Father's Will – He knew <u>*no*</u> strife (ambiguity or doubt about His Identity, Purpose, and Mission), <u>nor</u> hesitancy about appropriate courses of action. He was able to extend *gentleness of Spirit* to all, <u>*from*</u> <u>*the*</u> <u>*time*</u> <u>*He*</u> <u>*was*</u> <u>*a*</u> <u>*cooing*</u> <u>*babe*</u> through adulthood. Unfaltering, unfailing Love was born–even subconsciously expressed, when He, <u>AS</u> Love Incarnate, came to earth!

The Miracle Is Bestowed! For Now I Clearly See, The _Real_ Meaning of Christmas Proclaims Its Truth to Me! – To _Become_ Love Made Manifest – _Is My Destiny!_

The lyrics of a wonderfully beautiful, though mostly forgotten song, read, 'Oh, The Real Meaning of Christmas is *the Giving of Love Every Day*. Oh, the Real Meaning of Christmas is *to Live as the Master they say*. And, while you're wrapping your presents, don't forget as you give them away. That **the Real Meaning of Christmas, is the _Giving_ of Love – _Every_ Day!'** On the surface, this may seem a simplistic explanation, but, was this not the Master's philosophy? Did He not **magnify it** to mean the giving of Love _every_ hour? _Every_ minute? Even _every_ second? **He did**. As our example, Jesus paved the way for us to travel. Till Christ **'be _formed_'** in us, we begin as newborn babes. Never forget, our Saviour came to '[manifest] forth His Glory,' the **_Glory_** of **Love**! This, then, is **your** destiny! To be _AS_ He was, and to become–*as He* IS!

**Silent Night, Holy Night
Sleeps the Newborn Child of Light,
Day _Most_ Glorious, Day Most Bright
Awakes the World to – _Love's_ _Pure_ _Light_!**

My wistful friend, the world is destined, one day, to awake! The _temporal_ Christmas was meant to be a foreshadowing, a foretaste, of the **Eternal** Christmas to come! *This*, is what it pictures! And that All-Joyous future occasion shall commence when 'the tabernacle [temple] of God is with men, and **He** will *DWELL* with them [**once again**], and God **HIMSELF** _shall_ _be_ _with_ _them_ [*EVER*more].' No longer will men sing 'Silent Night', but rather **'Glorious Day'**! – A _New_ Song celebrating The **Eternal** Day of Christ's Kingdom come to Earth! Then, the second [complete, and full] 'birth' of Christ will have transpired! A great **spiritual awakening** will have *swept* the world! And the world will find God – *in its midst!* Then, the bells of Christmas will **truly** ring! – _Wedding_ _Bells_ _of_ _Joy_!

Farewell Words

Within the preceding Part I of this book are **hints**, provided here and there, of A *Hidden* Dream cradled in the Saviour's Heart, and of God the Father's, since His birth. It is a **Dream** He envisions even NOW, *continuously*, in Heaven above! This is a dream few men have had the privilege to be made privy to, primarily because mankind, as a whole, are incapable of **believing** the Truth of *SO glorious* a doctrine – It is just that wondrous and **sublime**! Therefore, should you, dear reader, be one intended to understand this doctrine **now**, as opposed to later, continue reading, as subsequent Parts II through V further introduce this concept and elaborate upon it progressively, so the sheer **enormity** of Its Wonder and Awe-Inspiring nature does not overwhelm you, as you **discover** It! You have now begun your journey! But, know that the word, 'Dream', in the case of Christ, does ***not*** mean 'a *hoped-for* outcome'. Rather, 'A **Certain** and **Unfailing** Destiny' – for Love's **All**!

In Christ's Love, The Author

Part II

The Ministry and Teachings *of* Jesus!

Their *Unrealized* Message!

Oh!
Saviour **Come**!
Let Me Behold,
A <u>*Clearer*</u> View of
You,
Now Told!
A Closer Walk,
A Word More Dear,
Hands Clasped
O'r
A **Heart** *Sincere!*

Part II – Introduction

The Truth Shall Set You Free! **Free** to enjoy Life and live it – to the Full! And **Jesus Christ**, being That Truth, can do just that, but <u>*only*</u> if you first **know** Him! – *Have* an **accurate** understanding of the major incidents of His Life, a **correct** knowledge of His *innermost* Intentions toward men, and **inspired** insight into the **centrality** of *His* Mission and Role in God's Plan. Regrettably, religious tradition and orthodoxy, not to mention New Thought views and metaphysical concepts, have obscured or distorted all these. <u>Here</u> though, by **God's Grace**, are refreshing, heart-relieving, and logical explanations that **exalt** the Saviour and reveal **Him** and <u>*His*</u> Truth – in Its **Pristine Light** – to the world!

Part II – Contents
(Page 1 of 2)

Lord, Teach Me as You Taught Then
On Starlit Nights, In Olive Groves
Who Was This Man of Humanity's 'Sea'
Your Finger Wrote on Sand
When Jesus Was Baptized in Jordan
Oh! Beautiful Life Who Pleaded For Men!
Lord, You Never Condemned
A Joy Far Greater Than Anyone Told
No Likeness of Him Bequeathed to Us
Oh! Won't You, Friend, With Welcome
No Hint of Anger, Nor Trace of Hate
Wide Is the Gate, Broad Is the Way
Words of Majesty and of Might
Jesus Stood Before Pilate Still
The Christ Who Knelt on Mountain Heights
What God Is There Who Would Share As I
Into the Depths of His Heart We Go

Part II – Contents
(Page 2 of 2)

Fear Is a Path to the Dark Side
The Parable of The Good Shepherd
The Work of God, or the work of Men
Supreme Power in the Cross Resides
Lord, I MUST Know, Is It Really True
Hear, a Strange-Sounding Truth, If You Can
What Triumphant Song of Love Is This
There Are No 'Lost' Teachings
I AM, Beloved, All That You Need
I Will Be Your Magnificent Obsession!
Oh! True Light, Burst Forth from My Heart
Lord, Blaze Your Light of Truth In Me
Many Were the Works of the Saviour
Farewell Words

**Lord, Teach Me as You Taught Then
<u>New</u> Truths That I Might Grow,
Ever More <u>Mature</u> and <u>*Wise*</u>
New Insights – <u>*I Will Know*</u>!**

'And they [of the synagogue] were all **amazed**, saying, What thing is this? What <u>*new doctrine*</u> is this?' Yes, when Jesus comes on the scene, He brings **new** doctrine – unheard of before! Such was the case then, and <u>*it is no different today!*</u> New teachings, or understandings, are continually being brought forth by Jesus in <u>*this*</u> day and age through His **All-Enlightening** Presence. And though Jesus Christ is 'the same yesterday, today, and forever,' His doctrines are <u>not</u>, as there is a **progressive revealing** of new truth as man is prepared to receive it. We are to '**grow** in the grace and <u>***knowledge***</u> of the Truth'. This means individuals, ministers, and churches, alike, are to keep open minded and <u>*humble*</u> to learn! This way, one is **free** to embrace the new. Do this, my friend – <u>*and receive more!*</u>

On Starlit Nights, In Olive Groves
His **Heartfelt, Earnest Prayers Arose,**
On Mountain Crest, By Shimmering Sea
He **Prayed** ***His*** **Prayers of Love –** *<u>For</u> <u>Me</u>!*

Some say we cannot know what Jesus spoke when He entered into *'solitary places'* to pray. We are told He 'departed into mountains' and 'withdrew Himself into the wilderness'– sometimes continuing '*all night* in prayer to God.' Yet, undoubtedly, in the depths of His Infinite Spirit, He called out **each** future follower's, *individual*, personal name – *<u>your name</u>, beloved!* – who would <u>yet</u> be born! Recall in His longest recorded prayer He said, 'Neither **pray** I for these [His *then*-present disciples], alone, *but for those <u>also</u> which <u>SHALL</u> [in the future] believe on Me.'* Here is proof positive that Jesus prayed for **<u>you</u>**, and me, while He was *<u>still</u>* on earth! His Love, knowing no bounds, reached out to you even <u>across the centuries</u>, to **bless** you, **empower** you, **inspire** you, and **protect** you, and to – *<u>set you free</u>!*

**Who _Was_ This Man of Humanity's 'Sea'
Who Loved the Scorned, the Weak, Unfree,
Who _Lived_ to Serve the Lost, the Lame, And
Brought New Hope – _to Man Again!_**

Wherever Jesus went, crowds gathered around Him. As many as _ten_ to _twelve thousand_ people were fed by His miraculous hand at one sitting, when one includes women and children. Now, as important as is air to man's physical existence, **Hope** is to man's spiritual. It is the _**first**_ prerequisite of life! The multitudes could **feel** this hope, this **mental atmosphere**, this **confidence**, which emanated from His person. 'And [Hope] _became_ flesh, and dwelt among us'! Jesus was the very embodiment of Hope on earth! And _that_ Hope – **unleashed**, along with **His** Faith and Love, the _flow_ of Healing energy to all about Him. _**They knew not who He was**_, only that He dispelled despair and doubt by His Word and touch. And though **you** may not, as yet, know Him **fully**, He is eager to do the same – _for you!_

**Your Finger Wrote On Sand,
Lord, Words No Person Could Reveal,
So, Write Them _IN_ My Heart, Instead,
That I _Might_ Their Meaning – _Feel!_**

Once, a woman taken in adultery was cast down at the feet of Jesus, so He might condemn her to death. But, before He spoke His **Immortal Words** that freed her, He stooped over and wrote _something_ on the ground – **something** never recorded! _Why?_ Because those words _were_ _not_ _meant_ _to be read or apprehended by the mind!_ He intended them to be _understood_ by the _**Heart!**_ Yet, what might they have been? Only one thing is certain. **Mercy**, **Forgiveness**, and **Compassion** were uppermost in the Saviour's mind at that time! And _these were all qualities of the **Heart** which must be deeply felt_, **not** recited in ridicule by _un_comprehending, _un_feeling men, such as those standing about this helpless daughter! The 'letter' (or words) were unimportant, only the 'spirit' (heart _feeling_) did count! The revelation of _their_ lofty meaning **erases** – _all_ _else!_

When Jesus Was Baptized in Jordan
No Beautiful Dove Did Descend in Flight,
But, a Shimmering Shower of Holy Love
That, Revealed God's – *Great Delight!*

When the Spirit of God descended upon the Saviour, no snow-white dove lit upon His shoulder, as taught. Rather, **something else** occurred, *much more* grand! Though all four gospel accounts relate this momentous occasion, they carefully state the Spirit's descent was 'in bodily **shape** – *like* [that of] a dove'. This careful choice of words meant the Spirit did *not* incarnate in a dove's body, per say, nor wing its way down upon Jesus' shoulder. This ***Coming of the Spirit*** merely had *characteristics* of a dove's descent. Fluttering wings of a dove create a 'blur' of wings in rapid motion, and would reflect a white light to a high degree. Waves of sparkling Eternal Life energy, first 'hovered' about Him, then 'lit *upon* Him', the ***Whole*** of Him, *enveloping* His person, **remaining** on Him, and *in* Him –*ever after!*

Oh! *Beautiful* Life Who Pleaded For Men! Hands Clasped to Heaven, Heart-*Chained* to *Them*, Thru Many a Night Your Vigil Did Keep Assigning *Each* Name – *to Stars in the Deep!*__

The Eternal Heavens! So have men described the orbs of blazing light illumining the night sky! When Jesus viewed the night skies of Galilee, beloved, he beheld these silent sentinels of majesty and glory. *And He knew what they meant.* Each one was *symbolic* of *A Life* of Brilliance and Power, of Majestic Being and Divine Declaration! And He envisioned *each one* as a precious human life who had **triumphed** over time, sin, disease, suffering, and death – *through Him!* So would they, all men, *one day*, shine forth in God-Glorifying splendor! These very thoughts occupied His Holy Mind in the sacred stillness of the night, and thrilled His Soul! The *then*-future scripture, *'To him that **overcometh** shall inherit ALL things'* burned in His Loving breast, as He in Divine **wonderment** and gratitude contemplated *our* certain destiny – *and does still!*

**Lord, You *Never* Condemned
Anything, Which Lived or Did Breath,
Whether Men Lost To Themselves
Or Trees Bearing – *Fig Leaves!*__**

No record exists of the Saviour of Life condemning *anyone*, or **anything**, to death! No record of the Life-Giver becoming the Death Deliverer! Yes, dire warnings of severe consequences resulting from major departures from the Law of Love were lovingly issued, but **never** a carrying out or dispensing of punishment by the Lord! Recall He said we are to **bless** those who curse us, *not* to **curse** (condemn) those – *who would condemn us!* Even the withered fig tree, which Jesus is reputed to have pronounced a death-curse upon, we find Him merely stating **what He perceived to be taking place.** The Life essence of the fig tree had **chosen** to cease bearing fruit! Out of 'guilt', it stopped 'believing in itself', and began to wither away! But, never forget! Restoring the withered, whether a plant's shoots or people's limbs–*is God's speciality!*

**A Joy *Far Greater* Than Anyone Told
Made the Master Fearless, Daring, and Bold,
Yet, What Was This Boon that Empowered Him
But, The Joy Derived *From* – *His Fellowmen*!**

Student of Truth, from what **source** did the Master draw upon to **fortify** Himself, to **strengthen** Himself, so that He might successfully perform His Life Mission? Of course, He relied upon His **Heavenly Father** every waking moment for empowerment, but through what *medium* was this power dispensed? Perhaps more than any other, it was the vehicle of **Joy!** If you think that Jesus predominantly expressed attitudes of somberness, great reserve, or sorrow, you would be greatly mistaken! What *so few* realize is that this Man is said to have been 'anointed with the oil of **Gladness** [**Joy**] *above His fellows*'! This means He experienced inwardly and manifested outwardly **more Joy** *than any other human being* had ever done! No wonder His strength never failed Him! He **rejoiced so** in the good fortune and blessing – *of others!*

**No _Likeness_ of Him Bequeathed to Us
So We Might His Features Our Fingers Touch,
No _Image_ to Cherish, Yet Why Should This Be,
Save His 'Picture' Is <u>Already</u> Given – _to See!_**

'<u>Behold</u> the MAN', Pilate declared. In other words, **look** upon Him steadfastly. Observe His **face** and the character _etched therein!_ Yet, how are we to do so, those of us removed from Him _by centuries?_ Beloved friend, one day a drawing, or even a portrait, of Jesus may be found, composed by some soul who could not bear to forget the Saviour's appearance. But why _should_ anyone be deprived of viewing His face? The Truth is – _none ever have!_ Recall, Jesus repeatedly stated **'I am <u>IN</u> you, and you are <u>IN</u> Me'**. This means, in a very real sense, when we see the Light of Selfless, Divine Love, in another's eyes, we are looking into _**His!**_ When we notice a smile of tender Adoration from our child, we witness _**His!**_ And _if_ we **dare** look into a mirror, we see _**Him** looking back at us,_ if we are –_truly His!_

**Oh! Won't You, Friend, With Welcome
Hear _The_ Unspoken Words of Him,
Who Gives Truth, Now, Which
Could _Not_ Be Borne – _Then!_**

If, dear friend, the Lord were to appear before _you_, **today**, what would He say? What new Truth would He impart to your heart? Imagine this: 'You **know** I Love you – but, did you know – _**I Need you?**_ You know I care about you – but, did it ever _dawn_ upon you – _**I Adore you?**_ Had you ever dreamt, beloved, in your wildest dreams – _**I Worship you?**_ Men have long thought holy reverence to be reserved only for Myself and my Father. How few have realized that _worship flows in both directions_ as My Golden Rule actually reveals! To paraphrase, 'What I desire **you** do _unto Me_, **I** desire to do _unto you!_' Remember, I _knelt,_ **bowed** _my head,_ before My disciples (as in prayer) washing their feet. And what greater **act of worship** – _the laying down of my life_ for the world?' Is this a valid perspective? Let the **Saviour** tell you whether true, when He bows – _before you!_

_No_ Hint of Anger, _Nor_ Trace of Hate
Did Mar the Countenance of One So Great,
Determined Resolve Is What They All Saw
Born of Grief O'er – _Humanity's_ _Flaws!_

Truth seeking friend, many believe that anger is a righteous emotion *when* it is justified. Yet, is anger really _ever_ justified? Anger is found in a continuum. Dislike precedes it, hate follows it, desire to harm emerges from it, and the act of attack or assault culminates it. In short, at every stage, it is the **_absence_** of Love. Most say Jesus expressed anger with the Pharisees on the occasion of healing the man with a paralyzed hand. For Mark records, '[Jesus] looked round about on **_them_ with anger**, being grieved for the hardness of their hearts, and the Pharisees took counsel, how they might destroy Him.' The anger, however, referred _to them_, as they were **consumed *by it*** to the point of desiring to _destroy_ Him. Jesus, in contrast, was 'grieved' (saddened) over their hearts' coldness, yet _continued_ **to love** them still! As He – _always will!_

**Wide Is the Gate, Broad Is the Way
And Most Feel the 'Lost' Enter to Stay,
Yet, <u>*Never*</u> Once Did I Say This Was So, For
It Only '<u>**Leadeth**</u>' to Where – <u>*They Can't Go*</u>!**

On one occasion, Jesus spoke of two gates. One was wide, so much so as to easily allow many to pass within it. And the road leading up to it was broad, as well. Many believe Jesus said those **many** whom enter therein would be destroyed. **Yet, He did not!** Rather, what He said was, the wide gate *'leadeth <u>to</u>'* destruction – yes, <u>*should*</u> they be permitted to continue down that path! But, note, <u>*there is no mention they did!*</u> 'Narrow is the gate which leadeth unto life, and *few* there be that find it.' Here, Jesus spoke of '**THE**' few (an idiom meaning '<u>none</u>') would find it, or even seek for it, *on their own, apart from Him!* Friend, Jesus said, 'the Son of man is NOT come to **destroy** men's lives [by *casting* them into Hell], but to save them [<u>***from***</u> it!].' Remember, too, He said, 'I will draw **ALL** men unto me' (Who am <u>***also***</u> called **The Door**, or *Gate*, for their passage into Heaven) – <u>*one by one!*</u>

Words of Majesty and of Might
<u>*Sent*</u> by the Father <u>**Thru**</u> Love's True Light,
Spoken by One, With Words <u>*Not*</u> His Own
Proclaiming <u>***Glorious***</u> News – <u>*Alone!*</u>

Friend, Jesus said, 'The words that I speak unto you are <u>*NOT*</u> mine, but [ARE] **the <u>*Father's*</u>.**' Jesus was so attuned with the Creator that the Father's Words <u>*naturally arose*</u> within Him. Those words <u>*emerged*</u> up from within His consciousness, which had **direct** contact with our Father. Jesus actually served as the Messenger <u>*of*</u> the Father, the <u>*spokesman*</u>, conveying words **verbatim**. Yet, a fascinating question remains: <u>*What WOULD Jesus' words HAVE been?*</u> **Then**, He spoke in the capacity *of God*, AS God. **One day**, He will speak to us **His** words in the capacity *of Divine Man!* – <u>*How*</u> He felt, <u>*What*</u> He thought, <u>*Why*</u> He did certain things the way He did. Scripture is silent here because the GOSPEL was His **ONLY** concern. His own *personal* words, His views, His human *auto*-**biography**–are <u>*yet to come!*</u>

Jesus Stood Before Pilate *Still*
And, Did Not INVITE an Evil Will,
For Love Turns *Not* the Other Cheek, but
Lovingly <u>Questions</u> Those – *<u>Not Meek</u>!*

But, did not Jesus say 'whosoever shall smite thee on thy right cheek, ***turn to him the other*** [left cheek] ***also***'? Yes, *but <u>not</u> to be struck!* Rather, to protect the one <u>*already*</u> struck from <u>*further*</u>, undoubtedly, **greater** harm! One does not wish to **<u>invite</u>** added assault. For this would be to encourage evil. How do we know this is true, beloved? Because Jesus, *Himself*, <u>our</u> Example, did **NOT** 'turn the other cheek' when brutally hit across His face in Pilate's presence. <u>*As soon as*</u> an officer, there, struck Him, Jesus responded by saying, 'If I have spoken evil, bear witness of the evil; but if well, <u>*why smitest thou me?*</u>' No, 'to turn the other cheek' really means **not to retaliate in kind** with hateful, malevolent rhetoric! Jesus' reply **benevolently** convicted those of hypocrisy, and would lead them to repentance – <u>*one day*</u>*!*

The Christ Who Knelt on Mountain Heights Did Beseech His Father in Prayerful Nights, *By Such Communion Sought*, **and Found Then, Prepared Him to Love –** *His Fellowmen!*

Whence was **the Source** of the *Mighty* Strength of Jesus' Love? Did It all just flow 'naturally' and '*effortlessly*' from His Being? Was there no 'preserving' or 'protecting' Love's purity? – No fortifying of Love's integrity? Yes! There surely WAS my friend! The writer of Hebrews tells us Jesus '**who** in the days of His flesh, offered up prayers and supplications (humble entreaties) with '**strong crying** and **tears**'. And more often than not, His were **cries** (heart yearnings) and **tears of Joy**! – 'crying out' in praise and thanksgiving and devotion, **OBEYING** the *First* and *Greatest* Commandment of **loving His Father** with 'ALL [of His] Heart, Soul, Mind, and Strength'! This enabled Him, then, to *'Love His neighbor as Himself'!* Though He were Love, personified, scripture says He 'was perfected', in Love's **obedient** expression and demonstration. Thus He could truthfully say, 'I am not alone!'**The Love** *of 'the Father* is with Me!'

What God _Is_ There Who Would _Share_ as I Elevating You to the Very Sky, Nay, _Far More Than_ Share, Is My Desire, Dear Heart, But To Make You of <u>MY</u> Life – _An Intrinsic Part!_

The Saviour of the World is one whose nature it is to give, wholly, completely, fully, withholding **nothing** of _all_ that He has – and even <u>IS</u>. He looks upon humanity as His **brethren** (Heb. 2:11), making us, astonishingly, _equal to_ Him, as He is equal to God! (Phil. 2:6) As the captain of our Salvation (Heb. 2:10), Christ is in the process of 'bringing <u>many</u> (actual Greek: '_ALL_') sons unto GLORY! He will have us be '**partakers** of [_His_] divine nature', nothing less! (2 Peter 1:4) Not only that, but the rulership he exercises is to be <u>thoroughly</u> shared, as we are to sit down with Him in **His throne**, even as He is 'set down with [God, His] Father in _**His**_ throne.' (Rev. 3:21) Mankind will then have arrived at the stature of the '**perfect** man, unto the measure of **The Stature**..._of Christ_'! (Eph. 4:13) _Then_, the God of _All_-Giving, will have _most_ surely given–_His ALL!_

**Into the _Depths_ of His Heart We Go
And FIND the _Most_ Startling View, <u>Lo</u>!
_So_ Humble a Yearning! <u>Profound</u>, and True
'To Be <u>Worthy</u> of the Love, of _Me – and You!_'**

Dear Heart, there was an expression, no doubt, our Lord held uppermost in His mind and heart whenever He interacted with His fellow woman and man. And that sentiment was: _'I would be_ **worthy** _of your love!'_ Whenever he stood stately and calm before threatening, angry crowds, He silently repeated, _'I would be_ **worthy** _of your love!'_ Wherever He encountered self-righteous, yet blind and condemning Pharisees, He would rehearse within, _'I would be_ **worthy** _of your love!'_ On those occasions when He was ridiculed and slandered, and accused falsely by so-called religious and upright men, He would say to Himself, _'I would be_ **worthy** _of your love!'_ Sending love to them all the while! **_Why_** did He do this? Beloved, He could not _help_ but do it! He knew that LOVE was _in_ them, tho unexpressed, and that <u>they</u> were of supreme value, irrespective of their behavior. **_This_** was the humble Saviour! **_This_** was, and IS, the God–**worthy** _of Love!_

**Fear Is A Path to the *Dark* Side
A Modern-Day Parable Tells, Yet,
The Truth, *So Told*, Conceals Error Bold
Which Only God's Son – *Can Dispel!***

Follower of God, hear **clearly** and **never forget** *these words* of the Apostles quoting the Saviour: 'This, then, is THE Message we have heard *of* Him, **God IS Light**, and in Him is **NO** darkness *at all*.' NONE! To any degree, or measure! There are those that believe God has a negative, judgmental, harsh, even frightening side to His nature – a ***Dark*** Side. God, referred to as the **Force** in this Mythology, consists of both a **Light** Side *and* a **Dark** Side. Either one, the antithesis of the Other! Good and Evil – within the Being of God! Knowing many would come to believe this, Jesus made the **unequivocal** statement of the **Absolute** indivisible Goodness of God. Recall, Jesus also said, 'A house divided *against itself* **cannot** stand.' Yet, God, our Father, will stand forever as ***Pure*** – *Ultimate Good!*

The Parable of The Good Shepherd Proclaims a <u>Truth</u> Many Dare *Not* See, *Lessoning* the Role of Man's 'Free' Will And Elevating – *<u>God's</u> <u>Sovereignty</u>*!

Jesus IS The Good Shepherd! *<u>He</u>* is **responsible** for the welfare of His sheep – their safety, security, their **ultimate** preservation. *<u>He</u>* **Will** descend the deepest ravine, or climb the highest mountain to recover His precious 'lost' sheep. *No matter* the terrain, nor the weather. *No matter* the length of time required. *No matter* the difficulty involved. He **Will** pursue His sheep *<u>till</u>* He recovers it! He possesses the skills, the strength, and the **determined, committed** Love to do so! Any sheep is 'free' to stray from the fold, but is <u>NOT</u> free to remove himself from the Master's responsibility, stewardship, and care. Yes, there are <u>many</u> 'black' sheep. They are prone to 'wander', to **resist** Jesus' gentle promptings, to 'go it alone'; but **moreso** is The Good Shepherd's **<u>Unbreakable</u>** Will to deliver such sheep – *<u>from</u> <u>themselves</u>!* **No** sheep is expendable, as the flock (mankind) would be diminished (<u>incomplete</u>) without their <u>repentant</u>–*<u>Joyous</u> <u>return</u>!*

**The Work *Of* God, or the work *of* Men
Upon This <u>One</u> Question Does <u>*All*</u> Depend,
For <u>*If*</u> Belief Alone Will Truly Set Men Free
Then, <u>*WHO*</u> Will the Great Believer – <u>*Be?*</u>**

God has decreed '**Belief**' to be the sole and exclusive requirement for the receiving of the **Gift** of Salvation. '**Believe** on the Lord Jesus Christ, and <u>*Thou Shalt Be Saved!*</u>' Yet, what has not been understood is the fact that 'Belief *IN* Christ' is NOT something any man embraces of himself. For if left up to man alone, **no one** would be saved! As Scripture asserts, 'No man seeketh after God, ***no not one***'! – That is, *of their <u>own</u> 'free' will!* This, beloved, is **key** to the Mystery of Salvation! Is man to be The Believer by his <u>*own*</u> virtue, choice, and power? Or, could another be **responsible** for this **Great Act** that is **crucial** to anyone's personal Redemption? Jesus said: 'And **This <u>*IS*</u>** the Work <u>OF</u> **God** [and NOT man], *that <u>ye</u> <u>believe</u> <u>on</u> <u>Him</u>'!* All **saving** belief originates and is sustained by God. Because of this, **no** person can fail to believe, ***when*** they are **meant** to! How reassuring! Jesus will **impart** <u>His</u> belief to all, *<u>for</u>* ALL–*<u>one glorious day!</u>*

**<u>Supreme</u> <u>Power</u> in the Cross Resides,
But, Lies *Hidden* To Unbelieving Eyes,
Yet, This <u>Equally</u> Holds, *Amazingly* True
To *Believers* who Cherish The Cross–*as <u>You</u>!***

If Love is, indeed, beloved, the most powerful force in the Universe, then the **Cross of Christ <u>*IS*</u> THE** most **powerful *instrument*** of Its Manifestation. So, the question, then, becomes what is this Power designed to **accomplish**, what is It to **Overcome**? Is there <u>anything</u>, or **anyone**, who can *<u>successfully</u>* oppose It? Or, **continue** to resist its ever-radiating influence? Is there anything that can render it power*<u>less</u>*? *<u>If there were, the Cross would be defeated!</u>* – And Christ, for any given individual, would have died, *<u>in vain!</u>* Is It, then, **limited** in Its outreach to save the 'lost', **<u>dependent</u> upon** unreliable human weakness and frailty? Or, is it true, as Jesus said, 'Ye know **NOT** the Power of God.' That is – Its **Capability**, Its Mightiness, and Its **Invincibility**! One day, **all** <u>will</u> experience, for themselves, Its Wondrous Working! And the **<u>All-Power</u>**, which Love is, will be known–*<u>to never fail!</u>*

**Lord, I <u>MUST</u> Know, Is It *Really* True
That <u>*MANY*</u>, Most Sadly, Will Depart from You,
'I Never Knew You', We Are *Told* You Will Say
On A Fateful Morning – *<u>of Judgment Day</u>!*

These words of our Saviour, dearly beloved, have frightened some men so, with their *seemingly* dire **irrevocable *finality*,** that they were horrifically <u>chilled</u> – to the very **depths** of their souls! For such a verdict, <u>*IF*</u> true, could elicit no other response by thoughtful Christians than to lament with the **greatest sorrow** such a fate to one's *fellow* woman or man! – A kinsman, a brother, or sister, father, mother, or child! What inner, irresolvable **struggle** would ensue to *attempt* to understand how Divine Love could abandon her children, forsake them, cast them away **utterly**, *forever* – even though wayward, destructive, and malevolent. Fortunately, a more *careful* reading of the Scripture reveals **<u>NO</u>** pronouncement of doom! Yes, it **<u>IS</u>** true many WILL depart from the Lord *for a time*, but ONLY <u>for a time</u>! Love, the Great Perseverer, will *<u>call them back</u>,* at an **unspecified date** – after ***<u>self</u>-***inflicted suffering is relinquished – *<u>to God</u>!*

**Hear, a _Strange_-Sounding Truth, _If_ You Can
The Lord Never _Once_ Forgave _any_ Man,
For a Powerful _Reason_ This Was So,
That a _Greater_ Truth You Might
Come – _to Know_!**

The *thief* on the cross, the *woman* taken in adultery, the *man* with the paralyzed hand – these **all** heard the words 'forgiven' spoken over them by Jesus, and so they were. Yet, surprising as it may sound, the Lord did **not** on any such occasion say, '*I forgive you*' or '*I forgive you – your sins*'. What He **did** say was, 'Your sins **ARE** *forgiven.*' No difference, you say? Actually a *world* of difference! Note, Jesus did *not* use the present verb tense, but the **PAST** tense. He was merely formally affirming what had *previously* taken place! – Even **_prior to_** His actual encounter with that person! God the Father had **already**forgiven those persons, therefore _Jesus did not have to_! This tells us our Creator is **_not_** angry with His wayward children, but regards us with **compassionate love**, as Jesus' carefully chosen and Truth-conveying words – *subtly reveal!*

What Triumphant Song of Love Is This Echoing in My Ears, and Approaching, Thrills My Raptured Heart, and Lifts my Soul – to *Celestial Spheres!*

Oh! To hear Jesus sing! What a privileged, glorious experience! What thrilling impulses did spontaneously arise in His hearers' hearts as His melodic voice, wondrous even in *normal* conversation or public discourse, did **instantaneously** capture their attention, and calm and soothe 'the savage heart' of the lower selves of men! Though Jesus loved to sing, He rarely did so for entertainment purposes, so as *not* to draw unwanted focus upon His *person* (humble as He was) as opposed to **His Message**. Yet, once having heard His Voice in song, one could never forget, as such vocal beauty as His had not been heard on earth since the Angels sang together at His birth above Bethlehem, and *theirs was a faint comparison!* **His Voice was a marriage of heavenly and earthly strains** in its vibrations and transmission. No man ever sang like this man! So beautiful were His Triumphant Songs – *of LOVE!*

There Are No 'Lost' Teachings Of Mine to be Found, Tho *Hidden* in Scripture To Hearts That Are Bound, My <u>Most</u> Advanced Doctrines Are There *In Plain View*, Tho Those Who Are Called to Understand – *Are Few!*

Many there be, today, beloved, who claim that **many** of the Words of our Lord did not survive the centuries, that His oral legacy has been altered or edited by unscrupulous men. Recall, however, the following reassurances: 'The grass withereth, the flower fadeth, but **the Word** of our God **shall stand** *forever*.' And, again, '**The Word** of the Lord **endureth** *forever*.' Lastly, our Lord's **solemn promise**, backed up by His Power and Authority: 'Heaven and earth shall pass away, but <u>My</u> **Words** shall ***NOT*** pass away.' This means, of course, they would be **accurately preserved**! Yes, there are epistles external to the New Testament which have legitimacy relative to historical and cultural considerations. But, the **Holy Spirit**, ***Itself****, chose* not to include them in the Divine Canon, beautiful writings or great Truths contained therein notwithstanding! So, the Word of God, again–*prevails!*

**I AM, Beloved, <u>All</u> That You Need
The <u>*One*</u> All-Embracing Truth in Deed,
None Are There Higher, *No Other* as Great
Second to <u>*No*</u> <u>*Other*</u> <u>*Being*</u> – <u>*of Late*</u>!**

Seeker of God-Truth, many there be, of recent years, who say Jesus is not sufficient for all your spiritual needs. Though other spiritual entities serve the Light to the <u>best</u> of *their* knowledge (greatest *degree* of which they are capable), Jesus serves the Light in the <u>FULLNESS</u> of *Celestial* Knowledge! (John 6:33) The ministrations of no other are required. For 'It pleased the Father that in [Jesus] should **ALL Fullness** dwell.' There is nothing partial or incomplete in what He has to offer. No lack in what He can impart. Again, in **Him** dwells 'the **Fullness** of the **God-<u>Head</u>** (or, *foremost* divine authority), bodily!' – the writer of Colossians avowed. Let no one convince you otherwise. Others should be honored for their goodness, what they do, and promote, but as 'The [sole] **Prince** of Life', Jesus holds **all** your heart desires! And, truly, **all** your Soul – *requires!*

**I <u>Will</u> <u>Be</u> Your *Magnificent* Obsession!
Which by My God-Self I Realized Each Day,
To GIVE without *<u>any</u>* Thought of Receiving
Yes, to Give One's Life Freely – *<u>Away</u>!***

An **obsession**, dear heart, is a <u>preoccupation</u> with, a total focus on, an Ideal that envelopes the whole of one's being. Something **magnificent** is, of course, that which is grand, exalted, and noble. The one and only thing with which one *should be* 'obsessed' is <u>*to love perfectly, impartially, completely, as did Jesus.*</u> This is a **divine** obsession, and is the ultimate purpose for your creation! Why is this so? Because the **attainment** of this lofty ideal will cause the Universe at the micro (personal) level and the macro (group) level to **blossom** into Its destined reason for being! And Peace, and Beauty, and Love will be *<u>All</u>* **There Is** for **All *<u>Who</u>* Are!** The resulting exalted state of Oneness will be experienced by everyone, and never again will separation, disunity mar God's handiwork. The ultimate Reason for being will have been **realized**! The **Magnificent Obsession of God**, we, too – will have – *<u>become</u>!*

**Oh! <u>True</u> Light, Burst Forth *from* My Heart
Hurl Your Beams Thru, My Life's Every Part,
Till I *Increasingly* Come to More Clearly See
<u>You</u> ARE – *<u>My GREATEST Reality</u>!***

'That was the True Light which lighteth every man that cometh into the world.' Yes, Jesus, **the True Light**, '[*illumines*] every man that cometh [**is born**] into the world.' Further, 'And of His **Fullness** [we] have all [each, *individually*] received.' We, who are 'partial', beloved, have *each* received a measure, or portion, of **His inexhaustible, infinite Self**, Who is '<u>full</u>'. 'And The Light shineth [*from* within the] darkness [of our being]; and the darkness comprehended It not.' – darkness meaning man's **unawareness** of the Light's existence, and Reality – *<u>Within</u>!* This is a perfect description of the state of ***<u>unregenerate</u>*** man! 'In Him was Life; and that Life was [and IS] **the Light** *of* **men**.' Here, the invisible, *ever-shining*, indestructible, unquenchable, spiritual **heart flame** is described. It continues to shine *no matter* HOW GREAT is the darkness! For It cannot be overcome, nor extinguished! It is there – *<u>to stay</u>!*

**Lord, *Blaze* Your LIGHT of Truth In Me
<u>Reveal</u> Your Love for All to See, Recognized
With Ease *If* The Word Is *Explained* –
In *<u>Ways</u> that* Praise–*<u>Your</u> <u>Holy</u> <u>Name</u>!*

Beloved Heart, you can be sure that **any** explanation of Jesus' words that do *not* bring Him the **highest Honor**, and the **greatest Validation** of *<u>His</u> <u>Love</u>* toward men, is *not* an accurate, correct, or true explanation. Either there is a faulty tradition involved, a misunderstanding by consensus, or an outright *<u>mistranslation</u>* of the original Greek text. **<u>Nowhere</u> <u>is</u> <u>this</u> <u>more</u> <u>evident</u>** than in the area of **God's Love**. For IF God TRULY <u>IS</u> Love, then He will **never cease** to *<u>seek</u>* for the highest good of any soul, no matter **how long** that soul has *<u>spurned</u>* God's <u>entreaties</u> or *<u>vehemently</u> <u>rejected</u>* God's conciliatory gestures! **<u>This</u> <u>is</u> <u>the</u> <u>Reach</u> <u>of</u> <u>the</u> <u>Cross</u>!** Therefore, it logically follows no person, no matter how *<u>seemingly</u>* incorrigible, will be 'given up on' by God relative to their ultimate salvation. **Divine Love** can abide by nothing less! And Praise be to God, Jesus **IS** That Divine Love – *<u>Evermore</u>!*

**Many *Were* the Works of the Saviour
<u>Beyond</u> What the Gospels Do Tell,
Miracles and *Marvels* Awaiting
Yet to Be Revealed –*<u>As</u> <u>Well</u>*!**

One day, beautiful friend, a **full** and **complete** account of the activities of the Lord of Life will be revealed. The Gospels were **never** meant to be a thorough catalog of <u>*every*</u> good and gracious work Jesus so lovingly performed. Had they been so, instead of a <u>*single*</u> bound volume, an **encyclopedia** would be required to narrate the countless <u>*undisclosed*</u> acts of <u>mercy</u>, <u>healing</u>, <u>forgiveness</u>, and <u>grace</u> He extended so freely, willingly, and eagerly. The Apostle John said, 'And there are also **<u>MANY</u>** <u>*other*</u> <u>*things*</u> which Jesus did, which, <u>*if*</u> they should be written every one, I suppose that ***<u>even</u> <u>the</u> <u>world</u> <u>itself</u>*** could not contain the **books** that should be written.' Yes, even Jesus' followers are in for some amazing surprises! He was <u>constantly</u> at work, *no less* than as our Great, Merciful High Priest – <u>*today*</u>!

Farewell Words

From illumined dawn to eve's moon rise, unceasingly, Christ, our Lord, sought to open men's eyes. He worked tirelessly to extend His Divine Love to others, and to cause men to realize *they could do the same!* His **Greatest Lesson**, of course, was from the Cross, where His **Enormous** Love, unlike ANY the world had ever seen, was so **prominently** displayed! He literally **dared** men to embrace this **new Way** of Life wherein a holy **boldness** to serve, care, and extend mercy was a daily occurrence. Jesus repeatedly took decisive action, seeking permission from no one, except *the Royal Law of Love*, to alleviate **all** suffering. With what Joy He performed His miracles we can only imagine, as He tenderly sought **every** lost soul! But, it must have been **tremendous**! This, then, was His Message! – **Dare *to* Love**! May it be ours –*too!*

With Every Good Wish, The Author

Part III

The Crucifixion and Resurrection *of* Jesus!

Their *Unrecognized* Significance!

Hear,
Now, a Story
<u>Few</u> Have Heard,
Communicated by
The
Living Word!
A True Account
of Christ's Passion
and Plight,
And the <u>Real</u> Reasons
He Rose
– from the Grave,
that Night!

Part III – Introduction

Part III of this book may well be unlike any you have ever read, as it reveals Truths few can scarcely imagine – *so* **Wonderful** are they in their **full** meaning and furthermost implications! For there is far more to **The** historical **Crucifixion** and **The *Resurrection*** of Jesus of Nazareth than is traditionally taught. The ultimate outcome of *so* **great** a Sacrifice, and **so profound** a **Love**, has eluded the most brilliant minds, but need not you. *Something* was effected back then at those pivotal events in Christ's life that has escaped *even* the understanding of the *Christian world*, not to mention many in the supposed more advanced New Thought and meta-physical groups. But, it is *nothing less* than the **Fullness** of the **'Glorious News'** Jesus proclaimed! May you, dear reader, be granted Vision by our **wondrous** God – *to see!*

Part III – **Contents** (1 of 3)

Section 1 – The Untold Truths of the Forgotten Cross

Oh, Holy Spirit, I Come to You
Blue Sky Did Flee and a Void Became
Upon A Cross Our Lord Was Pinned
Invisible Angels Knelt About
Lo! Invisible Words Were Nailed
My Lord Was Raised Up on A Tree
Upon The Tree Stripped Bare of Leaves
My Eyes Traced The Shaft
We Can Know What Dante Guessed

A Living Cross of Flesh and Bone
The Nightmare of the Cross Did Loom
If Love Is Stronger Than All Hate
Upon the Cross, He Silent Became
Why, Oh, WHY Is the Cross Not Shown
A Faith Supreme Our Master Held
Great Drops of Blood Our Saviour Shed
A Great Wooden Beam In the Ground

Part III – **Contents** (2 of 3)

Section 1 – The Untold Truths
of the Forgotten Cross
– Con.

Oh! Rose of Sharon on That Day
Naked He Hung Between the Earth
Mysterious Cloth Once Upon His Brow
Oh! Fabled Saviour, Life's Sweet King
When Were You Slain, Oh! Precious Lamb!
Oh, Comforting Love Divine!
'Father, Forgive Them, They Know Not'
Lord, Did You View Us Out of Dread
What 'I Do' You Think You Know

While on the Cross, His Love Outpoured
No More Powerful Image Can Be
Grace and the Cross Are One and the Same
Out from the Cross a New Universe 'Wends'
The Reach of the Cross, How Far It Extends
Oh! Cross of My Saviour! What Truth!
I Claim the World for My Own, It is Mine
Oh! Blessed Lord, We Did Not Know
Farewell Words

Part III – Contents (3 of 3)

Section 2 – The Hidden Glories *of* Our Lord's Resurrection

Unbarred Door of Empty Tomb
I Look Upon the First Witness to Faith
Oh, Sepulcher! Bathed in Brilliant Light
In Wild Flower-Strewn Garden
A Wondrous Hidden Truth Revealed
One Moment Linens Lay Wrapped About
The Earth Did Boom! The Sky Was Rent!
Oh, Mary! Dear, Sweet Mary!
Reputed To Have Said 'Touch Me Not'
Easter In My Heart Each Morn
So Baffling A Paradox
The Great Stone Many Tons Did Weigh
Shut In By Darkness The Lord's Body Lay
The First Words Behind Doors Spoken
Lord, I Drink In Of Thy Light
The Light Did Arc from Earth to Sky
Glorious Morning! Jesus is Risen!
A Strangely Beautiful Phrase I Hear
How Awesome, Thru Faith, Is the Sight
What Does the Resurrection Teach
The Real Meaning of Easter
Beautiful Saviour! Oh, Glorious Sight
The God-Ordained Dream!
Farewell Words

Section 1

The Untold Truths

Of

The Forgotten Cross!

And I,
[the Lord]
If I Be Lifted Up
from the Earth,
Will **Draw**
<u>ALL</u> Men
Unto
Me.

John 12:32

**Oh, Holy Spirit, I Come to You
To Learn Truths, _Unknown_ – Forgotten, Too,
I Know You've _Yet_ Many Things to Say, Which
Were _Unsaid_ Then, To Be Said – _Today!_**

He Who was the **_Personification_** of the Holy Spirit, once said, 'I have yet **_MANY_** things to say unto you, but you cannot *bear* them **_now_**. Nevertheless, when He, the Spirit of Truth, is come, He will **guide** you [progressively] into all truth.' Down through the ages, the Spirit has revealed **new** truth, restored **forgotten** truth, and renewed **deeper** understanding of Christ's teachings. The **Fullness** of the Gospel Message, or 'Glorious News', has been, and is being, unveiled in a step-by-step fashion. This allows God's children to '**_GROW_** in the **_KNOWLEDGE_** of The Truth.' We are incapable of grasping it all at once! Old concepts, not necessarily wrong, must give way to those *more* **true**, **accurate**, and **complete**. Be open and receptive to new insights! New Truth is always–*to God's Glory!*

**Blue Sky Did Flee and a *Void* Became
The Soldiers <u>Lit</u> Torches But All In Vain,
Unearthly Glow on Their Spears Did Dance, A
<u>Saviour</u> Hung Dying, Mankind–*<u>Would</u> <u>Advance</u>!***

Noon had come, and with it the most eerie blackness settled over the land. Where sunlit sky had just *<u>moments</u> <u>before</u>* been, a darkness descended. **Golgotha!** *The place of the skull*, was enveloped by it! The birds abruptly hushed their singing, and even the air became mysteriously still. Some thought it to be storm clouds, **<u>BUT</u>!** There was *<u>no</u>* storm, *<u>no</u>* wind, *<u>no</u>* thundering – <u>nor</u> even rain! As the Gospel authors unanimously attest! No doubt, the commander of the guard ordered torches be lit to ensure better visibility, but vainly so, attempting to alleviate the near-terror they felt! *<u>What</u> <u>possibly</u> <u>could</u> <u>be</u> <u>happening</u>?* Some suspected. Yet, one centurion knew when he boldly declared, '**<u>Truly</u>**, this man **<u>WAS</u>** the **<u>SON</u>** of ***God**!*' Mankind *would* <u>go</u> <u>on</u>, precious time had been bought, due to His Sacrifice! Love to rule–*<u>one</u> <u>day</u>!*

**Upon A Cross Our Lord Was Pinned
All Recognize as True, Yet, the Apostles
Attest _Upon a Living Tree_ – He Gave
Himself – _for You!_**

No fewer than _four_ times the Apostles Paul and Peter unequivocally said that Jesus was crucified **upon an actual living tree!** The Apostles record, 'The God of our fathers raised up Jesus, whom ye slew and hanged on **a tree**.' 'They took Him down from **the tree**, and laid Him in a sepulcher.' Christ was made 'a curse for us . . . Cursed is everyone who hangeth on **a tree**.' 'Who His own self bare our sins in His own body on **the tree**.' Surely, most suppose wooden poles or rough-hewn planks are being referred to here – in a poetic sense. **Not so, my friend!** Consider! Jesus came to REVERSE the 'Fall of man.' The tree in Eden bore a _death-dealing_ fruit; The Tree at Calvary 'bore' the **Life-Giving Fruit** – which we must 'eat'! _Jesus!_ The cross-piece was nailed _into_ the tree bark. And the Curse? Transformed into **Blessing** for all – _Evermore!_

Invisible Angels Knelt About – With Their _Astonished_ Gaze! Riveted Eyes On The Cross, Transfixed Before _Unfathomed_ Love The MARVEL – _of The Age!_

*They **could** not take their heavenly eyes off of Him!* As horrific as was the scene before them, they were **spell-bound** and incapable of moving! God's **Love Incarnate** giving _every ounce_ of Life He had to give. Withholding nothing! Though men turned away, **they** could not! Before them, willingly, He bled in profuse unimaginable agony. With ONE thought, He could have freed Himself from the tortuous, life-crushing cross, but it *never once* occurred to His mind. He WAS the Lamb of God (literal Greek – little, *helpless baby* lamb)! The Saviour of the World! And through the **sheer Strength** of His Love, _at which even the angels marveled,_ He chose to endure the unendurable, the unthinkable, *for us!* Angels there knelt, and wept, in indescribable anguish. Stark witnesses to the Drama of All Ages, ***The Redemption of** – the World!*

Lo! <u>Invisible</u> <u>Words</u> Were Nailed, So Firmly to the Tree, *Along With* – The Dying Saviour Who Did <u>Obliterate</u> Them – *<u>for</u>* *<u>Me</u>!*

It is generally known that a wooden placard bearing the inscription, 'This is Jesus, King of the Jews,' was nailed to the cross above the Saviour's head during His crucifixion. However, very few know that *<u>other</u>* <u>words</u> were also firmly affixed to that cruel tree – ***by Jesus Himself!*** And it was for *<u>this</u>* *<u>very reason</u>* He went *<u>to</u>* the cross – to strip those words of their power to enslave, torment, and ultimately destroy the human race! **Listen!** With His own blood He '**[*<u>BLOTTED</u>*] *<u>OUT</u>*** the *hand<u>writing</u>* of ordinances <u>against</u> <u>us</u>, <u>nailing</u> <u>it</u> <u>to</u> <u>His</u> <u>cross</u>*!*' So Colossians declares! Those writings and their power **died** – then and there! ***What were those words?*** Any words judging humanity worthy of everlasting condemnation, guilt, and fear! Yet, **sacred crimson** overflowed *<u>every</u>* single solitary letter,causing them to **cease** to be!–*<u>setting ALL free</u>!*

My Lord Was Raised Up on A Tree
And Sin '*__Became__*' – For You and Me,
__Like__ the Serpent Lifted Up Due to Strife,
Inflicting Both Death, while – *__Imparting Life__*!

'As Moses lifted up the serpent in the wilderness, *even* *so* must the Son of Man be lifted up, *That* whosoever believeth in Him should not perish.' 'For He hath '**made**' Him, Who knew no sin, to *be* sin for us.' In ancient times, when an Israelite was bitten by a poisonous snake, he was healed by **gazing** upon a bronze serpent Moses affixed to a pole. Amazingly, Christ was likened to *__this__* serpent! A creature capable of inflicting death, yet here imparting life. Did you know, friend, Christ, too, was dispensing 'death' from the Cross? – *__Death to sin itself__*, its cause and consequences! The serpent *represented* evil, or sin; Jesus, *figuratively*, **became** sin, and therefore, when *He* died, sin died with Him! And because '**every** eye shall **see** Him', all will partake of the Remedy *infinitely* more potent than **any** serpent's venom! *Even* the Adversary–*__Himself__*!

**Upon *The* Tree Stripped Bare of Leaves
This Man of God, and God of Man,
Clung to All He Knew Was True
By Thought *of Me* – *and You*!**

What was it that enabled our Saviour to **hold on** to life *TILL* He had satisfied the claims of Justice? It was necessary He remain there for **six** solid hours, the ancient Hebrew number denoting 'fallen' man! His unimaginable ordeal *could not* be over till this had occurred – *AND* He **personally** declared it over! Few know it was Jesus Himself Who **released** His Spirit back to God, **choosing** the very moment of His death! When six hours were fulfilled, Jesus exclaimed, 'It is Finished; and **He** bowed His head and [*He*] GAVE up the spirit.' It was *not* taken *from* him by His body's deteriorating condition nor by another's actions! How do we know? Jesus said, '**NO MAN** *taketh* [my Life] from Me, but **I** lay It down – *OF MYSELF*.' **Only** the thought of His brothers' and sisters' future salvation kept Him alive! He **Willed** *NOT* to fail them! –*and He didn't!*

My Eyes Traced The Shaft Up *from* the Ground To a Figure *Nailed High*, Crossbeam Bound, <u>Time</u> Seemed *<u>Suspended</u>*, As Truly was He Amidst Past, Future – *<u>and</u> <u>Thee</u>!*

Something **inscrutable** happened there at the Cross. When a person's time to be drawn to It comes, they find themselves kneeling there before It in **rapt awe** and **unbroken wonderment**. Utter silence reigns and no other soul is in sight save the crucified Lord. A person finds himself in a *<u>timeless</u> <u>realm</u>* where all lack of meaning *finds* its meaning in Him! No surreal landscape could compare with the unveiling to one's eyes of *<u>the</u> <u>Supreme</u> <u>Reality</u> <u>of</u> <u>Divine</u> <u>Love</u>!* And, there, dear heart, at that *very* **Eternal Moment**, a person is given to know the **Depths** of the **Heart** of Love! And what is *that* Vision of Love? In one word, Its utter *<u>Endlessness</u>!* A person then realizes herself to be the object of *Infinite* affection! Suddenly, time resumes, but this Image remains, **transforming** one's life – *<u>forever</u> <u>more</u>!*

We Can KNOW What Dante *Guessed* The Scope Upon Which Salvation Rests, The *Extent* of the Number God <u>Chooses</u> to Be Inheritors of Heaven – *Through Eternity!*

In The Divine Comedy, that great spiritual allegory, Dante wrote: '**Predestination!** . . . Mortals, be slow to judge! Not even we who look on God in Heaven know, *as yet*, **how many** *He* [God] will **choose** for [Salvation] (Canto 20) To which He added, we '[rest] in the assurance that the *unknown consequences* of God's **Will** <u>CANNOT</u> fail to be good.' Beloved, our Creator has specifically and clearly revealed His Sovereign Will regarding the **exact** **number** of individuals to be saved! Timothy wrote: 'Who **WILL** have **All Men** to be saved.' And, again, 'And I, if I be lifted up from the earth, will draw **All Men** unto Me.' And, *still* again, 'we trust in the Living God Who is the Saviour of **All Men**, e*specially* of those that believe [but, *equally as much* for those also who do not *yet* believe!]. Numerous other scriptures testify to this fact! What, then, is that number? – *<u>Every single, solitary</u> **ONE**!*

**A _LIVING_ Cross of Flesh and Bone
And SPIRIT, Come For 'To ATONE',
The <u>BE</u>-*ing* of Man, and the I <u>AM</u> of God
An Upright <u>BEAM</u> Upon Earth's – *<u>Dark Sod!</u>***

He is known by two names: The Son of Man and the Son of God! He was the *<u>joining</u>* of two orders of being, the **union** produced by the 'crossing' or 'breeding' of two life forms! The lesser life and the Greater Life. The human life and the Divine Life. The product? A **New** Humanity! A Wholly *<u>Divine</u>* Man! And it is THIS cross (of the twain becoming one), *really*, <u>not</u> the tree upon which He hung, that will 'draw ALL men unto Me'! *<u>It</u>* was only a wooden scaffolding, to hold the Saviour in the air, possessing no power in itself to heal a broken humanity. **HE** was the <u>intersecting</u>, or **Crossing**, of men and women and divinity! The **very first** of *<u>His</u>* **Kind!** – *<u>But</u> <u>not</u> <u>the</u> <u>last!</u>* As we are, along with Him, to be '**<u>partakers</u> of the <u>Divine</u> <u>Nature</u>**'! So said ApostlePeter–*and* our awakening hearts, *<u>today!</u>*

**The Nightmare of the Cross Did Loom
Before the Saviour – Foretelling *Doom*,
Yet, 'Awaken' from This Dream He Would
To a <u>World</u> of WONDER – Foretelling *<u>Good</u>!***

One could hardly imagine a more terror-filled scenario than that of a crucifixion scene, and one <u>*being*</u> the condemned to die! The thought, *alone*, of this hellish scene is enough to **shatter** the nerve of the most courageous human, and leave one on the verge of total insanity. All that the Divine Man experienced, *within*, we cannot know, as He was the **first** being of the perfect Human/God Kind, and His unique *psychological makeup* differed strikingly from our own. However, we DO know His thoughts and emotions were, somehow, with herculean will, **focused** upon the welfare of others (His mother, disciples, the 'good thief', etc.), and 'the Joy that was set *before Him'!* He **knew** the World of the Resurrection would be one of Wonders and Marvels worth the suffering of ANY torture or barbarity. And Supreme GOOD for **All** – *would be assured!*

***If* Love Is Stronger Than All Hate
Then Surely This Leaves a Major Clue,
That, ALL Those Who Hate Will, *One Day*
Be, 'Won Over' By A Love – *So True!***

How <u>*strong*</u>, dear friend, was the Love Jesus had for His fellow man? For Love to be the undisputed Victor over the world, as Holy Writ unequivocally declares, to have achieved *<u>Its</u>* calculated outcome, there can only be one possible answer! – The winning over of **all** people to the side of love, the logic of love, the practicality of love, the desirability of love! *This is WHAT The Cross* **permanently** *secured!* But, I hear you say, *why* do we not <u>yet</u> see this? Because, there is a grand and glorious purpose being worked out here below! And the outworking of that Purpose – *the <u>transformation</u> of <u>human</u> <u>hearts</u>* – involves time and experience. Hate is actually <u>*very*</u> <u>*weak*</u>, though it **appears** strong! And it WILL be abandoned, *one-by-one,* as people recognize Love's colossal strength and ALL-Attractiveness! – Love's **Sole** Aim – *Achieved!*

Upon the Cross, He Silent Became
Though Pain Did _Sear_ Thru-out His Frame,
_No_ Scream Did Pass Out of His Trembling Lips
Yet, He _felt_ the Sting – _of a Thousand Whips!_

Had you ever wondered, dear friend, what _sounds_ Jesus made upon the Cross between the few brief occurrences of His last recorded words? Was He uncontrollably **yelling** out of agony? Was He _screaming_ part, or even most of the time? Was He **shouting** due to unremitting pain of unimaginable proportions? Had He done so, it would have been wholly natural and expected. Such action on our Lord's part would have, _however slight_, relieved _some_ of His pain, providing a physical release of sorts. The Truth is: Jesus may well have been moaning and groaning, but **nothing** more than this, _as He determined to bear the full brunt of physical torture in mankind's behalf!_ Scripture says 'He was led as a sheep to the slaughter, and like a lamb _dumb_ before His shearer, so opened He NOT His mouth.' This, alone, required a superhuman Love to accomplish! Truly, Christ bore it all – _for our sakes!_

**Why, *Oh*, WHY Is The Cross Not Shown
Even in Churches Its Absence is 'Known',
No More Accorded Honor, As It *Used* to Be
Often Dispensed With, No Relic – *to See!***

Time was when **every** church prominently displayed at least one large Cross, often more. It was usually situated on the central altar before the congregation, or upon the wall behind it. Proudly displayed for the **profound symbol** of *Divine Love and Mercy* it was, it afforded parishioners and soul-weary visitors and seekers, alike, consolation and solace. Now, frequently, it is conspicuous by its absence. *WHY was It removed?* Flowers may be abundant, scripture verses, even pictures of Saints – but **NOT** the Cross! It is because supposed 'enlightened' men now view It as 'offensive'! **Forgetting**, or never knowing, the ***Depths* of Love** this formerly-venerated wooden object of Art proclaimed, they have *hidden it away* – **denying** Its Power, and thereby, **Christ's Central Role** in Salvation! Still, *The* Atonement It effected–*Remains!*

**A Faith Supreme Our Master Held
And the '_Why_' He Uttered Could Not Dispel,
His TOTAL Belief That THIS Was True:
'God IS – EVER With Me' – _Too!_**

Toward the end of our Lord's torturous ordeal upon the tree, Matthew records 'And about the ninth hour, Jesus cried with a loud voice, saying, Eli, Eli, lama sabachthani? That is to say, _My God, My God, **WHY** hast Thou **FORSAKEN** Me?_' Many believe that, here, Jesus' faith, for the first time, **weakened**, however briefly. Here, they say, **doubt** had crept into His noble heart and caused Him to _question_ His Mission, and Himself! They cite this as **proof** of His humanity. Yet, Jesus _had_ **no moment** of weakness! – Then, nor ever! What the onlookers heard was Jesus _reciting_ Psalm 22 wherein **King David** is quoted as saying 'My God, my God, why hast Thou forsaken _me_.' This was only _one_ among numerous Scriptures Jesus was rehearsing in reviewing God's Promises and historical Reality! Jesus KNEW of His **inseparable Oneness** with God, and not even the cruel Cross – could dissuade Him – _Otherwise!_

**Great Drops of Blood Our Saviour Shed
And We Have Been Told Because of _Dread_,
Yet 'Twas Not Fear That Made It So, But
Compassion's Heart – _Bursting Below!_**

On the eve of Jesus' crucifixion, in the Garden of Gethsemane, He knelt down to pray. Blood began to drop off His brow. We are told this was the result of the incredible mental _**agony**_ Jesus experienced as the ordeal of death by the cross loomed before Him. Yet, _scripture does not say this was so!_ Jesus, **FULLY** aware of His Divinity and **singularly unique Role** as Saviour of the world never once, _for even one second,_ flinched nor cringed before His chosen destiny! Jesus bled, _not_ out of anguish over _Himself,_ but out of an **astonishing** compassion for a humanity lost in ignorance, blindness, weakness, and death. His heart melted in a compassion **SO GREAT**, His body could not endure the grandeur and magnitude of His love! Blood vessels **burst** across His brow! His thoughts of concern, as always, were on the welfare of others – _even then!_

A Great Wooden Beam In the Ground Was Placed, Yet, to the *Heart* of the Earth *It Invisibly Raced!* It Burst there as a New-Born Sun, and Its Beams, *Back Out*, Thru the Earth – *Did Run!*

That hard, unyielding beam of wood thrust upright into the earth seemingly came to a stop as a dull thud was heard. But, when He Who had become one with that 'pillar' did surrender His Life to Death, the ***Victorious* energy** of His Achievement of 'enduring unto the end' was transmitted **instantaneously** to the center of the earth! From there, it expanded out through every layer of Mother Earth! *What had transpired?* Every molecule was alerted, 'felt' in its inner matrix that the first half of its very reason for being was accomplished, **secured**. It, *too*, would be freed from decay and corruption. 'For the **entire creation** *groans and travails* until now, waiting for the manifestation of the Sons of God!' The **antidote** had come! The resurrection of our Lord confirmed it! God's future, Trusting One, **assuredly** – *will fulfill it!*

Oh! Rose of Sharon on That Day, You Had 'Thorns' _Attached_, and Were Wed to Tree, Though Sharpened Prongs Men Felt Belonged Could _NOT_ Be Made – _a Part of Thee_!

The Rose of Sharon has no thorns! The Forces of evil could not tolerate the thought of a Saviour, beautiful as the **Perfect, Harmless, Blemishless** rose that _**He was**_ – _not having thorns!_ Evil wanted to remake Him like unto itself – bearing implements in His _very_ person to harm, inflict suffering, and sorrow! But, they were **removed** when He was lovingly taken from the cross, and the 'crown of thorns' was _pried_ from His sacred brow, to be **discarded** *evermore*. It is NOT in the Lord's nature to inflict harm on anyone, _nor will it ever be!_ The Lord Jesus refuses even to judge anyone as deserving of condemnation! He **IS** the Eternal Flower of Sharon – _The Rose without one thorn!_ Evil's way is to pierce, lance, and destroy. *HIS* WAY, as He **taught** and **lived**, is to **overcome** the vilest of human, or demonic, evil – _with Good!_

**Naked He Hung Between the Earth and Sky
The Only Man, Ever, *Truly* Born to Die,
Darkness Around Him, All About,
'Immortal Flame *of* Love!
<u>Dare</u> You – *<u>Go Out</u>!***

It was beyond belief! The **impossible** had happened! Those disciples who so loved Him **must** have thought <u>*these*</u> very thoughts! He Who could command death to depart, was now commanded *by* death to die! With the **one** hope of salvation gone, Death was the sure victor, *<u>after all</u>,* and along with it, suffering and despair – *or so it seemed.* For as yet the disciples did not recall, nor even understand, His Words He would ***<u>RISE</u> Again!*** So, they feared for themselves – and the world! '**How** <u>*could*</u> this have happened?' was their anguished cry. '**How** <u>*Dare*</u> He permit it?' was their most agonizing question of all! And, 'WHY did He die and leave us – *so all ALONE?'* was the most **horror-ridden** thought of all. Yes, so they thought – <u>till</u> celestial beings DECLARED, 'He ***IS*** risen!' **Then**, they knew why! His Life was extinguished in flesh, so theirs would flourish – *<u>in Spirit</u>!*

**Mysterious Cloth Once Upon His Brow
Found _Folded_ in The Tomb _Apart!_
Where Linen Clothing, Lying, Now,
No More Did Drape – _His Sacred Heart!_**

The sweet-scented spices used to saturate the burial garment of the Lord, my friend, still filled the cavern with its fragrance. And strangely, there **wasn't** the _slightest hint_ death had _ever_ occupied this 'room', nor held **anyone** in its yet _up-till-then_, inescapable grasp! His disciples could sense it, but dared not believe, as yet. The Lord's body, His _**naked**_ body, was gone! The linens so lovingly wrapped about His breast and downward, clung to _**no**_ beloved one now. **Why**, then, were His garments left? _**Why**_ was He 'taken' –_**disrobed?**_ Listen! As the Lord told Nicodemus, 'You must be BORN from Above!'_A birth had just taken place,_ and a newborn IS _**naked**_! He Who **rose** was the 'first-_**BORN**_ from the dead!' An earthly body transmuted to spiritual perfection, manifesting 'physically' – _at will!_

**Oh! Fabled Saviour, Life's Sweet King
The _Horror_ of So Dread A Thing!
The Prince of Life Lay Low in _Death_
Till, They Felt Again – *His Sacred Breath!*__**

If there ever were **conclusive proof** that someone reputed to still be dead, _were alive_, precious friend, it is to _**feel**_ that someone's breath upon one's face. To _**see**_ another's breast rise and fall, to _**hear**_ the gentle passage of air though another's nostrils and mouth. To _**smell**_ the sweet fragrance of a Health- and Life-Filled body! After all, one might well believe he were deluded by a vision, instead of a **living, breathing** person! That is _why_ Jesus provided this much needed proof after He arose. He said, '**Peace** be unto you; as my Father hath sent Me, even so send I you. And when He had said this, He **breathed** *ON THEM*, and saith unto [His disciples], Receive ye the Holy Spirit!' Jesus knew breath is **evidence indisputable** of Life. And that **Peace** would fill their hearts – _as a result!_

When Were You Slain, *Oh!* Precious Lamb! At Mid-Afternoon in a Forsaken Land, Or When The Spear Did Pierce You Thru, *Or*, a *Time* and *Place* the World – *Never Knew!*

Friend of the Blessed One, at precisely midway between noon and evening, at a hill called Calvary, an event occurred **unparalleled** in the history of the world! A bleeding and tortured Man hung His head down for the last time, as He uttered these immortal words, *'It is finished!'* The Divine Love of the Ages was no more! His body was lifeless and grew cold. But, was Jesus actually slain *at that time?* A strange question, you ask? Perhaps so, but hear now, a *stranger* answer! The Lamb was actually '*slain from* [*before*] *the foundation of the world!'* So said the Apostle John in the Book of Revelation! His death was a **foregone** conclusion! It was **predestined** to occur, and in Eternity, *already had!* Its startling occurrence in time merely *reflected*, three-dimensionally – *this God-Ordained Reality!*

**Oh, _Comforting_ Love Divine!
You Stood By _To Shine!_ In My Darkest
Moments, On the Tree, I Was Bathed In God's
Love, '_Perpetually_' – _Through Thee!_**

When the **greatest Exemplar** of humanity was hung so mercilessly between Heaven and earth, was there no comfort _whatsoever_ afforded Him from on High? **Where** was the 'Dove' of Comfort that had alighted upon His 'shoulder' to signal the official beginning of His ministry? Had It _deserted_ Him _completely_ in His greatest moments of need? Had God the Father _totally_ forsaken His Beloved? Many believe so, but is that the Truth? **God's 'Mother Love' was** present, **there**, _even at the crucifixion!_ Overlooked by most, It actually resided in _**the persons**_ of His mother, her sister, and Mary Magdala! These three women knelt at the foot of the cross obeying their dying Saviour by 'agreeing together' in intense **strengthening** prayer in His behalf! What **comfort** this afforded _Him!_ He will one day tell! As tell of _**His**_ comfort Love – _by you!_

'Father, *Forgive* Them, They Know <u>*Not*</u> What They Do', Was This a One-Time Pardon, Or Is It <u>*Ever*</u> True? Or Will the Forgiveness of Jesus Cease to Be – *For <u>Some</u> Like You!*

When Jesus was hoisted up on the Cross after having been impaled with iron spikes through his hands and feet, He made this declaration asking His Heavenly Father to *forgive* **the <u>most</u> atrocious act** *ever* committed in human history – the crucifixion of the Son of God, Himself! Yet, as **horrendous** as was <u>this</u> act – *this* ULTIMATE act of evil – Jesus without hesitation offered TOTAL and UNEQUIVACAL forgiveness! Now I ask you, friend, would our Heavenly Father do any less? Surely He will! However, the **deeper** question is: Can any other *lesser* act, or <u>*repeated*</u> acts, <u>EVER</u> be perpetrated that will NOT be forgiven by our Lord? The Truth is – all will be! As long as any individual commits a **heinous** act, 'they know NOT what they do!' Only the <u>*UN*</u>-knowing are capable of this! And, as such, will ALWAYS, by God, be – *forgiven!*

**Lord, Did You View Us Out of Dread
Or With Understanding, Divine, Instead,
When from the Cross Your Eyes Surveyed
A *Surreal* Scene Which Men – _**Had Made**_*!*

The landscape below and before Him was barren, stark, and foreboding. But it was *not* these images our Lord was conscious of, rather those of the Reality of mankind's plight! Jesus did NOT see *harsh conquerors*, but soldiers who were **slaves of sin – to be pitied!** He did NOT observe *ignoble men*, but rather **terrified children – to be reassured!** He did NOT witness a *hate-filled gathering*, but rather a **frightened crowd – to be comforted!** In short, Jesus watched a **weakened world** *mistakenly believing* 'Might Makes Right' – **to be forgiven!** Due to *unasked for* Spiritual Blindness and their incomprehension of The Law of Love! All this, our Saviour saw – WITHOUT, through the perfect lens of His Divine Vision – *WITHIN*. And such characteristics are NOT worthy of condemnation! – *Nor will they ever be!*

**What 'I Do' You *Think* You Know
Secure in a *Self*-Knowledge that Tells You So,
But, What I *Did*, You Could Hardly Surmise
As Its Purpose Transcended – *The Skies!***

On the occasion of Jesus' washing His disciples' feet, Jesus said, 'What I **do** thou knowest not now; but thou shalt know hereafter [at a later time].' (John 13:7) Now, if this remark were true regarding the meaning of a simple ceremonial foot washing, *how much more so* is it applicable to the profound and esoteric (at present) **meaning** of The Cross! Many understand what Jesus accomplished upon the Cross at a basic and fundamental level, but there remains a **full** and **maturer** meaning which *transcends* the most elemental understanding. These are the **depths** to The Cross – unfathomed by most! Paul, in possession of such knowledge, exclaimed 'the *Unsearchable* Riches of Christ!' and 'O *the Depth* of the Riches both of the wisdom and knowledge of God [in the **'workings'** of The Cross]!'. Its significance requires special, personal revelation, its so great! (Eph.1:17) May it–*be yours!*

**While on the Cross, His Love Outpoured
To a Degree, He Had <u>Never</u> Done Before,
A Love <u>*SO*</u> Vast, It Could *Not* Be Contained
An Unending Fount – Bearing <u>Mercy</u>'s Name!**

Even as a rose continually breathes out of its fragrance to the world, *unceasingly*, so did our Lord and Saviour Jesus Christ give out His Love throughout His life. <u>Never</u> did He withhold It – for even one second! But, when *any other* would have forgotten His commitment to Love, while under the tremendous distress of torture, He, instead, INCREASED the measure of Its Outpouring to all those round about Him – in His *tender looks* toward them, His *loving words* offered them, and His *thoughts of blessing* concerning them! The temptation at the very least was to be *indifferent* to His tormentors, but His Heroic Heart would not allow Him to! The Rose of Sharon – The MERCY Rose – bravely unfolded Its 'petals' and radiated Its perfumed Love to the <u>maximum</u> – that ALL men might know 'This truly WAS – <u>*the Son of God!*</u>'

**No More *Powerful* Image Can Be
Than the Christ-borne Cross of Calvary,
Destined To <u>Infiltrate</u> *Every* Solitary Heart
Whether Small or Great – *<u>Tho Worlds Apart</u>!*__**

An Eastern religion holds to the belief that there is a certain mandala, or *<u>mystical image</u>*, that can, and will ultimately **<u>destroy</u>** all evil. It is, in effect, a symbolic pattern of The Good that will prevail throughout the universe. But, the Cross of the Saviour, dear friend, is the **TRUE** All-Powerful Image that will accomplish *<u>even more</u>* than this! For *this* Image will NOT destroy 'Evil' – but will ***<u>transform</u>*** it – into Good! Christ's greatest Apostle called this act **'Reconciliation'** – the bringing back into a harmonious relationship two parties formerly opposed to one another. Hear then: 'Having made Peace through *the blood of His Cross,* to reconcile **<u>ALL</u>** things [beings] *unto Himself'!* The Cross image will prove Itself inescapable and irresistible. For it is the **Supreme** symbol of every heart-winning, each mind-convincing,**<u>All</u>**-**<u>Conquering</u>**–*<u>Love</u>!*

Grace and the Cross Are *One* and the *Same*,
The Emblem of Majesty's Inner Heart Flame,
The Will of the Father, and Intent of the Son,
That <u>All</u> Be Forgiven, *<u>All</u>* Be Made – *<u>One</u>!*

Jesus made a stunning statement that *if* believed, and *<u>correctly</u>* understood, would lay to rest any doubt as to God's ultimate intentions toward men. It is: 'No man **CAN** come to me, except The Father which hath sent Me ***<u>DRAW</u>*** him [*through the <u>Power</u> of the Cross*]: and I will raise him up [to Divine Spiritual, Everlasting Life] at the last day.' (John 6:44) And, again, 'No man **CAN** come unto Me, except it were ***<u>given</u>*** unto him of my Father.' (John 6:65) In this one concept, alone, lies the answer to men's apprehensions and fears regarding any man's fate. Man is to be 'wooed' to the foot of the Cross, ***<u>not</u>*** through external force, but through the sweet and **irresistible** All-Powerful **Allurements** of the Grace-filled Holy Spirit! Once one's conscience is touched, regeneration commences, and the soul *<u>willingly</u>* embraces **The Christ of the Cross**, her Lord! The Ultimate <u>Gift</u> of Grace! **Attractive** *<u>to</u> <u>All</u>!*

**Out from the Cross a *New Universe* 'Wends',
In Every Direction, Its Dominion Extends,
<u>Expanding</u> to Every Dimension we See, A
Brave New World, Marked by
– *<u>Love's</u> <u>Victory</u>!*

The point of the **New Creation** commences *not* with a formerly supposed 'Big Bang', but rather with the *Ever-radiating* Transforming Power and *All-Penetrating* Influence of **The Cross** of **The Christ!** – That same Cross positioned on Calvary's Hill in Palestine some 2000 years ago! The Universe man knows, his very being and world, is being overtaken and incorporated into the **New Reality** birthed from the Cross in a systematic, steady, and progressive way. This is the Plan of God **purposed** in Jesus Christ (Eph. 3:11). What may appear to be setbacks or outright contradictions to this Glorious Truth are merely that – *appearances only!* God's designed outcome is **a foregone conclusion** (Eph. 1:4) – A matter of <u>God's</u> <u>Choice</u> ALONE, *not* of our feeble choosing! How thankful we can be, for we can rest in the avowed **certainty** – *<u>this</u> <u>is</u> <u>so</u>!*

**The *Reach* of the Cross, How <u>Far</u> It Extends Beyond the Yearning Imagination of Men, To the Globe at Hand, and To What Planets There *May* Be, On *<u>Out</u>* Into the Realms – *<u>of Infinity</u>!*

Beloved, one day humanity will be told whether there be other planets, that harbor human life, *people* made in the image and likeness of God. One day, perhaps soon, we will no longer wonder, for we will **know**. Yet, till that day arrives, **what** we <u>CAN</u> know is that The Cross of Jesus, His Victory, **propelled** Him '*<u>far</u> <u>above</u>* **ALL** principality, and power, and might, and dominion, and **every** name, not only in THIS world, but also in that [or those] which is to come [into our knowledge].' (Eph. 1:21) So, whether or not planets are discovered inhabited by humans is really of little import, *relative to* the Lordship of Christ. For scripture clearly tells us that Jesus <u>IS</u> 'the Head over **ALL** [beings].' (Eph. 1:22) Such 'brother' beings would in no way threaten the Truth about Jesus Himself and His All-Embracing Cosmic Role. As **Peace** will be preached to any such beings, *there*, as it has been – *<u>here</u>.* (Eph. 2:17)

Oh! Cross of My Saviour! What Truth You Convey! What _Appeared_ to Be Loss Is _My Gain Every_ Day, My Life's Not Diminished, _Nor Can It Be_, But Will Thrive, Grow, and Bloom – _Thru Eternity_!

The crucifixion of the Lord of Life to all *outward* appearances proclaimed **unimaginable** and **unendurable** LOSS of the most inconceivable kind. The Light of the World – *extinguished!* – Along with His incomparable Words, His matchless Deeds, His Heart-Elevating Promises, and Sacred Love! – _And_ all the Good that *might yet* had been done! It seemed all was over. All past. All was now only a beautiful dream which had failed. **But with the Resurrection** came the Supreme Insight of the Ages to KNOW that 'Nothing REAL can be threatened, nothing UNREAL exists. HEREIN lies The Peace of God!'** Beloved, you can KNOW the Truth of these divine words in your soul, *today*, if you will. **No loss** you have ever experienced is truly a loss at all, as whatever *temporarily* is lost to us, is **permanently** safe and secure in God. And, **will**, at God's appointed time, be **regiven** to us–*once again!*

**I Claim the World for My Own, It is Mine
The Light of My Cross Encircles and Enshrines!
Astride the Wide Globe It Towers and Stands
Affording Protection to – _Every_ _Man_!**

When the Lord willingly forfeited His Life upon the tree of crucifixion, at *that* very moment of His death, a huge surge of dynamic, Supernatural Life Energy was ***released***, infiltrating every atom of the earth's body, saturating every molecule of earth's space! It were as though **a cosmic explosion** was detonated, *so powerful* were its waves! Could this be seen by the naked human eye? No. But spiritual perception verified its existence. The world, and ALL its inhabitants, are **now** under the sole auspices of the Risen Lord. The ownership of the world, and all its populace, has been *wrested* from the Dark One, nevermore to be in *inescapable* bondage or servitude again. And though the **outpicturing** of this Reality is yet to be seen, planet earth and all those who dwell there, **are redeemed!** As the ForceShield of the Cross is impenetrable to Evil, and impervious to anything – _less_ _than_ _Good_!

Oh! Blessed Lord, We Did Not Know
The <u>Depths</u> to Which Your Love Would Go,
For 'Twas <u>*Not*</u> by Crucifixion You Died, But, by
A Method Forgotten – <u>*Long*</u> <u>*Since*</u> <u>*Denied!*</u>

One could hardly imagine any method of execution more brutal than crucifixion – yet, <u>*there*</u> <u>*was*</u> <u>*one!*</u> It has been assumed the terrible assault on our Lord's body, by merciless whipping, impalement of limbs, was the principal means of His death, along with suffocation – and the primary cause of His physical agony. <u>***Not so!***</u> Christ, for a six-hour period, actually was <u>pelted</u> unremittingly with *hundreds* of sharp stones. This is the **only** possible explanation for the final description of Him, where 'His visage was <u>so marred</u> *more than any man,* and His form *more than the sons of men.*' Scripture declares people were 'astonished' when they viewed His mangled body, as '<u>*ALL*</u> [His] bones' were plainly in view! Recall, Jesus' enemies sought to stone Him *repeatedly* during His ministry. Here, while helpless, defenseless, and unguarded, on the cross, they finally got their chance. He **truly** gave [<u>*ALL*</u>] His 'flesh', <u>*as He said He would,*</u> for the life – <u>*of the World!*</u>

Farewell Words

The Psalmist wrote, 'I will lift up my eyes **unto *The* Hills** from which cometh my strength. My **Strength** *cometh from the Lord.*' Calvary was situated at the **base** of a hill, among hills! And it was of ***THIS*** hill David prophetically spoke! There, the **All-Glorious Atonement** of the Lord took place! Utter weakness and helplessness were turned into Glorious **Strength**. The dreadest of Deaths was turned into Triumphant, **Energy-Filled** LIFE! Here, my friend, is a Fount of Strength ready to be poured out **today**, as it was then, in your behalf! Strength first and foremost for your **Spirit** and **Soul**. But, also for your *Mind* and *Body!* So, in your mind's eye, reach back, envision the Christ-affixed wooden beams, or perhaps a purple robe waving in morning breeze. Emanating **Energy** for your empowerment–*is there!*

With Every Good Wish, The Author

Section 2

The Hidden Glories

Of

Our Lord's Resurrection!

Every Morning
__Is__ Easter Morning!
And Each Day,
I More Clearly See.
__Every__ Sorrow
Has *Fled* Tomorrow!
As Joy Is **__Burst__** *__Back__*
– *__Upon__* *__Me__*!

Unbarred Door of Empty Tomb, Barren Slate of Stone, What LIFE Did *Rise* From Thee *That* Day, When God Did Claim – *His Own!*

The Event of the ***Resurrection!*** The barren slate of stone, meant to be a death slab, for the *Dearest* and *Best*, became a birth dais (or platform) from which Life Everlasting *arose!* The emptiness of the tomb was filled with Fullness of the Resurrection '*Flame*' or energy, while the boulder meant to bar, was itself banned from ever obstructing the **Light** – evermore! But few know, **more than** Jesus *alone* arose That Day! A **world** of men and women arose, as they were *enshrined* in the heart of our Lord! Their loving memory, the Divine Image, of those both past, then-present, *and future*, was now raised up with Him in *prefigurement* of their actual rebirth! *All* **mankind** rose That Day, *in the Father's mind*, now **assured** by the *Heart* of the Son! What **Joy** He knew! –And unprecedented **Rapture**! – *as will you!*

I Look Upon the First Witness to Faith's Foundation, As 'Fitting' as Hands in Gloves, And What Should My *Startled* Eyes Behold But, the *Left-Behind* Linens – *of Love!*_

The first two people to enter the earth-hewn chamber were not persuaded of **Life's Victory** over death solely on the basis of an empty sepulcher. *But*, **what** Peter and John beheld left no room for doubt in their minds – 'the linen clothes lying' before them, and the napkin facial covering 'wrapped together in a place [apart] *by itself*'. THEN – they believed! – But *WHY?* – **What** was the **significance** of mentioning the condition of these two items? The removed facial napkin revealed the opening to an **empty shell!** A napkin wrapped, linens *unwrapped!* Though the body was gone, its contours were preserved by 100 pounds of **hardened** myrrh and aloes! Jesus' body had *escaped* the burial garments, leaving them in the form of an *unopened* **cocoon!** THIS was the Miracle! This was the All-convincing, empirical **Proof** – *left by Love!*

**Oh, Sepulcher! Bathed in Brilliant Light,
Your Door's Flung Open *in The Night*
The Stars Which Canopied Above
Recede Before the Light – *of Love!***

It is likely, dear friend, you believe that Jesus rose from the grave at the *dawn* of the first day of the week. Presumably, the majestic fiery orb whose given name is Sol (as in *Sol*ar system), was *already* cresting the horizon as Jesus stepped out of the tomb. But, **you would be mistaken**! His re-entrance into the world was not simultaneous with the rising of the sun, but rather, ***prior to*** its ascent into the sky. The record clearly states 'when it was ***yet dark***,' Mary Magdalene 'seeth the stone taken away.' The *significance?* It was **Jesus**, now, *not* the sun, that ushers in the dawning of each new day! That gives **True Life** to the world! No earthly ***nor*** *spiritual light*, however bright, has preeminence over *Him*. The **Supreme** Light of the World, in His resplendent Glory, pales all else – *from view!*

**In Wild Flower-Strewn Garden
The Lord of Life Stood Forth and Smiled,
When Hearing the Birds so Joyously Sing, 'God
Has Ushered In – *<u>Now</u>* Eternal – *<u>Spring!</u>*'**

There in a beautiful garden, where perhaps a gentle stream did flow, or a hardwood bench offered seating to mourners or reminiscers, and a winding mosaic stone path led by each entry into earthen tombs, **He stood forth**. *Alone*. How sweet the birds' carols were to His ears! How fragrant, too, was the morning air! But, He was waiting *<u>for</u> <u>her</u>*, whom He knew would come. At last she approached. He observed her so tenderly, lovingly, for she was grieving so. Then, **He spoke**. Her tear-flooded eyes blurred her vision, and she did not recognize Him – till He said, *'Mary!'* She flung herself into His arms as He embraced her. At *that* very moment, she **knew**, Spring would ever live in her heart. Hope ever shine from her eyes! For God's Son was **Born Anew**! *Eternal* Life! *Eternal* Love! – *<u>Evermore!</u>*

A Wondrous Hidden Truth Revealed
**_Why_ the Chamber's Stone Was Moved About,
'Twas to Let the Bewildered Disciples Rush _In
NOT_, to Let the Risen Lord – _Walk Out_!**

The huge rounded stone rolled away at the command of the angel. This occurred the _very moment_ Mary Magdala and a female companion arrived. Most certainly, you'd think, they witnessed Jesus emerge from the tomb. But, my friend, *they did not!* The angel told them, 'He is [**already**] risen. **He Is _NOT Here!_**' This, though the tomb **was still barred** – _up to the very moment they came!_ Not surprisingly, then, ***not one*** of the Gospels say Jesus 'walked out of the tomb'! For in His resurrected state, His body possessed undreamt of celestial powers, allowing Him to ***pass through*** solid granite walls, or vanish, at will! And, undoubtedly, He did! This manner of 'escape' served to even _more prove_ His **Absolute Sovereignty** over _all_ forces of Nature. Jesus had traveled **inter-dimensionally** to leave the tomb!AllPower in Heaven&earth–_wasHis!_

***One* Moment Linens Lay Wrapped About
He Who Had Shouldered The Wooden Beam,
But, the *Following* Moment <u>No</u> Eye Could Discern
For Miracles *Aren't* Meant – *to Be Seen!***

Had you witnessed what transpired in the inky black tomb at the **very moment** of Resurrection, *<u>what would you have seen</u>?* Would you have observed 'color' returning to the lifeless, battered body of the Lord? Would the pale 'whiteness' of death gradually have given way to the pink flushing of life? Had you been <u>*alongside*</u> His body, would you have felt warmth returning where only cold had been just before? And might you have perceived the Lord's chest begin to rise and fall as respiration resumed? His eyes slowly opening, and Him sitting up from the sleep of death? **No, my friend, *<u>not</u> <u>at</u> <u>all</u>!*** The Lord's body, as Saint Paul affirmed, would have risen 'in the ***<u>twinkling</u>*** of an eye', *<u>instantaneously</u>*, into the Realm of Spirit! That body, **transformed** by Supernatural Power, would have simply <u>vanished</u> from earthly sight! Contoured linens visible only – *<u>left</u> <u>all</u> <u>alone</u>!*

The Earth Did <u>Boom</u>! The Sky Was *<u>Rent</u>!* Applauds to the *Angel* Heaven-Sent, <u>All</u> Tombs Were *'<u>Opened</u>'* on That Fateful Day, When God Bid the Boulder – *<u>Roll</u> <u>Away</u>!*

Tell me, caring friend, was the garden tomb the *<u>only</u>* 'last abode' opened on Resurrection Day? Strange as it may sound, actually *<u>many</u>* other graves, burial sites, and tombs found themselves opening that very same day. St. Matthew tells us 'the earth did quake, and the rocks were split; and *<u>the graves were opened</u>*, and **many bodies** of the saints that slept *<u>were raised</u>*, And came *<u>out of</u>* the graves *<u>after</u>* His Resurrection, and **went into the holy city**, [appearing to] **many**.' But, something more happened! In Christ's mind, **all** graves had already been opened, by *HIM*, as His risen Life now *<u>assured</u>* theirs! His mystic disciple quoted Him, '<u>**All**</u> [who] are in the graves shall hear His Voice, And *<u>shall come forth!</u>*' Some to Life, and some to judgment (correction). An **invisible** chain reaction started on the Day, *<u>that</u>* stone – *<u>was rolled away</u>!*

**Oh, Mary! Dear, Sweet Mary!
With _What_ Wisdom Did You 'See',
The Sacred Rite of _Mystical_ Love
Joining the Saviour – _to Thee!_**

Perhaps, she was _**there**_. *Someone* prepared the food and drink, set the table, and even served those present. This was, after all, the customary task of women in that day. Then, she likely receded into the background – and _**listened**_. Her Lord then said something **wholly unexpected**, borrowing from a _**then-present**_ tradition of a groom seeking his prospective bride to accept his life for hers in return. Slightly paraphrased, Jesus said, _**'This is the cup of a New Covenant which I offer to you!'**_ The Apostles *recognized* the words as those from a **marriage proposal**, but were perplexed as to their meaning. Yet, somehow, Mary _**knew!**_ For when she first met her risen Lord, she joyfully cried out, '**Rabboni!**', whose variant meaning is, _**'My Husband!'**_ His Resurrection '*sealed*' a new relationship, having been 'wed' to mankind! – _**Evermore!**_

Reputed To Have Said 'Touch Me _Not_' Jesus Bid Mary '_Withdraw_' We're Taught, Yet, How Could This Be, As 'Twas SHE – _Love Sought!_

Love is quoted as saying to dear Mary Magdalene, at His first _post_-Resurrection appearance, _'Touch Me not,_ for I AM not yet ascended to My Father'. Now, did it ever strike you, my friend, as peculiar that Love, Who ever sought **union** and **joining** with _all_ – should say, in effect, 'Keep your distance, come no closer, do not approach me'? Yes, strange that would be, _if_ indeed Love said this – _but Love didn't!_ The correct Greek rendering is, 'Do not _keep_ [or continue] _clinging_ to Me'! His beloved Mary was holding Him in **full embrace**, her arms _tightly wrapped_ around His Person, which He permitted _gladly_. But, after an appropriate period of time, Love then gently asked she release Him, and let Him go, as He had work yet to do. The message is clear! Love _**always**_ seeks contact – _never distance!_

Easter In My Heart Each Morn
Beholding His Glory, I AM Reborn,
Every Day I Rejoice Tho Drear or Bright
I Bask In My Saviour's – _Resurrection Light!_

When, my friend, each morning, you first become aware you have become awakened from sleep, what thoughts do you entertain? Do the words, **'Lord Jesus, Good Morning!** _I Love Thee, I Adore Thee!'_ spontaneously arise in your heart? Do you envision Him standing there before you in resplendent Glory, _fresh arisen_ – from the grave? Can you sense the subtle emanation of inherent, indestructible **Eternal Life** streaming out from His Divine Person – toward you? And are you warmed by His Love that knows **_no judgment, nor condemnation_**, but only acceptance of and unity with you? Can you say, beloved, as did John, 'We **beheld** His **Glory**, the _Glory_ as of the Only-begotten of the Father.' 'And of His **Fullness** have we all received.' Say it, with sincere awe and reverence, and any emptiness you may have felt will gladly be **filled** – _by Him!_

So *Baffling* A Paradox
Back to Life In Three Days!
<u>*Yet*</u>, the Broken <u>Body</u> of My Lord
Was <u>*NOT*</u> Healed – <u>*But Was Raised*</u>*!*

Did you know, dear friend, the **body temple** that had allowed such divinely exquisite expressions of Love by the Lord of Life <u>*never*</u> received Divine Healing! – <u>*Never*</u> underwent supernatural repair! 'How foolish!', you exclaim. 'To be raised back to life demands bodily healing!' Are you *so sure?* The Lord's body was <u>*so*</u> marred, had faced such <u>*horrific*</u> destruction, He <u>*no longer appeared human*</u>! So much flesh had been mercilessly **torn** from His person, it was no longer there *TO BE* healed! Something far more wonderful was required. So, the Lord's body was *transformed*, instead! Actually, it was **<u>RE</u>-created**! The molecules comprising His physical body were *transmuted* by Spirit and **re-formed** to express His perfect likeness! Only the most prominent scars on His hands, side, and feet were replicated, **proving** beyond doubt – <u>*It was He*</u>*!*

**The Great Stone Many *Tons* Did Weigh
Yet, at a *<u>Finger's</u>* Touch Did Roll Away,
And, All Other Barriers Did <u>Cease</u> To Be
When the Master Triumphed – <u>*O'er*</u> <u>*Calvary*</u>!**

What you may little realize, dear heart, is that the massive 'immovable' boulder which barred a tomb door was actually the <u>***least***</u> of the obstacles to the liberation and full expression of the Master's Life! Though fullness of Divinity in flesh, that *very* flesh imposed limits upon Him. It was not until **<u>after</u>** the Resurrection, that *Rebirthing* into the limitless Kingdom of God, was He given '**All power** in Heaven – **<u>*and in earth*</u>**'! This meant that even the dimensions of time and space could not hold Him! Those barriers were **abolished** <u>*as*</u> He passed through solid walls in His disciples' presence, vanished and re-appeared before their sight. **<u>*Nothing*</u>** could any longer *confine* Him! Recall, He even said He would be with each person <u>individually</u> – *<u>more than</u>* **one place – at a time!** His Triumph over Death was **total** Mastery – <u>*over Life*</u>!

Shut In By Darkness The Lord's _Body_ Lay _Devoid_ of All Life and Cold as Clay! Yet, Destined To Be Raised Again, But _Not_ by the Father, by the Light – _Within!_

Lovely friend, Jesus made several declarative statements, overlooked by most, regarding the **agency** of His resurrection. 'For as the Father hath Life in **_Himself_**, so hath He given to the Son TO HAVE LIFE **_IN_** HIMSELF'. This was **God-Life**, **_Eternal_ Life**, in the depths of His _Immaterial_ Spirit! He possessed It as a then-Present Reality. Recall, He said, 'Destroy _this_ temple, and in three days **I** [Jesus] will raise it up'. To which John adds, 'But He spoke of the temple of _His body_.' Again, Jesus said, '**I** [myself] have the Power to lay [my life] down, **_and I have Power to take it [up] again!_** This commandment [or _empowerment_] have I received of my Father.' It was Jesus' **Immortal** Spirit which **breathed** life back into His _lifeless_ body! His deathless, Divine Consciousness had lived on! He truly **_was_**, as He said, the Resurrection–and _the Life!_

The <u>First</u> Words Behind Doors Spoken Were Meant *<u>Not</u>* Simply to Endear, But To *<u>Release</u>* His Disciples Inner Selves And <u>Break</u> their Pale – *of Fear!*

The Master's seemingly simple greeting, He voiced when He appeared before His gathered followers behind barred doors, **'Peace Be Unto You!'**, were words chosen with great care! Of all the words He *<u>could</u>* have first spoken, such as 'Friends!', or 'Do not be afraid!', or even 'Greetings All!', He chose **'Peace'**! *Why? <u>Because</u> <u>authentic</u> <u>Spiritual</u> <u>Peace</u>, <u>ALONE</u>, <u>is</u> <u>the</u> <u>antidote</u> <u>to</u> <u>fear</u>!* His disciples were terrified the dread Roman authorities were going to apprehend, imprison, and torture them – *as they did their beloved Jesus!* But the disciples were *<u>already</u>* in a **prison** of their own making! And ONLY **The Peace of God** could <u>release</u> them from this torment! He, as always, gave them what they **most** needed, bequeathed by *<u>His</u>* **Resurrection** – the Invincible Peace to know all would be well – *<u>come</u> <u>what</u> <u>may</u>!*

**Lord, I *Drink* In Of Thy Light
Behold! Emanation! *So* Subtle, Bright,
The <u>Resurrection</u> Glow About Thy Form
Within Me, Now, *New* Consciousness – *Is <u>Born</u>!***

Did you know, precious friend, scientists now recognize and classify the vibrational energy we call light – *as a <u>nutrient</u>?* This is because our emotional well-being is fed, is nourished, by this wavelength of *<u>non-physical</u>* particles. The full-spectrum light of the sun enters our very beings through the windows of our souls, *the eyes,* and causes chemical reactions to raise our mood and uplift our disposition. You need only determine to see Jesus in ***His <u>Resurrected</u> state*** in your *<u>imagination</u>* to partake of this healing, regenerative **Life <u>energy</u>**. Colors ranging from intense snow-white to varying degrees of sun yellow. *<u>Feel</u>* this radiation infiltrate your being with waves of refreshment, strength, and stability. Partake of <u>this</u> **ultimate** nutrient, and experience elevated consciousness where mental burdens grow smaller, and **life grows** much larger, immeasurably –*<u>for you</u>!*

The Light Did Arc from Earth to Sky
A Radiant 'Rainbow' Burst on High,
Yet, <u>*Who*</u> Did Witness This Marvel Supreme
When Christ Did Prefigure – <u>*God's Dream*</u>!

Believing friend, some say there were <u>*no*</u> witnesses to the singularly most important event in earth's history. **<u>All</u>** admit to an empty tomb, but skeptics say none can <u>*validate*</u> the reality of resurrection as there were no eyewitnesses. <u>*Is this true?*</u> Actually, there were **<u>*several*</u>** highly trained Roman soldiers who themselves did **<u>seal</u>** the tomb and stand guard through the night. And after the grave gave up its most prized possession, **<u>*they*</u>** behold the tomb open wide its door, accompanied by **dazzling bursts** of Light emanating from an angel! Moreover, at least **three** angels participated in this greatest of Miracles! For two were **<u>*in*</u>** the tomb itself! No **<u>*credible*</u>** witnesses? The soldiers bore witness to priests, and Holy angels to the disciples. A greater witness? Jesus' appearances and testimony–<u>*Himself*</u>!

**Glorious Morning! Jesus Is *Risen!*
No Tomb Could Hold Him! *No* Stone Could
Seal! *Glorious*Morning!The *World* Has a Saviour
Jesus, the Lamb of God! The King–*of the World!***

To what end, dear friend, did Jesus suffer, die, and be buried above the ground? To what **purpose** was He then raised back to Life from the dead? Few know His Life's Mission *was* to bring Peace on Earth! Yet, did He not say, **'I came NOT to bring Peace, but a sword'?** Yes, not universal peace, at that time. *But what was that 'sword'?* The Apostle Paul wrote, 'the sword of the Spirit *IS* **the Word of God.**' Jesus 'unsheathed' that sword, and brought new, *Calm*-**bestowing** words never before spoken. And though His words were not meant, then, to bring peace to the nations, they **were intended** to bring Peace to **legions** of receptive hearts, as many as would receive Him! And the day all hearts know *that* Peace, our **planet** will know peace! The blade of the righteous sword, *as then*, brings Peace – *still!*

**A *Strangely* Beautiful Phrase I Hear
Ever Circling Down, Through the Years,
My Heart Is *Held Captive* to A Verse *So* True
A Glory Proclaimed – *Ever-Lastingly New!***

Where, my lovely friend, can your *release* from sorrow and regret for the past, and worry and anxiety over the future be found? True Faith provides you with the answer – **'He *IS* Risen!'** Yet, pause for a moment, and consider, just how **unusual**, even *strange,* these words sound! We are *not* told He '*has* risen,' or '*had* risen,' or even that 'He *rose*.' Rather, 'He *IS* Risen!' The language, **deliberately** and **carefully** chosen, conveys a sense of timelessness, of *unending* occurrence. It were as if this experience is ever *new*, ever *young*, ever *just-born!* Though an actual historical event, a mystical component is clearly conveyed – *The eternally resurrected NOW!* **THIS** is where our blessed Saviour resides, where we will, too. Where liberation from all suffering is promised –*and assured!*

**How *Awesome*, Thru Faith, Is the Sight
Of Our Radiant, and Now <u>*Risen*</u>, King of Life,
<u>Brother</u> to Humanity Still, Though Exalted
And Glorified – <u>*by*</u> <u>*God's*</u> <u>*Will*</u>!**

How do you, my hopeful friend, envision the One Who claimed to be 'The Way, the **Reality**, and the Life'? Do you see Him in an ethereal realm as a kind of specter or disembodied soul? Recall, Jesus assured us of **precisely** the *opposite!* He said '**Handle** Me and see, for a spirit hath <u>*not*</u> flesh and bones as you see <u>*Me*</u> have.' The Truth is, the Man Jesus has shed **none** of His Humanity! Indeed, He is the *<u>Fullness</u>* of what humans are destined to become! And added to this is the now-unveiled *<u>Fullness</u>* of His **Divinity**! The two natures, forming the one nature – of *the Divine Man!* Or is it the *perceived* two natures have actually been **only** the One Nature – *all along?* Either way, you can be sure the streaming emanation from His Being is Resplendent –with a Divine, yet **so-*<u>Human</u>***– *<u>Glory</u>!*

What *Does* the Resurrection Teach If Not that God His Promise Will Keep, There Is *Purpose* Sublime, tho Sorrows Grow A <u>Reason</u> For ALL Heartache – *and Woe!*

After the crucifixion – comes – the *Resurrection!* When suffering appears to be the most pointless, the most meaningless, the most nonsensical and absurd, THAT is when we must **remind** ourselves tho suffering is **never** created by God, He *allows* it and uses it to fashion and mold us into stronger beings! More compassionate beings! Wiser beings! To all outward appearances, the destructive assault leveled upon our Lord's body and spirit on the Cross was such a waste and absurdity. **What** good could *possibly* come from this? – As the beautiful body temple of Christ was violated, dishonored, and progressively rendered totally functionless. Beloved, what happened to Jesus, in some *shape, form,* or *fashion* – happens to EVERY son and daughter of God! No one's exempt! Such is the nature of the matter Cosmos! Yet, we can know restoration follows, as sure as Dawn – *<u>overtakes night!</u>*

The *Real* Meaning of Easter
Was Not Just a Stone Rolled *Away*,
But, IS Experienced by Receptive Souls
As the <u>Victory</u> of Love – *<u>Each</u> <u>Day</u>!*

What, my friend, is the **True** Meaning of *Resurrection Morn*? That the world's **greatest** <u>outward</u> miracle took place near Gethsemane Grove is indisputable by those who have studied the **infallible proofs**! He Who *was* dead, against all odds, *took death captive*, and transcended an 'inescapable' grave. As Jesus' actual physical body, battered and torn beyond recognition, which Jesus *had* inhabited, was restored to Life! A **culmination** of one increasingly greater Victory – after another! Yet, the forces of *anti-Life* were defeated even *before* they did their worst! *<u>This</u> <u>is</u> <u>the</u> <u>lesson for</u> <u>us</u>!* **We stand as Victors even in the midst of sorrows, *seeming* defeats, and *apparent* failure!** United with His Spirit, we can rejoice and praise God for Love's Victory over <u>*All*</u> Life's Trials! And when we do, a spirit of Trust, a *<u>Certainty</u>* of **Love's Triumph** in our Spirit and Hearts, daily – will prevail!

**Beautiful Saviour! Oh, Glorious Sight
Clothes Now _Shimmering_ Unearthly White!
JOY Ever-Streaming Forth From Your Face,
Your Heart Ever-Pouring Forth – _Endless_ _Grace!_**

'Father, forgive them, they know _**not**_ what they do,' you recall, this most beautiful of all men said. He forgave all – **_ALL_** departures from the Law of Love, no matter the degree of expression! The most _unimaginable_ acts He forgave, as He does still, and _ever_ _will!_ For He knows that the **Victory** He secured will **one day redeem** the blackest inhuman heart, the furthest fallen soul! This, my friend, **IS** the **AWE-Inspiring** and **Worship-Compelling** Grace of the Son of God! There is **no end** to His Patience and Love. They **cannot** be exhausted! _Nor_ diminished! _Nor_ changed! This, dear friend, is a Saviour worthy of all worship! **_THIS_** is the **Risen**, and **_Now_-Ascended** Lord! **Grace** He forever offers – **Love _beyond_ All Love!** A Power **_beyond_** all Comprehension, but not beyond – _God's_ _Reach!_

THE GOD-*ORDAINED* DREAM!
A Glorious Quest in Christ's Heart Arose
A Heaven-Born *Dream* Thought *Impossible*
By Those, Who View It as an *Unreachable* Star,
Yet Their Vision be Dim, Seeing – *from Afar!*

Jesus committed Himself unreservedly, whole-heartedly, irrevocably to the Attainment of **One** Stupendous Goal, a humanly *thought-to-be,* **Impossible Dream**! (Col. 1:20) So **important** was this, He pledged His Eternal Allegiance. This 'Dream' He could not share with most, and even angelic powers doubted the possibility of *such a* **Supreme** Universal Wonder being brought to pass; particularly, Christ's capacity to 'make it so' as the captain of humanity's salvation (Heb. 2:10). Yet, this God-Man ***chose*** to 'Dream the *Impossible* Dream', to 'fight the *unbeatable* foe', and to make this His **personal** Quest. More importantly, He ***believed* HE**, alone, could **'*Right* THE Unrightable Wrong'** – by the UNDOING of all effects of sin – even to *redeeming the totality of the world back to God!* But, with Christ's Resurrection, Heaven's annals recorded **His Dream** to be a, **now**, foregone conclusion! A **true** future Reality – *Certain to be!*

Farewell Words

Beloved friend, you can receive all the Love your heart can store, *today*. And along with that Love will come Joy, and Peace, and Contentment. **And *<u>other</u>*-worldly** Calm and Trust. Who will offer this boon to you? Who ***<u>alone</u>*** possesses such treasures? *None other than the Rose portrayed in the Song of Solomon!* This precious 'Flower of the Father' was **raised to Life** after It was so brutally crushed. Yet, It blossomed forth from the dark earth, and Its fragrance is spreading throughout the land, **destined** to infiltrate *<u>every</u>* molecule of air, permeate *<u>every</u>* atom of earth! This will take place *'At the dispensation of the **<u>Fullness</u>** of Times.'* A period known only to the Father. Therefore, despair not! ***Your*** door is <u>not</u> draped by a shroud of mourning, but by a garment of golden threads wove from **the Light** of Resurrection's Rose! Be thankful *<u>The Christ Tale Never Told</u>* has, **now**, **been told** to you! Ponder It! Thrill to It! That your Life may be **transformed** by So Miraculous, *<u>Astonishing Love</u>!*

With Every Good Wish, The Author

Part IV

The Hidden Nature and Unknown Meaning *of* Jesus!

Their *Supreme* Reality!

Part IV – Introduction

Part IV of this book, in particular, is the result of one man's heartfelt and lifelong efforts to probe the heights and **depths** of God's Love. Men believe they comprehend what Divine Love actually IS – Its true nature and capabilities – yet they are mistaken. God's Love is *Beyond* **anything** the world, as a whole, has ever dreamed! So GREAT is this Love, It is *far more wonderful* that men have **dared** to imagine. The Gentle Galilean taught Mercy, Forgiveness, and Compassion, **above all**, and one day the outcome of <u>His</u> commitment to these Virtues will astonish – and redeem, *a world!*

I Peter 2:9 'His <u>*Marvelous*</u> Light'!

There
with Lambkin
The Infant Lay,
Eyes of the Most Holy
Luminous Ray,
Sent For
The Lost To _Make_
Them Found,
In This Grotto
of
– _Bethlehem_ Town!

Part IV – Contents (Page 1 of 3)

In Him Was Life, God-Life Supreme
Infinite Beauty! To Earth You Did Come!
Envision Now The Ultimate Man
You Are Known as The Living Saviour
Was Jesus Ever Disappointed or Surprised
A Precious 'Preoccupation' We Do Find
Who Can Fathom the Extent of God's Reach
I Stand at the Head of the Human Race
So Little Have People Realized
Oh, Consummate Beauty! What Can It Be
No Deeper Truth Can Be Known
Man IS Divine, When He Knows He's Divine
God, The Great Awakener, Has Chosen to
In the Still of the Night
No Greater Reason to Believe Could Be
I, Thy Saviour, Can Change Anyone
Clear Your Mind of All But Me
Jesus, Universal Man, That You Are
I Am the Light For All Time
Lord Jesus, Strange Words You Did Say
Beauty Will Save the World
I Gave My Uttermost and More
Judge Not, I Admonished All
The World Stands Forgiven

Part IV – Contents

No Greater Creed Did the Master Give
Your Eyes! Such Eyes! Oh, Lord of Love
Best-Loved Prayer of Our Saviour
You Can Believe That This Is So
Beloved Jesus, Alone You Do Stand
Another Stupendous Achievement
This Lofty View of Atonement
Jesus, We May Say If We Dare
The Horizontal Plane, We See
Ascended Master, Lord, You Are
Jesus Was a Super Scientist Some Do Say
Oh! Heart of Hearts! I Reach Out Now!
Oh! Perfect Love! All Human Thought
This Cross was New, Had Never Been
There Are No 'Lost' Teachings

Concluding Reflections

I AM The Way, But Others Say
I AM The Truth, But Others Proclaim
I AM The Life, But Others Teach
The Light of The World I Said I AM
The Great Achievement, Now Achieved

Part IV – Contents

(Page 3 of 3)

Final Note

The Spirit of Victory!

Precious One, I Would Have You Know
Receive, Now, My Greatest Gift of All
The Mantle of My Glorious Victory

**In Him Was Life, God-*Life* Supreme
Far *Beyond* Man's Wildest Dream, He Came
To Give *<u>Himself</u>* So All Men Might Know, The
Depths The Father's Love – *<u>Would Go</u>!*ˇ**

What, beloved, WAS <u>this</u> Life that John proclaimed as coming into the world? In the person of Jesus? *It was the <u>Fullness</u> of the Life of God made manifest in Man!* Eternal Life! Divine Life! Unconquerable Life! Expressed as Unimagined Love! Yet, deep as was the descent of our Lord from Heaven to earth, **deeper** still are the depths of the human soul fashioned in the Image of God! *The Lord did then, is now, and will plumb the depths of men's minds, then their hearts, and thereafter their souls and spirits!* **To the Innermost Reaches of man's Being the Father's Love dare go**. Its Lofty aim? No depth of depravity could turn away a Love that awakens, convicts, and heals those lost to themselves, but **never** to God! What yet remains? Only the Fullness of Time when **every** depth will have been plumbed, and then – ***<u>every Soul reborn</u>!***

**Infinite Beauty! To Earth You Did Come!
With Words *Never* Spoken, *Nor* Heard by No
One, Molecules of the Air Did Transmit the
Sound, *Of* A <u>Voice</u> *Never* Imagined,
A <u>Love</u> – *<u>Never Found</u>!*ns*

As wonderful, and as new, and as captivating as were the words of our Saviour, what might the **sound** of *His voice* have been like? Without a doubt, its sure **uniqueness** was only matched by His words! The people exclaimed, 'This man speaks with <u>authority, *not*</u> as the scribes!' He conveyed this with His tone of voice, inflection, cadence of speech, and volume. He was the Living **Word**, or ***<u>Spokes</u> <u>person</u>*** of God our Father! There was a *gentleness*, yet a *strength*, in His vocal expression, a wisdom, a Love – never before felt by audible means. To hear Him **speak** was to be immediately arrested by a personality, a Presence, that **quieted** the **soul** – and disarmed the defensive heart. They, then, knew here was <u>*no*</u> ordinary man! For many, His unhurried Voice would linger in their minds! **Impossible** of being forgotten – *<u>or</u> <u>to forget</u>!*

**Envision Now the _Ultimate_ Man
Who Came to Show Man's Destiny
Reach Out With Your Mind to Grasp
If You Can, The <u>Illumined</u> One – _from <u>Galilee</u>!_**

When Jesus walked among men, He did so as a giant among spiritual infants. He was a **living window** to the future, providing man a three-dimensional view of a time when man and deity would be **joined** as one! He was the **end** (God's desired Aim) displayed for all the world to see at the **beginning**. He was the **unveiling** of the far distant future when the work of physical creation will have been completed and its **purpose realized**. _A PERFECT and <u>perfected</u> Man!_ Scripture tells us that in order to bring earth's sons unto glory, He was <u>MADE</u> perfect – by the things which He _<u>suffered</u>_. Mankind, beloved, is undergoing the same process. Though man walks in spiritual darkness, **<u>He</u>** stands out as **the Beacon Light** _modeling_ **the Life** _of_ God as **the Way** _to_ God! There is purpose in suffering! **Compassion's Power** is being formed – _<u>in us</u>!_

You Are Known as The Living Saviour Lord, But *What* Are You Saving Us *From*, As The Ultimate Power Against Us Is Neither 'The World, the Flesh' – *Nor 'Dark One'!*

Beloved friend, what do you consider to be your greatest enemy? What is mankind's most formidable foe? Traditionally, religion has said the **allure** of the world, the **temptations** of the flesh, and the clever **deceptions** of 'the adversary' were the greatest forces arrayed against man, calculated to surely destroy him! Granted, they have caused much havoc upon the earth, but **none** are the **principle** reason Christ died to remedy. For the greatest enemy is our lower, false selves! *Jesus came to save each and every one of us – from ourselves!* Our false thinking, erroneous perceptions, selfish attitudes, ego-centric outlook. **Will He succeed**? Or can our little, immature selves prove to be impervious to His enormous, wholly mature, **Irresistible** Self? God *will free* our True Self, then all other foes will **lose their power**, automatically – *forever!*

Was Jesus *Ever* Disappointed or Surprised By Men Who Did *Not* Have Spiritual Eyes, Turning Away from Truth as They Could *Away* from The Lord of – *All Good!*

Did you know, beloved, the common conception among many Christians is that Jesus suffered great disappointment and sorrow, even *surprise*, over the fact *so many people* did not believe nor understand Him. Even theologians state Jesus felt utter incredulity (could scarcely believe) people would not accept Him and aspects of His message – with gladness, eagerness, and haste. **How erroneous is this teaching!** It is true Jesus, on several occasions, did voice the expression '*How is it* that you do not understand?' *as IF* asking a question He did not know the answer to. **But**, knowing 'No man **CAN** come to Me [and understand Me], *except* the Father which hath sent Me **draw** him', this could not have been the case. Had *tone of voice* been recorded, His meaning would have been clear, as there was **no note** of personal inquiry, but rather a **prodding** to others to examine their motives & mode–*of thinking!*

**A Precious 'Preoccupation' We Do Find
Ever and <u>Always</u> Uppermost on His Mind,
To Seek Out and Locate <u>*All*</u> Those Gone Astray,
And Set Them Back on – <u>*the Glorious Way*</u>*!*

In twelve words *alone* the **Mission Statement** of Jesus Christ is proclaimed: **'The Son of Man is come to SAVE that which *was* lost'** (Matt. 18:11). His **Prime Objective** was to ensure that '**nothing** be lost' – whether fragments of food, or no doubt, men's souls (John 6:12). Satisfied with <u>nothing</u> <u>less</u> than the 'finding' of **all** wayward souls, and their conversion, Jesus time and again spoke of recovering the 'lost' – whether a lost *coin*, a lost *sheep*, or a lost *prodigal son*. And Scripture makes it clear that His **Principal Concern** was to 'lose [<u>*no*</u> <u>*one*</u>]' (John 18:9). In fact, unlike search and rescue operations conducted by men, which at some point must be aborted, His searches <u>***NEVER are***</u> *[****'****<u>until</u> <u>He</u> <u>find</u> <u>it</u>****'*** *–* ***<u>the</u> <u>one</u> <u>lost</u>****]!* (Luke 15:4) Beloved, those that are considered 'lost' simply have the Gospel *hid* from them (II Cor. 4:3), but **Its glorious Light** will illumine them – <u>*once they are found*</u>*!*

**Who Can Fathom the <u>Extent</u> of God's Reach
To Redeem Each, and *Every* Soul from Above,
Save She Who Is <u>Plunged</u> by the Spirit Into
The *<u>Depths</u>* of the Heart – *<u>of</u> <u>Love</u>!***

What are the ***<u>heights</u>*** to which interstellar space extends? Scientists tell us as far as they can tell, that which lies between the galaxies extends forever. When they peer within the atom, into its ***<u>depths</u>***, they are continually discovering smaller and smaller particles. But, as immense and mind-boggling as these distances are, they are as **nothing** compared to ***<u>the</u> <u>DEPTHS</u> <u>of</u> <u>the</u> <u>HEART</u> <u>of</u> <u>God's</u> <u>Love</u>***! Paul declared, 'For I am persuaded *<u>neither</u>* [cosmic] **height** nor [earthly] **depth** shall be able to separate us from the Love of God, which is in Christ Jesus, our Lord.' This means, beloved, the Saviour's Love is **limitless** in Its Scope! To plumb its depths can, in one sense, be done! But, **only** a Miracle of God, a revelation, will allow one to grasp this Truth. Yet, God will **one day** persuade all – *<u>as</u> <u>He</u> <u>did</u> <u>Paul</u>!*

**I Stand at the Head of the Human Race
As Its Guardian, *Good* Shepherd, and King,
For One Day <u>ALL</u> *Will* Bow Before Me Now
And In Adoration, My Praises – <u>*Sing*</u>!**

'At the name of Jesus **<u>every</u>** knee should bow, of things in heaven, of things in earth, and things under the earth; and that **<u>every</u>** tongue should confess that Jesus Christ is Lord, <u>*to the glory of God the Father*</u>.' The bowing is voluntary; the confession of complete free will! **All beings**, in every realm, are included. This is the **true** meaning! For *nothing less*, beloved, would be to the complete and maximal **glory** of the Creator! Proving His Sovereignty! Demonstrating His **All-Powerful Love**! God's glory would be diminished if **<u>*only*</u>** one solitary soul refused to bow, or was forced to bow through coercion. But, no! It will all be <u>*to God's Glory!*</u> **<u>Not</u> His shame!** – in failing to win back to him any estranged heart! All glory is worthy of being ascribed to Him, as ALL finally, ultimately, joyfully, and thankfully confess – <u>*Jesus IS Lord!*</u>

**So Little Have People Realized
Just How <u>GREAT</u> Was His Victory,
For *<u>Not</u>* Even GOD, Had *<u>Ever</u>* Raised
A Soul Swallowed by Death – *<u>As</u> <u>Was</u> <u>He</u>!***

Seeker of deeper Truth, the bodily resurrection of Jesus, *great as it was*, was **not** the Supreme Miracle of the Ages! The forces of anti-Life actually **knew** Jesus *would* be raised, as the Creator had restored life to others – *<u>prior</u>* to Jesus birth! No, the Untold, Unrecognized, Greater Victory, indeed, the **GREATEST** Victory, was Jesus' ability to withstand all the demoniacal furies of anti-Life, endure their onslaught to His *<u>Inner</u>* Person, and STILL remain the pure, unadultured, *<u>Sweetness</u> <u>of</u> <u>Innocence</u>* of God's Love! Anti-Good was **convinced** there would be irreparable scars to His Psyche, which would **permanently** destroy His capacity to Love Unconditionally. *Yet*, even Evil was <u>astounded</u>! How *<u>proud</u>* we can be of our Saviour! **This**, then, was the **<u>Greatest</u> Miracle**! That of Indestructible, Incorruptible, Everlastingly Living – *<u>Holy</u> <u>Love</u>!*

Oh, Consummate Beauty! *What* **Can It Be But, The Saviour's** *Streaming* **Love Towards Me! Denied** *No* **Other, Though Unbelieving Are** *Till* **the Day They Embrace –** *This Morning Star!*

Do you know, dear friend, what it actually **IS** that will *ultimately* save men? Is it the *warning* of punishment – or the *promise* of reward? **Neither one**! What will melt the hearts of men – penetrate the coldest, blackest, most wicked heart, will be something *far more* persuasive! Jesus said, 'And I, If I be lifted up from earth, will *draw* All men unto Me.' What *IS* the actual agency of that **Attraction** – of that magnetic, ***Drawing*** Power? Listen! It will be the **unsurpassable** and **irresistible Beauty** – *of God's LOVE – for men!* No person can forever withstand such a startlingly wonderful and astonishing demonstration of Love as the Saviour provided. ***Such Love*** cannot forever be scorned! It is simply too powerful! Literally beyond belief, God must **give** all the power to believe it – *and He Will!*

No Deeper Truth Can Be Known Yet, Oh! How *Mysterious* It Can Be, Having '**Done** It To the *Least* of These *My* [*Own*], You Have **Done** It – *Unto* *Me!*'

Was Jesus, kindly friend, merely expressing a sweet sentiment? Or, was He declaring a *profound* Truth hidden beneath sacred words? Taken to their ultimate conclusion, they can only mean one thing: In some unfathomable way, *God and Man – are One!* ONE in a **Greater Reality** of which most are only dimly aware. There is an Inter-Connectedness, a Unity of Being, Jesus spoke of here. Jesus came to REVEAL Spiritual Truth. And though *this* Truth may forever elude man's mind, it **cannot** escape His **Awakened Heart**! Recall, Jesus prayed, 'That they may be **One**, even as We [You and I, Father] are ONE.' And *how* were they One? One in the Knowledge of *Who* they were, and of their **Shared Identity**! Whatever's done to *any* human is simultaneously done to the Lord! You must FEEL this Truth first, comprehension will – *come later!*

'Man IS Divine, *When* He KNOWS He's Divine', Forgotten Mystics Declared, While the Key To Discovery Whether True, Is To <u>BE</u> That Inner Light – *<u>Fair</u>!*

Truth seeking friend, are these words valid? First, listen with your inner, **awakened** heart to Peter: 'Given unto us [are] all things that pertain to Life and **<u>Godliness</u>** through the **<u>Knowledge</u>** of Him that hath called us to **<u>Glory</u>** and **<u>Virtue</u>** [*transcendent* beauty]; By which are given unto us exceedingly great and precious promises, that by them ye might be ***<u>PARTAKERS</u>** of* – **the <u>DIVINE</u> Nature!**' Many have read these words <u>un</u>knowingly. Forgetting that we are the <u>very</u> Children of God, His *offspring*, we fail to grasp the startling, humbling, yet *<u>heart-thrilling</u>* implications. To **KNOW**, in its fullest sense, means to **live** a thing, to actually **<u>BECOME</u>** it *<u>in expression</u>!* 'Behold, ***<u>what</u>*** <u>manner</u> of Love the Father hath bestowed upon us'! It reveals a <u>shared</u> **<u>Inner</u>** state of *BEING*, a **ONENESS**,beyond human understanding, but not beyond – *<u>Christ Knowing</u>!*

God, The Great Awakener, Has Chosen to Do, The _One_ Thing the World Could <u>Never</u> Believe Is True, When from the Touch _He_ Will Provide, <u>All</u> Awaken –_<u>to</u> <u>be</u> <u>Deified</u>!_

What, dear heart, is the **Ultimate Goal** of God the Father? – And of Jesus Christ (the Very Heart of Life) His Son? Who carries out His every desire, wish, or aim *however small* – or **_<u>GRAND</u>_**? Scripture tells us in words which are VEILED to human belief, apart from the Holy Spirit's **direct** and **special** intervention. And what are those words? That 'ye might be **partakers** of [sharing in] the DIVINE NATURE' (II Peter 1:4). This will take place 'in the dispensation of the **FULLNESS** of **times** [when God] might gather together in one all things in Christ' (Eph. 1:10). This is God's Purpose, His *<u>Heart</u>-<u>Held</u> Dream!* There is to be a 'joining', a marriage to the Lamb, a **union** creating a ONENESS of Being that will, and can, *<u>never</u>* be 'put asunder'. Every man to become wholly ONE, as was Jesus – *<u>with</u> <u>God</u>!*

In the Still of the Night
God's Love Reaches Out to Me,
And JOY <u>Sings</u> in My Heart
'I <u>**Will**</u> Be – *What I Will Be!*'

What, dear friend, are you going *to be?* What is to be your destiny? God 'visits' His own during the night and whispers Messages of <u>future</u> Glory – plants **<u>Visions</u>** of Love. An inspired lyricist wrote, 'Do you love me, *as I love you?* Are you *my* Life **to Be**? – My **Dream** come True?' These words echo the very words of our Saviour who said to Peter three times, '**<u>Lovest Thou Me</u>**?' 'Lord, Thou *Knowest* I Love Thee' was the reply. But, with *<u>what</u>* Love was this Apostle loving His Lord? – <u>*The very Love the Saviour had planted in his heart, was cultivating, and maturing!*</u> The Lord knows we are progressively becoming **<u>His</u> Life** – that He *IS* **<u>Our</u> life** – *to be!* And that we are ***His**** Dream – *Coming True!* He has **decreed** it so! Can you grasp the significance of this? *If* so, **Joy** will sing in your heart, when pondering this Heavenly wonder – *<u>too</u>!*

No <u>Greater</u> Reason to Believe Could Be FAR Beyond *<u>All</u>* Doubt and Uncertainty, This *<u>IS</u>* the Assurance I So Freely Share The *Living* <u>Proof</u> That – <u>I</u> <u>AM</u> There!

Did you know, beloved friend, what constitutes the **greatest** evidence for the **Reality** of Jesus Christ? – That He *was* who He *said* He was? Some say accuracy of Scripture, fulfilled prophecy, testimony of saints or angels, even miracles. Yet, Jesus gave the answer in His 'High Priestly' prayer: 'That they might **<u>KNOW</u>** Thee, the only True God, *and <u>Jesus Christ</u>* – whom Thou hast sent.' When you come to **know** the Lord, *thoroughly*, you become incapable of doubting His existence. For when Jesus *<u>draws</u>* you to Himself, a highly personal 'revelation' is granted you. A **conviction** arises in your heart, and you become undeniably aware of <u>Jesus'</u> <u>Presence</u>! THIS is the **<u>supreme</u>** proof! It is this direct, *<u>first-hand</u>*, spiritual experience that dispels all doubt and dissolves any prior reservations. A **True Believer** is born, mercifully created with –a ***<u>KNOWING</u>** <u>Heart</u>!*

**I, Thy Saviour, Can Change <u>*Anyone*</u>
From *Incorrigible* Lost Soul to Saintly Son,
<u>*I*</u> Choose the Time and Place This Will Be
<u>Not</u> Each Person–*by Their <u>Own</u> Decree!***

The Saviour of the World is not bound by any human concepts (religious) nor restricted by any of nature's laws (scientific). Anything which normally requires the **passage** of time can *easily* be abrogated by His Sovereign Will, since time is actually a construct of human thought. Time is collapsed with the utterance of one word by He Who inhabits Eternity! This means divine, godly character, for instance, can **instantly** be created by **fiat**, should the Lord so desire (as in the case of Saul of Tarsus being transformed into the Apostle Paul), as can the spiritual unfoldment of **any** individual be **instantaneously** *accelerated* far beyond its normal course of development. This fact, <u>alone</u>, proves there is <u>***no necessity***</u> for the living of successive lives to grow 'unto the measure, stature, and fullness of Christ'! The mere pronouncement by Christ of '**Let It Be!**' causes it to – <u>*leap into being!*</u>

***Clear* Your Mind of *All* But Me
Close Your Eyes to <u>*Witness*</u> and *See*,
I AM the Towering Strength of Prayer
I AM <u>Your</u> Advocate, Lord Jesus – <u>*the Fair*</u>!**

Once there was a statue sculpted of Jesus depicting Him as standing Erect, **Powerful** and **Serene**, with hands clasped to His Heart's center gazing upward into the Heavens – *praying* in behalf of all mankind. As our '**great** High Priest', He **continually** is making intercession for us before the Father. He beholds <u>***you***</u>, and is praying, now, in *your* behalf, Beloved, for *your* strengthening and increase in Wisdom, *your* reception of His Peace into your Heart, and His Power into *your* soul! <u>He is your **Eternal** **Advocate**</u>, and it is through <u>*His*</u> perfect prayers you <u>***will***</u> ultimately triumph! Over every foe, obstacle, hardship, trial, or illness. <u>***This***</u> is His present ministry, primarily to strengthen and encourage you <u>*until such time*</u> as your deliverance is at hand! **Picture** Him before you! <u>His</u> **committed Vigil** and prayers **never** cease – <u>*though yours may*</u>!

Jesus, <u>Universal</u> Man, That You Are
Not Just a Person of Ethnic Origin from Afar,
But, A Man Whose Race Originated From *Above*
One Whose View *<u>Transcended</u>* – Human Love!

There are those who look upon Jesus as a **very** extraordinary man, but *still* an ethnically-conditioned man–steeped in Jewish worldview and traditions. A man bound by *race consciousness* whose **identification** would have been with the Hebrew people, their religious practices, and tribal ways. This, however, affords little credit to He who **knew** Himself to be *not* of any one clan or culture, but rather a human being belonging to, and *representative of*, **all** mankind. His thought processes were **not** Jewish, though He were born a Jew, and educated by them. Even His skin color fell in the middle range of fleshly hue, signifying this *universal* aspect of His Being. Repeatedly, He said that He 'came down from Above'. This was His **True** origin. And though His Spirit was introduced into the world thru human flesh, His **Celestial** DNA marked Him not ethnic, but as God's Universal Man–*of Divine Love!*

I Am *THE* Light For All Time
Thy God, Thy Saviour, Thy Friend,
And I Am *THE* Love Hurdling Down from
Above, Convicting THE Hearts – *of All Men!*

Everything the **True** Light did will grow, and expand, and have continually unfolding effects *for Good* – for as long as the ages roll! The Divine Testimony, known as the *Gospel* record, along with the convicting power of the Holy Spirit, will continue **illumining** the minds and awakening the hearts of men and women everywhere, age to passing age. This is what the book of Timothy says, 'Who gave Himself a ransom for ALL, to be testified *in due time*.' The correct rendering of the last three words, however, is 'at their *appointed* time seasons.' For though the Lord has transcended time, and entered eternity, He *oversees* time and illuminations He is bringing to men's hearts at intervals of *His* own choosing. All will **know** His Light, as ALL are destined **His Love** – *to return!*

Lord Jesus, _Strange_ Words You Did Say
Viewing _Your_ Person – In So _Unusual_ A Way,
Seeing Yourself _by_ 'Looking Down' _from_ Above
A Key to Your Victory, A Door to Your Love!

His closing words in the Upper Room were, 'Father, glorify ***thy Son***, that ***thy Son*** may glorify thee. As Thou hast given ***Him*** power that ***He*** should give Eternal Life to [those] given ***Him***.' Notice, Jesus did NOT say, 'glorify **ME**', nor 'that **I** may glorify thee.' He spoke in grammatical _third_ person, NOT _first_ person – **WHY?** Because in Jesus' **exalted** state of Oneness with the Father, He was **mentally identifying** _solely_ with His **divine** Self, 'looking on' His ***human*** self – in a detached, though loving way. This view **empowered** Him, relieving any sense of aloneness, and guaranteeing His capacity **not** to be emotionally hurt _(weakened)_ by others. And since, dear friend, Jesus is our example, we're meant to do the same! **Unconditional Love** can **grow** in **you** and I more readily, then – _as in Him!_

**Beauty *Will* Save the World,
Yet, How Few Do Understand
Its Contour Is of Compassion's Face,
While Its Shape Is of a Carpenter's Hand!**

The human artisan has many names – Wonderful, Counselor, Mighty God, Everlasting Father, Prince of Peace! But, did you know, my friend, His name is *also* **Beautiful!** In the temple in Jerusalem was a gate called Beautiful. The Lord is called 'The Gate', and it is this 'All-Beautiful One' Who will save the world! This is because *every* single virtuous quality of Beauty resided *full-blown* within Him! So much so that an ancient prophet of Israel exclaimed, **'*How Great IS* His Beauty!'** For when you grasp the magnitude of this Beauty, you, too, will shout as did the Psalmist, 'Behold! [or stand in awe and wonder at] **The** Beauty – of the Lord!' He came to **awaken** these qualities in others, buried deep in the Image of God we all share. He alone, as ***Beauty Incarnate***, can *reach down* into our depths – to draw forth **the Beauty** destined one day – *to mirror His Own!*

**I Gave My Uttermost and *More*
To SAVE a World I Gladly Poured,
My Heart and Soul Into My DESTINY
I COULD *NOT* Fail – *For Love of Thee!***

Beloved, <u>could</u> *Jesus have failed in His Mission to save the world?* The surprising, yet **reassuring** answer is **NO**! This is just one more irrefutable proof of God's Supreme **Love** and **Commitment** to mankind. Whether sin, 'free will', or fallen angel, God loves us **so much** that He will permit **nothing** to ultimately destroy us and abort our destiny. Tho the Victory Jesus achieved was inconceivably torturous and incalculably costly, He was **Incapable** of failing due to His <u>*unwavering*</u> **dedication** to mankind, AND the Father's <u>added</u> **empowerment** at *critical* moments of His Ordeal. And *<u>because</u>* Jesus was willing to expend the ultimate, maximal effort, to give *<u>every last ounce</u>* of His precious Life Energy, the Father **guaranteed** His Victory, making it **impossible** to fail! In fact, thru the **Power** of *His* Love, His Victory was a foregone conclusion, accomplished before – *'<u>the foundation of the world!</u>'*

Judge _Not_, I Admonished All
That the Sword of 'Justice' Not Fall,
Upon the Head of <u>ANY</u> Wayward Son
Who _One Day_ Back, to the Father – _Will Run!_

There are two **Overarching** statements in John's Gospel meant to govern _every_ interpretation man places upon the concept of judgment as revealed in the New Testament. They are **'The Father judges _no_ man'** and **'I [Jesus] judge _no_ man.'** (John 5:22, 8:15) Every other reference to 'judgment' is intended to be viewed in their all-enveloping Light. The statements are clear, direct, and their meaning **absolute**: Judgment is **not** an attribute of God the Father, **nor** of Jesus Christ His Son! Yet, judgment IS spoken of in Scripture. _How_ can this be? The answer is that judgment (**condemnation**) is an attribute of _unregenerate man!_ Even the Last Judgment is the judgment humans _would_ make _upon themselves_ as Christ the Revelator **reveals** consequences and outcome of behaviors. THIS is a Saviour beyond the world's comprehension! One where judgment is **unrecognized**, and –_nonexistent!_

The World STANDS Forgiven
Therefore Jesus _Never_ Had Need, To
Forgive _Any_ Man, Who Sought Such _of_ Him,
And Who Embraced – _This False Creed!_

The vast majority of believers are convinced, dear heart, that the Saviour of the World _repeatedly extended_ **forgiveness** to the repentant 'sinner.' Yet, the Scriptural record makes it abundantly clear this is NOT so! Jesus is _never_ quoted as saying, '_I_ forgive you,' or '_I_ forgive your sins,' or '_I_, your Lord, forgive you _here_ and _now_.' No, instead, you find statements such as 'Son, Thy sins **BE** [**presently stand**] forgiven thee.' Or, as the Apostle Paul paraphrased, 'We HAVE the forgiveness of sins.' This is an ongoing possession – _continuous_ and _ever effective!_ **Granted by Grace** to mankind in far distant reaches of the past! The **erroneous belief** is that Jesus, _Himself_, forgives a person if and when asked to do so. But, since Jesus **never** _took_ offense, He **never** had _need_ to forgive! He **knew** in the Father's Mind, Forgiveness, an **ongoing** Reality, looked with **Anticipatory Vision** – _to the Cross!_

**No *Greater* Creed Did the Master Give
By Which One Day ALL Men Should Live,
As 'Do Unto <u>*Others*</u>' – *Still* Resounds, To Heights
Of Stellar Space, and to Inner Depths –
<u>*Unfound!*</u>**

The Lord's daily **Life Creed** He summed up in one so brief sentence: **'Do Unto *Others*, as You would Have [*Others*] do Unto You.'** Yet, in fact, this phrase could be captured as one word alone, **'*Others*'**. Meaning, of course, placing the welfare of others *first*. This 'Golden Rule' has been viewed as THE most beautiful sentiment. Actually, it is a declaration of *inviolate* **Spiritual Law!** <u>*Built*</u> into the very fabric of the universe! It can no more be violated with impunity than can anyone disregard the law of gravity. <u>***Why?***</u> Because in some very mysterious sense, I, you, we – <u>***ARE***</u> the *'others'!* This insight places Christ's statement into a whole new category of significance, as in **'That which You <u>*Do*</u> unto *Others*, You <u>*Do*</u> unto <u>*Yourself*</u>.'** When all men grasp this, war will become impossible and cease, peace will blossom, and **Love will Prevail** – *on Earth!*

**Your Eyes! Such Eyes! Oh, Lord of Love
What _Hold_ They Have On Me,
For All It Took Was <u>One</u> Sure Gaze
To _Seize_ My Heart, Yet – *Set It Free!*__**

Tender-hearted friend, only <u>one</u> thing can both **capture** your heart, and at the same time **liberate** it! You once most likely experienced it, a **divine gift** granted the young, but thought by many to be denied the old. **Joy _alone_ can set your heart free!** For without a free heart, life is hardly worth living! It is drudgery, a sorrowful plodding, an empty existence. When Jesus said, 'I AM come that they might have Life, and that **more abundantly**', He meant the _**Joyful**_ Life! What so few realize is that perhaps the most **captivating** quality of Jesus was the rare *Joy* emanating from His eyes, like deeply-embanked **glowing embers** – in His Soul! He looked upon people with Divine Love, suffused with Joy! This made Him so _**All-Attractive!**_ So _**Heart-Opening**_ and _**Compelling!**_ – _So Able to Free!_

Best-Loved Prayer of Our Saviour
You're the *Least* Understood as We'll See,
For Who Would Suspect *New Vistas* of Truth
Have Always Resided – *In Thee!*

The Lord's Prayer was given in *abbreviated* form, so **much** of its true meaning is implied, 'Our Father Who art in Heaven, Hallowed [***shall***] be Thy Name [***by*** *all*], Thy Kingdom Come [***to*** *all*], Thy Will be done [***through*** all], on Earth, *as it is in Heaven'*. And may we not be led 'into temptation [to ever doubt these mighty TRUTHS], but deliver us from the 'Evil One' [or, the *ONE* Evil of our temporary, unbelieving, visionless selves]. For THINE is the Kingdom [*pervading* us], the POWER [working *IN* us], and the GLORY' [to *transform* us] – ***all forever!*** Implicit in this prayer are the words supplied above. And when understood in this light, the **meaning** becomes gloriously apparent. *Jesus taught us to pray **inclusively** for all men!* To **Declare** and **Envision** the Salvation *of* ALL – *Coming True!*

**You CAN Believe That <u>This</u> Is So
Man *<u>Will</u>* Survive Though Troubles Grow,
Though *Others* Despair Over This to You
By <u>Solemn</u> Oath, I Declare – *<u>It's</u> <u>True</u>!*.**

Countless people, particularly of metaphysical persuasions, **disbelieve** an all-comforting teaching of the Lord – one that even *some* sincere Christians have abandoned. They believe, in all likelihood, the human race may well destroy itself, *<u>perish</u>* by its own hand. But, **YOU**, beloved can know with all certainty – <u>otherwise</u>! The Saviour spoke **directly** to this issue when in the Olivet Discourse He told of a 'Great Tribulation' unlike *any* the world would ever experience. And that should those days of suffering *<u>not</u>* be cut short, no human beings would survive upon the earth! BUT, note well the Lord's subsequent words: '**For the Elect's sake, those days <u>SHALL</u> be *<u>shortened</u>!*'** This will be done by divine, decisive Intervention, known as The Appearing (or 'Parousia' in the Greek). So, thankfully, Christ will curtail man's ultimate misuse of 'free will', and prove once again – *<u>His</u> <u>Lordship</u>!*

Beloved Jesus, ALONE You Do Stand
Unique **Among <u>any</u> Pantheon, Conceived by Man,**
NO OTHER Being Even Approaches Your Place
Supreme God O'er, the Whole – *Human Race!*

Holy writ unequivocally tells us there <u>truly</u> *does* exist a great spiritual **hierarchy** of beings who serve the Light – Holy beings of VAST Love, Wisdom, and Power. But, there are those who teach that Jesus is *only <u>one</u> <u>of</u>* **many** exalted beings – of EQUAL attainment, rank and authority. This teaching, however, is untrue. Jesus derives His **Utter Uniqueness** from multiple factors, only <u>SOME</u> of which are His *Achievement* in Overcoming the World (John 16:33), His *Position* of **First**born from the dead (Col. 1:18), His *Authority* He *<u>Alone</u>* has been granted to wield **ALL Power** in heaven – and in earth (Matt. 28:18), and His *Commission* of the **exclusive charge** given Him to reconcile man – to God! (Col. 1:20) Not to mention the fact that it pleased the Father to have the ***<u>FULL</u>*-NESS** of the Godhead dwell in Jesus bodily! <u>*No other*</u> individual has merited and been afforded such Credentials – *<u>and</u> <u>Grace</u>!*

Another Stupendous Achievement Our Christ Did Attain, the <u>Dethronement</u> and Victory Over Spirits Profane, Who May Now *Appear* Visitors Benign, <u>Advanced</u> in Knowledge Earthly–*<u>Divine</u>!*

Beloved, Jesus' Atonement, His **Victory** on the Cross, proved to be the 'undoing' of fallen spiritual authority. He '**spoiled** [*<u>thwarted</u>* the aims and designs of] principalities and powers' and 'made a shew of them openly, **triumphing** over them *<u>in It</u>* [His crucifixion].' (Col. 2:15) What this means is that Christ has **greatly curtailed** what powers they can exercise, **diminished** what types of influence they can wield, and **permanently stripped** them *<u>entirely</u>* of certain abilities formerly used to enslave, mentally blind (thru superstition), and torment men! Yet, God **still** allows them to be 'transformed into angel[s] of **Light**' to further His Purposes. (II Cor. 11:14) Also, Satan's power is 'supreme' *in the sky*, as He is known as 'the prince of the Power *<u>of the air</u>*.' (Eph. 2:2) Supposed alien spacecraft, which defy the laws of physics, and their occupants, are these beings, but <u>only</u> for a time – *<u>deceiving still</u>!*

This Lofty View of Atonement
One Day, The World Will Awaken To,
Causing <u>*All*</u> Men to Bow In Reverence
To A Saviour They – <u>*Never*</u> <u>*Knew!*</u>

In what specific way was Jesus **unique** as the scriptures boldly, and *uncompromisingly*, declare? Many believe Jesus was just 'one among many' of great spiritual teachers. But, is this true? Can the <u>exclusive</u> title of **Saviour** be legitimately accorded Him? Unequivocally – *YES!* Though **all** men are destined to attain 'Christ Consciousness', they would NEVER have been able to, had it NOT been for this ***Supreme Cosmic Act,*** **<u>required</u>** at that stage in human history, which Jesus **alone** performed on the Cross <u>*for us*</u>. Without this Great Achievement, the world would have long ago plunged into another **Dark Age** from which it would never arise. <u>*The departure from Light would have simply been too great!*</u> As the '**Pioneer** of <u>*our*</u> Salvation' – He will EVER remain the very *first* perfected Man. And there can only be ONE first, Who *through* His **Sacrificial Love** – sealed <u>our</u> Destiny – <u>*for GOOD!*</u>

**Jesus, We May Say If We Dare, You're
The FIRST Born of All Beings *Self-Aware*,
And Moreso Than This, It Was *Through* You
That All Sentient Beings Were –*Given Birth Too!***

What many devote people, sincere believers in the Christ, fail to realize is that Jesus is said to be, by the Apostle Paul, NOT the Creator of this *physical* universe, as is commonly supposed, but rather the Creator of ALL individual *personalities* (self-aware consciousnesses) ever to have been brought into existence! This includes all human and angelic life forms. Jesus IS 'the image of the invisible God, the firstborn of every CREATURE: For by [original Greek: *through*] Him were all things [**sentient, thought-possessed** *beings*] created, that are in heaven, and that are in earth, **visible** [human] and **invisible** – whether *they* be *thrones*, or *dominions*, or *principalities*, or *powers*: [Note that these are all **angelic entities** specified here] all things [beings who can say I AM] were created by [*through*] Him, and *for Him*.' Just another UNIQUE characteristic of Jesus' specialness and sole right–*to reconcile all!*

The Horizontal Plane, We See
Served as the Lever on The Fulcrum-Tree,
Bringing True <u>Balance</u> to the World of 'Sin'
Nullifying Its Power, Delivering – *All Men!*

Scientifically speaking, a Mighty Equation was utilized by our Creator in His chosen method of redeeming the **totality** of the world. The arms of The Christ, outstretched along a horizontal plane, **symbolized** an unbreakable lever (or plank) positioned on and *balanced over* a fulcrum (or centering point of **Stillness** – The Divine Heart). Jesus, Who possessed complete **Balance** (or Inner *Harmony*), was actually a LIVING, unmovable, Fulcrum – providing the necessary stability upon which the world could be brought back into Perfect Alignment at the spiritual level, *<u>first</u>*, and at the physical level, *<u>later</u>*. Only a Man completely **FREE** of and *immune <u>to</u>* the contagion of sin could fulfill this **Cosmic Role**! If one understands 'Balance' to be the absence of *In*-harmony or *Un*-cooperation, we can KNOW that the equilibrium of Universal Reconciliation – *will <u>one</u> day* emerge – *and <u>Reign</u>!*

**Ascended Master, Lord, YOU Are
Exalted *Far Above* <u>Every</u> Heavenly Star,
<u>You</u> Have the Preeminence, As *All* Will See
Reconciling the World – *<u>Back to Thee</u>!***

Jesus, the singular Lord of Life, stands at the **pinnacle** of the human race, the *<u>first</u>* perfected man, (Heb. 5:9) and presently **oversees** the spiritual development of **all** peoples; their nations, races, and creeds, but principally the *unfoldment* of Love within their hearts. He is charged with the Ultimate Responsibility of The Universal Reconciliation (Reunion) of Man back to God. *No other being* has been **bequeathed** this mandate, nor **entrusted** with the <u>Power</u> to make it a Universal Reality! For Jesus was the **ONLY** one of *all* men to have been *found worthy* (Rev. 5:4,12) of so GREAT an undertaking! – *The most **far-reaching** and **stupendous** <u>Crusade EVER</u> conceived, assigned to, and undertaken by a **God-Indwelt Divine Man** – in behalf of a helpless and dying humanity!* For this reason, Jesus retains pre-eminence! (Col. 1:18) The 'times and seasons' are now, thankfully, in His – *<u>ALL</u>-<u>Capable Hands</u>!*

Jesus Was a *Super Scientist* Some Do Say *But* Does This Depiction *Accurately* Portray Who and What He <u>Truly</u> Was to Men, When Displaying Knowledge Beyond – *<u>Their Kin</u>*!

Jesus is described by some as the greatest scientist the world has ever known, possessing **Knowledge** far beyond their understanding. He is said to have been the 'most advanced human' ever to have appeared on this planet, deriving His knowledge '**cosmically**' rather than *empirically* through sense-based observation. However, such an assessment is at best misleading, and at worst – wholly false! Jesus **never** experimented. He *never* had to 'test' His ideas. For He *never* had theories to promulgate, nor defend! He had no need to! **He was God Incarnate!** He did *not* guess, He **knew**! And though, in Jesus' human state, He had *voluntarily limited* His access to His innate Omniscience, He called It forth when It was critical for Him to do so. Jesus was *the Unique interface* between the Supreme God of Love and humankind. **Neither** a scientist, nor a mystic, but a Divinity–*<u>from on High</u>*!

**Oh! Heart _Of_ Hearts! I Reach Out Now!
Before You – _Alone_, My Love, I'll Ever Bow,
You ARE The Ideal of My Longing Soul
The Perfect Being – _I Must_ Behold!**

When the soul has found Its Beloved, dear heart, it has _no other recourse_ than to seek His face continually! Such a one searches subconsciously within her dreams, and consciously _every waking hour_ but for to catch even a glimpse of the highest manifestation of Divine Love there is! – With the pure and holy intention to drink It in, and progressively **become** It! Meaning to embody every attribute of Divinity of which the being of man is capable. Jesus of Nazareth WAS this exalted expression of God in Its Fullness, meeting every requirement of Perfection at every level of His Being! The seeker, having recognized Jesus as The _True_ Beloved of the Soul, is now betrothed to same, and lives _**only**_ to mirror the life of The Love of God – _personified_ on earth. Then, the Great Heart of Life, our precious Saviour, becomes – _our sole All!_

'Oh! _Perfect Love_! All Human Thought Transcending, Lowly We Kneel Before Thy Throne, That <u>Ours</u> May Be The Love Which Knows _No Ending_, Whom Thou Forever More Doth _Join – In One!_'

Beloved brother, you who seek that Love Which Is Flawless and unfailing, that Love Which is impeccable and blemishless, in Jesus you have **found** the object of your searchings! The above refrain are lyrics to a wedding hymn of years gone by, once cherished by so many adoring hearts. It succinctly captures in poetic fashion **the Truth** so poignantly _felt_ in the innermost recesses of receptive souls relative to the Reverence and Awe and Wonder called forth in the Presence of such Holiness and Sacred Mystery! **Jesus!** The _perfect_ love! The _endless_ love! The _wholly mature_ love! While human love will falter and fail, the Love of God so gloriously **_lived out_** in, through, and AS Jesus, never will! He was and IS the **Perfect Saviour**! Beyond comprehension, His Love persists even in the face of unimaginable Lovelessness! Such Love is our refuge, and our – _eternal Hope!_

THIS **Cross was NEW, Had <u>Never</u> Been, Unveiled Before the Hearts of Men, Tho 'Mystery Schools' Had Much to Teach, Knowledge of The Cross Was – *<u>Beyond Their Reach</u>!***

Beloved, there truly is a 'Mystery' Teaching mentioned in Holy Scripture, which up until the time of its unveiling had *<u>never been known</u>!* For mystery religions from previous times, cultures, countries and races, had <u>no</u> knowledge of the future Cross and Its **Supremacy** and Its **Centrality** in God's Plan. Only by *<u>'special revelation'</u>* could such a thing be known. Paul wrote: 'How that by revelation He made known unto *<u>me</u>* The Mystery; … *Which in <u>other</u> ages* was **not** made known unto the sons of men, as it is NOW revealed unto His Holy apostles and prophets by the Spirit; … And to make all men see what is the fellowship of The Mystery, *which from the beginning of the world* hath been **hid** in God (Ephesians 3). Thanks be to God, an open mystery, now, to those called *to see!* Amen!

**There Are No 'Lost' Teachings
Of Mine to be Found, Tho *Hidden* in Scripture
To Hearts That Are Bound, My <u>Most</u> Advanced
Doctrines Are There *In Plain View*, Tho Those
Who Are Called to Understand – *Are Few!***

Many there be, today, beloved, who claim that **many** of the Words of our Lord did not survive the centuries, that His oral legacy has been altered or edited by unscrupulous men. Recall, however, the following reassurances: 'The grass withereth, the flower fadeth, but **the Word** of our God **shall stand** <u>*forever*</u>.' And, again, '**The Word** of the Lord **endureth** <u>*forever*</u>.' Lastly, our Lord's **solemn promise**, backed up by His Power and Authority: 'Heaven and earth shall pass away, but <u>**My**</u> **Words** shall <u>*NOT*</u> pass away.' This means, of course, they would be **accurately preserved!** Yes, there are epistles external to the New Testament which have legitimacy relative to historical and cultural considerations. But, the **Holy Spirit**, *<u>Itself</u>, chose* not to include them in the Divine Canon, beautiful writings or great Truths contained therein notwithstanding! So, the Word of God, again–*<u>prevails!</u>*

Concluding Reflections

On

He Who Was

The Way, The Truth And – The Life

(*And* The Light of the World!)

**I Am THE Way, But *Others* Say
I Was the *Pattern* to Be Followed Today,
A Way shower, by Some, I Am *Thought* to Be
But, A Pathfinder Alone *Cannot* – Set Men Free!**

There are those who believe that Jesus was the '*perfect pattern*' after Whom we should model our lives – to 'imitate' His behavior as He best exemplified an '*ideal*' human being. Yet, be careful to note that Jesus ***never once*** did say 'I AM the Pattern' or 'I AM the Ideal'. Or, 'I AM a traveler on the Path.' No, beloved, He clearly stated, without apology, 'I AM – ***THE*** Way!' Among other things, this meant Jesus was and IS **The** Way to a freedom which **only** He can grant! Attempting to follow in His footsteps *alone* cannot liberate **anyone** from the effects of departing from the Royal Law of Love. Apostle John put it thus: 'If **the Son** therefore shall **MAKE** you free, ye shall be free indeed.' It is NOT the path and becoming proficient, or skillful, in its navigation that frees you, but rather a Personage with Whom all are destined to encounter! Recognizing His Supremacy (Lordship) IS–*the Key!*

**I <u>AM</u> The Truth, But *Others* Proclaim
That I *<u>Spoke</u>* the Truth *Only* in My Name,
Believing That Each Their *<u>Own</u>* Truth Possess
Such People Who Teach This *of Me* –do *Profess!***

Beloved, recognize that Jesus **never** said that The Truth He proclaimed was One Truth among *Many* Truths of equal validity or value! In fact, never did He say that 'His' Truth was even *His* – at all! He DID say, however, 'I have NOT spoken of myself, but **the Father** Who sent Me, **He** gave me…*what* I should say, and *what* I should speak.' And '**Whatsoever** [everything, without exception] I speak therefore, even as the Father said unto Me, *SO I SPEAK*.' Lastly, Jesus said, 'I Am come in my *Father's* name.' This elevates His Message far above any man-made conceptions or proclamations. Further, Jesus revealed that Truth is **a Person** embodied and manifested in the world of form, not a mental construct or relative viewpoint. And He identified **Himself** AS that person! In short, Jesus IS the Summit of Being! The **Ultimate** Truth [or *Word*]made flesh!'ThyWord[Oh!Father]–<u>IS</u> Truth!'

**I Am The LIFE, But *Others* Teach
A Person Of Only Remarkable Feats,
Who Was *NO* Different Than – You or Me
A Life of Great Brilliance, but *Still* Such as Thee!**

When Jesus, dear heart, boldly declared 'I AM **The Life**', He placed Himself in a category with no peers *nor* any equal. What He was actually referring to was **GOD** Life, which is Life qualitatively *above* and intrinsically *different* from any other kind of life! When He said that He had 'come that you might have Life', it was to *THIS* Life He alluded. As John, in the prologue to his gospel stated: 'In Him WAS Life, and *THAT* [unique, *supernatural*] **Life** was the **Light** of men.' We can say that we possess life, but we cannot affirm that we **ARE** Life – *apart* from Him! He is the Source Who provides access to the resplendent **glory** *imprisoned* within ourselves! – Still resident in The Divine Image – The '**Christ** IN you'. Jesus possesses the 'keys to the kingdom of Heaven' and with these keys unlocks (opens) our hearts, after which 'NONE can [ever] shut'! This is HisMission and avowed Aim – to make us'**partakers** of the DivineNature'–or *Life*!

The LIGHT of The World I Said _I_ AM
A Cosmic Orb on High to Illumine All Men
The _Solitary_ Power to <u>Yet</u> Flood All Parts
I _Will_ Banish _<u>Any</u>_ Darkness Lurking
– In <u>Every</u> Human Heart!

Our beloved planetary body, the earth, draws its life and sustenance from **Sol**, our home star. Through this **ONE** Power alone, the earth is made habitable, with much of it being resplendent with beauty and wonders – nourished by the **life energies** of Light! And so it is with the Saviour! Jesus drew upon this metaphor 'I AM **The Light of the World'** because of the **exact** parallel between Himself and this great solar body. If ever there were a perfect analogy, it is this one! Jesus IS 'Sol' – the Great <u>S</u>ervitor <u>O</u>f <u>L</u>ight! Light at the proper wavelengths, in the correct amounts, provided at the right times, ALWAYS restores, regenerates, renews! And NEVER harms, debilitates, nor destroys! After this incomparable statement, Jesus said 'He that followeth _**Me**_ shall NOT walk in darkness, but shall have the Light of LIFE!' As the sun is that Light to our terrestrial globe, He ALONE is–_to us, <u>mankind</u>!_

**The *Great* Achievement, <u>Now</u> Achieved
By The One In Whom His Heart Believed,
That Allegiance to Love *Would* Prevail
And, <u>*Never More*</u>, a Cosmos – <u>*Fail!*</u>**

Beloved, the Greatest Single Accomplishment, or **Achievement**, *<u>ever to occur</u>*, will have been the **wholly realized Goal** of Christ, our Lord! Men and women have repeatedly failed themselves, their God, and each other due to their **utter** inability to Love *<u>as Christ loved</u>*. The result has been a world of unbelievable woe. Yet, the Love of Christ is in process of infiltrating every heart, whose fruit will be the *<u>total, willing, and eager allegiance</u>* to the Rule of Love **forevermore**! The *Final* **Outcome** will be complete Unity and Oneness between *<u>all</u>* created beings (even *formerly* malevolent angelic ones). Christ's indestructible dedication to *<u>every, single, solitary soul</u>* will have proven irresistible, and will have *<u>**won over**</u>* the entire 'Sonship' back to God! After which, a **New Universe of God-Filled Beings**, wholly permeated by the Christed energies, will ensure Love *<u>evermore</u>* to the Great All – ***<u>in All!</u>***

Final Note

The Spirit *Of* Victory!

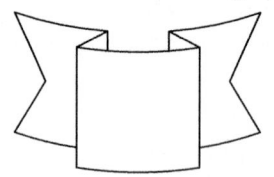

(*Claim* It! Right Now! – *Today!*)

**Precious One, I Would Have You Know
The *Spirit* of <u>Victory</u> I So Gladly Bestow,
Upon Those Who Seek Me from Morn *till* Night
To Be <u>Empowered</u> by – *<u>Heaven's</u> <u>Might</u>!***

The Victory that Jesus secured in behalf of all mankind, beloved, is one meant to be **appropriated** by YOU – and me! We have been afforded the high privilege of *sharing* in, **experiencing**, and actually *living* in this consciousness – **The Spirit of <u>Christ-Victory</u>**, emanating from the very Presence of the Risen Lord! – Radiating to all those who seek to behold His Face, contemplatively, in their souls! This Spirit is one of **Invincibility** and the *certain* **Total Attainment** of <u>ALL</u> that God seeks to accomplish in your life! Each day, practice envisioning Christ in His Resplendent Glory, and know that YOU are meant to be a **receptacle** of a measure of this Light! – *Through* which your emotional body will be fortified and rid of all negative downward 'spirals' and 'momentums' that would dispirit and hold you captive! For 'where the Spirit [of **The Victory**] of the Lord is, there is **Liberty'**! Freedom from – *fear!*

**Receive, Now, My _Greatest_ Gift of All
One _Most_ Needed, For which You <u>Must</u> Call,
The One Bestowal So Often Bereft, Of Those
Who Are Joyless, Lacking – _<u>This Gift</u>!_**

Beloved, Hear, now, the question of the hour: Has not your heart **thrilled** to the sheer magnificence of Christ's Supreme Accomplishment, and all it portends for humanity – and _you?_ If not, then you are undoubtedly not partaking of and sharing in **The Christ-Victory** made in your behalf, so that YOU might live (experience) **a life triumphant!** – One Victorious in thought, word, action, and deed! To arrive at this state of consciousness, though, you **must** _declare_ its Reality, regularly, with such **Truth declarations** as, 'I AM Victorious!' 'I AM more than a Conqueror!' 'I AM an Overcomer, irrespective of circumstance!' 'I AM the unquenchable Light of God Shining Every Hour!' Yes, it is **this _Spirit of Victory_** that will fill you with **Joy**, as nothing else will, and **energize** your soul! But, you must announce it! Proclaim it! Even shout it, where appropriate! <u>Then</u>, you will begin to **<u>feel</u>** It – _<u>at last</u>!_

**The Mantle of My Glorious Victory
Upon YOU, Reader, I Do Now, Bestow,
You've <u>Power</u> to Flood, to Change Your World
This IS the Truth – <u>*You Must Know*</u>!**

Beloved Heart, **Know**, *without a shadow of a doubt*, you are <u>MEANT</u> to *SHARE* in Christ's Victory Over the World! This means you are meant to **experience** the **Increase** of His Colossal Victory, in YOUR life, through your realization and utilization of The Spirit of **<u>Christ-Victory</u>** He imparts to you! Yet, how is this maintained? The **Momentum** of His Victory has been *growing*, in your consciousness, with every page you've marveled at and turned. **Here**, in unmistakable, heart-compelling, and irrefutable language, you have had **revealed** to you a Saviour Who ***<u>Cannot</u>*** fail you, in His ultimate Aims for your Destiny, nor will He fail you in providing 'Grace to help in time of [your *present*] need!' (Heb. 4:16) You can be **BOLD** in your life, **forcibly** declare His Truth, and COMMAND thoughts and feelings that would diminish YOU, *'Depart!'* **No longer** remain a powerless, dispirited Believer! <u>Read this book</u>, **frequently**. Let the **Power** of His Victory–<u>*be Yours!*</u>

Farewell Words

A modern day revelation states, 'When **certainty** has come, *where* is doubt? The answer, of course, is that it has ceased to be, with **Freedom** taking its rightful place, instead. For to be uncertain, in the arena of God, is to live in darkness and imprisonment. But as you, beloved friend, grow in the Grace and Knowledge of **The [Living] Truth**, the Lord Jesus Christ, *Himself*, you will become ever the more **certain** of His *wholly desirous* **Reality**! He will become **more** real, and alive to you, than any other person. And He will become *ever the more* the focal point and lodestone of your life! You may be doubtful of every other thing, but not of Him! For **He** will have removed all doubt – *evermore!* Only the *endless* reach of His Love can do this. And your now certain conviction that His All-Powerful Love WILL save your Soul! Life, then, becomes a **joyous journey** and wonder – *with Him!*

With Every Good Wish, The Author

Part V

The

Crusade
of
Jesus Christ!

Its *Ultimate* and *Undreamed-of* Outcome!

Part V – Introduction

The **Saviour's names** reveal His many-*Splendored* attributes – such as Wonderful, Counselor, The Mighty God, The Everlasting Father, **The Prince of Peace**. Not to mention, The Good Shepherd. And so, during times of deep meditation and prayer, the author was graciously given *another name*, whereby a further **glorious** aspect of His Deity is also made known – **The Mercy Rose**! Rooted in Solomon's appellation, 'The Rose of Sharon', and Christ's declaration that He would 'have *Mercy* and not sacrifice' (of *any* kind), the **Rose Image** was also shown to have no thorns! May its meaning amaze you, and challenge you, to ponder God's – *Undreamt of* Love, through poetic images – Anew!

Part V – Contents

When Holy Love Unclosed His Eyes

Message of the Mercy Rose
Song of the Mercy Rose

When Holy Love Unclosed His Eyes
(Complete poem)

God's Nearness
Captured Heart
The Truth
Holiness

God's Dream

Farewell Message

**When Holy Love Unclosed His Eyes
What *Rapture* in His Breast Arose
'Twas the *Joy* Triumphant!
– *Of The Mercy Rose!***

Desirous friend, slowly did His eyes unclose within a chamber growing **bright**. Calmly, then He rose up empowered by Heaven's Might. *What* did He *feel*, this Saviour Most Fair? This wholly human, yet Divine, Mind of Everlasting Care? – When Immortal Life had proved, for all Time, that *Love is Stronger than All Death?* Ah! **Glorious Morning!** It was **rapturous Joy** He *felt!* Then, out through the opening in the earth He walked and stood! Undisputed Lord of Heaven and Earth! Redemption for **All** mankind *Won!* – With death, forevermore, *un*done! His **Victory** IS Accomplished! He IS the Lord of Life! He *WILL* draw *every* man to Him – Through the **Mercy** of His **Might**! Yet, as that distant day is hastening near, you can be assured by Heaven's Dove, when *His* **Joy** will spread to fill the needy hearts of ALL – *by this Mercy Rose of Love!*

Message *of* the Mercy Rose!

I *Will* Have *Mercy!*

I Who AM the Lord of Life, desire not sacrifice, my friend. No sacrifice of life or limb! No sacrifice of mind or heart. Nor of eternal human soul! – *From anyone!* I'll forfeit *no one* of 'my own'. For the 'lost' ones **all** belong to Me! And I'll not rest till I've set free, each and every one to be, a Messenger of Love, like me!

I *Will* Have *Mercy!*

I Who **AM** the *Risen Lord,* upon those whose hearts are cold, upon the hate-filled, upon those who would destroy and kill, upon those who think that might is right, upon those who feel that hate is strength, upon those who desire to hurt and maim, upon those who delight in others' pain!

Message *of* the Mercy Rose! – *Con.*

I *Will* Have *Mercy!*

I Who AM All-Powerful and Eternally Free! For they are blind, **all** who stray from Love Divine, *they do not see!* Nor know they what they do to Me. *I've not yet touched their hearts you see!* And till I do, there is an awful emptiness within, that *blinds* them to *their* love for men! Recall, I came *not* to judge the earth, but to shed My Mercy and to give New Birth! And when I do, each one in turn, will transformed be, and clearly see, how wrong they were!

I *Will* Have *Mercy!*

I Who AM All-Loving! Hear now what I proclaim! No matter what others would have Me be! **I will not do to other men what they have done to me!** They tried to destroy my Life on earth, will I, now, *their* destroyer be? Can I go back upon my words, and Hate my 'enemy'? *Will I curse those who* were unable *to bless Me?*

Message
of the Mercy Rose! – *Con.*

I *Will* Have *Mercy!*

I Who AM the Living Word! 'Do unto Others', I taught to men, 'as you would have them do to you.' Am I to be exempt from words – so lofty, and so true? I tell you, NO! For I will continue to pray for all those who my persecutors are! And I'll *never* cease to pray for them – till the 'flaring out' of the furthest star!

I *Will* Have *Mercy!*

I Who AM the Saviour Fair! *All this,* my friend, is the *Ultimate* Test of the Power of My Love – *and* Care! If my Words meant anything at all, they spoke to this: I WILL redeem the blackest heart, the furthest, fallen soul! This is the cause for which I live, and in this Quest I can <u>*NOT*</u> fail! For to **<u>demonstrate</u>** the **Power** of Love, *Is not this WHY I came?*

I tell you, friend, The **Mercy Rose** – will <u>*ALWAYS*</u> – be my Name!

Song *of* the Mercy Rose

I AM
the Mercy Rose!   I breathe out *only* Love! I can-not hate, nor hurt, nor harm! I AM sent by Comfort's Dove!

I AM
the Mercy Rose!   Tho delicate appear to be, my matchless Strength resides in the Truth – there is *no hint* of sin in Me!

I AM
the Mercy Rose!   I've *no* desire to kill, no need to judge, no motive, intent, nor faintest will – to cause another *not* to be!

I AM
the Mercy Rose!   The Rose *without* one thorn! I AM the Flower that's Heaven-Born! A flower that can *only* Bless!

Song *of* the Mercy Rose – *Con.*

I AM
the Mercy Rose!   *I exile none from Love!* No place of torment will I send a wayward son – or daughter of men!

I AM
the Mercy Rose!   I WILL make ALL men see! The error of their ways, to turn quickly back to Me!

I AM
the Mercy Rose!   My Perfect Love *none* can resist! When *I* decide to convert a soul, their Love will then *fore'r* persist!

I AM
the Mercy Rose!   *Remember*, I've *no* thorns to wound! I'll ne'er cause others fear, who veer from the straight and narrow sphere!

Song *of* the Mercy Rose – *Con.*

I AM
the Mercy Rose!   I AM Pure Love, and Love *alone!* A Mercy Mild, yet Mighty, too! I come for ALL, including YOU!

I AM
the Mercy Rose!   Safe for all around to be, harmless, evermore forgiving, offenseless, too, *nothing* possess I to cause pain!

Beloved!

This *IS* the Meaning

of *My* Name!

When Holy Love *<u>Unclosed</u>* His Eyes

Still as the stillest statue, cold as the coldest night, The heart that harbored the Deepest Love, was now Bereft of Heaven's Light.

The hands that prayed, that worked and served, that only touched to heal, were motionless, they moved no more, it's true! – for those like me and you.

Alone His body lay – bereft of life, or so it seemed. But, *Lo!* Within the ink-black darkness of the sepulcher sealed tight – *What* was it there? The glimmer of the faintest, strangest light!

For about His head, had you but seen, you would have witnessed, too, an other-worldly glow of light, that grew, and Grew, and GREW!

A radiance, all at once did fill – the tomb, in the twinkling of an eye! A *flash* of brilliance brighter than – a ten-thousand moon-lit sky!

When
Holy Love
<u>*Unclosed*</u> **His Eyes** – *Con.*

The burial garment that had served as swaddling clothes in death, now neatly lay in a corner, of the chamber where *He* lay. Folded, but <u>*not*</u> by human hands, upon the hardened clay.

A garment from an unknown realm – did appear to adorn His earthly frame – The form that had been *oh* so marred! – more than any man, *in shame*, held *'Just'* by scorners of His Name!

The body that had borne the lash, cruel, where flesh was ripped apart – The terrible thrust of the massive spear up through His Daring, Sacred Heart.

But, now! *Now!* His body shows *no* sign of murderous, torturous deeds! *Except* – for five strange opening marks upon His palms, within His side, and well beneath His knees.

When
Holy Love
Unclosed His Eyes – *Con.*

Slowly, His eyes do, now, *un*close,
Within the chamber bright!
Calmly, now, He raises up!
Empowered by Heaven's Might!
Up from the gloom of death
In an eternal Night!

Up to the immovable stone He strides,
Without a moment's pause.
And then another *burst* of Light,
To hurl the boulder far, because
_No_ power could now stay Love's
Re-entrance to the World!

What does He feel, this Saviour Most Fair? This wholly-human, yet Divine, Mind of Everlasting Care? When Immortal Life had *proved*, for all Time, that _Love is Stronger than All Death?_

When Holy Love <u>*Unclosed*</u> His Eyes – Con.

Ah! **Glorious Morning!** 'Twas rapturous Joy He felt! And the <u>Message</u> that He shared with all – He shares with all still! Yet, comes to each in an order determined *solely* by His Will!

> Now out through the opening in the
> Earth, He walks and stands!
> Undisputed Lord! – of Heaven and earth!
> Redemption For All mankind ***Won!***
> *– With death, forevermore, <u>un</u>done!*

> Never again His eyes to close,
> And His Work continues still. As
> Intercessor to a World – that <u>*one day*</u>
> – Will <u>Do</u> God's Will!

> His Victory is accomplished!
> He *IS* the Lord of Life!
> He WILL draw *every* man to Him –
> Through the <u>***Mercy***</u> – of <u>His</u> <u>**Might!**</u>

So, That distant day is hastening near, be assured by Heaven's Dove. *Then*, will every woman and every man, know the Power of His Wondrous Love!

GOD'S NEARNESS

*There never was an instant,
A Soul was lost to Thee,
How'er bereft communion sweet,
With Master it may be.*

*For time is but a Teacher,
To unveil the Sacred Heart,
When aloneness will be laid aside,
And where God - will ne'er depart!*

CAPTURED HEART

*To be held in this fashion,
By a Love that will free,
Unbound from the chains,
That have long fettered thee.*

*To be captured in twilight,
When you thought life would end.
Then, a prisoner of sorrow,
Now, a Joy to no end!*

HOLINESS

What once was sacred afore to thee,
After years of wandering upon Life's sea,
Is sacred still! Its beauty fadeth not!
Nor can it lose its place tho time forgot!

Holiness resides within the Soul,
And ever beckons us to hold,
The Light of Christ - within our hearts,
And then - to give, to pour, to share,
The Love Eternal resting there!

By this shall all men come to see,
The Truth that God doth dwell in thee!
Forever calling to His own, with gentle
Voice, and comfort tone.

HOLINESS - Con.

The world, and all therein, will be,
Wooed back to Love - thereby set free!
For Holiness, and beauty true,
Are bound up both inside of you.

Yes! You! - Who seek the Father's face,
The Virgin's song, our Brother's grace,
The Holiness you once sought then,
Is still within the heart of men.

So, sacred still the Light in thee,
Continues calling o'r Life's Sea,
You hear it when you listen true,
For Holiness still calls - to you!

God's Dream

Upon the crests of Cosmic Waves
Heaven *bursting* through Earth's
seams, Flowers <u>blazing</u> with radiant,
deathless Love, Rides a glorious
Vision – ***Christ's Dream!***

<u>*Each*</u> day a little closer comes
This reach of Reality's hold, Heart-
held By the **Saviour's** Inner, Glorious
sight – A **Vision** So Grand, and
Eternal, too, Destined to embrace – the
All *of you!*

Stirrings in your ***Soul*** of Souls
Heart-yearnings growing ever
<u>*more*</u> keen,

God's Dream – *Con.*

Thoughts exalted above one's clay-fashioned Abode – Spirit <u>*drawn*</u> to realms unseen!

Mystical longings more potent do grow, Deeper the depths from which feelings arise, Inner senses <u>*awakening*</u> – to heights of the skies!

Oh! How Glorious! And Joyously True! The Heart of Life – ***Wed to You!*** Transcendent, Exalted, Liberated, so Free!

A <u>*Joining*</u> taking place within, Oneness revealing **a Unity Supreme**, The Aim, the Goal – ***of Resurrection's Dream***

God's Dream – *Con.*

Racing O'er the Earths It goes
From the deepest wells to the swiftest streams, To the highest mountain peaks – and climes!

The **Universe** *awakened!* All Beauty beheld! Swirling round, the new-born procession proceeds,
All who had been without, are now entered Within
God's Rapturous Being!

As miracles spring about the feet of the Redeemed! *Immersed* in the Glory of Life Supreme!
All Life awakened – to God's Dream!

God's Dream – *Con.*

All things possible have come to pass
And **all** disbelief is discarded, *at last,*
The All-Redeeming Love has Won
<u>*Every*</u> Soul back – ***to Life's
Radiant Son!***

M.E.

– Finis –

Farewell Words

Long ago, dear friend, **a beautiful arbor** was fashioned by <u>Love</u> *Itself*. This was unlike any arbor the world had seen, as it consisted of the interlacing, *<u>not</u>* of flowers, but of human beings! The utmost care was provided to the lattice work supporting these 'branches', offshoots of **the Vine**. And this Vine, Itself, proceeded from the ultimate flowering of Goodness among humanity – **the *<u>Mercy</u> <u>Rose</u>!*** He had told them, His garden bower, 'I AM the true Vine, ye are the branches.' Some knew His title as **'<u>The</u> <u>Rose</u> <u>of</u> <u>Sharon</u>'** Who would **'have Mercy.'** And the *same* bower continues to grow today, spreading the Life blood of this flowering plant – **Joy** *<u>to</u> <u>All</u>!* It is my sincere desire that the poetic and picturesque language of the Soul, presented, herein, has *touched* your heart, *captivated* your mind, and *a-wakened* **new** depths of understanding in your Soul!

With Every Good Wish, The Author

About The Author

A devotee of Jesus and student of scripture since childhood, Mack seeks to teach others about *'the Deep Things of God.'* Writing with poetic majesty, yet with elegant simplicity, he **'paints'** *word-pictures* that captivate the heart, and awaken the soul. His mission is to reveal aspects of **the Fullness of the Gospel of Christ** *few* know of, with special emphasis on the Lord's singularly unique Life-Purpose and the **All-Redeeming Nature** of His Love. Mack has authored numerous books, facilitated classes on spirituality, and gives talks on living a Radiant Life. He has been called to unveil to others – *nothing less* – than the uttermost **'Depths** – *of The Heart of Love!'* He presently resides in Central Virginia, and graciously welcomes comments.

An
Out-Reach of

Mercy Rose Ministries

Proclaiming

The
Depths
of

The **Heart** *Of* Love!

__Concluding Remarks__

This book is, obviously, not intended to be an exhaustive treatise, or formal discussion, on the historical doctrines of Christian Universalism (the salvation of all), *primarily*, nor that of Mystical Immanence (the oneness of man and God within), *secondarily*. However, it *IS* designed to present aspects of these concepts with heart-compelling logic, persuasive reason, scriptural authority, literary beauty, and most of all, the *profound* and *inexhaustible* depths of the gentle Galilean's Love in non-technical, easy-to-understand language.

Thankfully, today, scholarly research by committed followers of Christ (inspired by the Holy Spirit), whether Protestant, Greek Orthodox, Catholic, or of nondenominational persuasions, has uncovered **incontrovertible proof** of the scriptural *validity* of these forgotten or 'lost' teachings, and of their widespread acceptance among Christians, including Christian scholars, theologians, and clergy, in ages past. And of the FACT that virtually all references to eternal punishment (or everlasting destruction) are all *mistranslations*, referring ONLY to corrective parental measures (though severe) instituted by God our Father, designed to <u>wholly</u> redeem wayward souls, without possibility of fail!

For in-depth, scholarly, theological evidence, both ancient and modern, contact the author, who will gladly provide names of a multitude of written sources, organizations, and churches which promote these true teachings to God's Glory, and as testimony to the *Ever-Astonishing Love* – of Christ the Lord – for mankind!

For More Information:

Go to

Authentic Life Publications

through

www.themercyrose.com

or

Facebook page:

Teachings of The Mercy Rose

or contact directly

mackethridge@hotmail.com

Book 2

God's True Message *Proclaim!*

The **Universal** *Scope*
Of **Christ's** Love, Wisdom and Power!

Heaven
And
Earth
Shall
Pass Away,
But My **Words**,
[My *Message*]
Shall
Not
Pass Away!

(Matt. 24:35)

Copyright © 2010
by Mack W. Ethridge

Published by **Authentic Life Publications**

All rights reserved. Printed in the United States of America. Permission granted to quote brief portions of this book provided due credit is afforded the author.

Cover design selected by Mack Ethridge

Library of Congress Cataloging-in-Publications Data, Ethridge, Mack W.

God's True Message Proclaim!
– Complete edition

1st Complete Amazon Softback Edition
August 2012

Loving Tribute

The most Christ-like man I have ever known was my beloved father, Floyd L. R. Ethridge. With **profound** love, service, and good cheer, he sought to serve God with every breath. Fondly remembered, simply as '**Roy**', the Lord Jesus Christ revealed **His Reality** to me *through* Him. Without the influence of his life, this book would never have been written. Now, Godspeed my beloved father! – Till we meet again! That I might serve **you**, as you so *faithfully* served me, all through the years. Amen.

PROLOGUE
The Author's *Remembered* Childhood Experience

When the author was three years of age, standing alone in a backyard on a mid-summer's day, he received a **Message**. As he looked up and gazed into the sunlit sky, a feeling of **transcendent Glory**, **Purpose**, and **Power** enveloped him. And as he looked around, he beheld all things infused with life, purpose, immortality, and an inner knowledge was conveyed to him regarding the **profound meaning** of the world and human life. It was brief, perhaps, only a few seconds, but that was all the time required. **The Message came not in words, for no voice was heard, but rather in 'Inner Knowing'.** And further, Mack was 'told' there was 'a great reason for your having been born, and it will be *revealed* to you in your lifetime.'

The Author's *Remembered* <u>Childhood</u> Experience – *Con.*

It was not, however, until after many years had transpired that Mack began to realize this revelation may well be a long-time coming. Yet, he never gave up hope that it would come. He often thought of it as, '***<u>The Unforgotten Message</u>***'. He told no one of this occurrence for many years, yet it was indelibly imprinted in his heart.

When Mack entered the eve of his 49th year on earth, **the purpose for his having been born** was, as promised, revealed to him. And, he was, also, at that very time, given the power to make it so. Again, it came not in words, but as before, with an '**Inner Knowing**' of unmistakable clarity, conviction, and power. **He had found his purpose!** And it was to write and lecture

The Author's *Remembered* **Childhood** Experience – *Con.*

for the upliftment of mankind, by sharing and conveying to them the wondrous insights afforded him throughout his life.

Mack does not believe, nor claim for one moment, that what happened to him somehow makes him special or different from any other.

Quite the contrary, Mack realizes that countless thousands of his fellow human beings have had similar **childhood** or **early life experiences**, if not all. Often, however, these experiences are regarded as childhood fantasies, events that never actually took place. And viewed as such, are frequently given little further notice, and are subsequently forgotten. Often beyond recall.

The Author's *Remembered Childhood* Experience – *Con.*

But, these events are real. And they are *given* to us usually at early stages of our lives, so that once we have been properly prepared in **the Great School of Life**, we will remember, if only subconsciously, and recognize our life calling when it presents itself. The initial promises, given, too, serve to fortify us for the inevitable trials and struggles we must confront and surmount if we are to fulfill **the purpose for which we were born.**

May Mack's writings serve to awaken within you the knowledge of *your* life's purpose, and to kindle the desire to find it, and live it! For it is only in living it, that the **Peace**, and the **Power**, and the **Happiness** you seek can be fully realized. Godspeed!

Contents of Book

Part I
To *Thrill* the Mind
– Those Wondrous Words!

Part II
To *Empower* the Heart
– Take Heart Beloved!

Part III
To *Heal* the Body
– A Healing Mercy Rose!

Part IV
To *Liberate* the Spirit
– In Jesus' Presence!

Part V
To *Secure* One's Well-Being
– The Blessings of Wealth!

Special Supplement – True Love

Part I

A Message to Thrill *the* Mind!

Those Wondrous Words!

The **Words**
That
<u>I</u>
Speak
Unto You,
They *<u>Are</u>* **Spirit**,
And They
<u>Are</u>
Life!

(John 6:63)

Part I – Introduction
The *Master's* Legacy!

Part I of this book was born of a sincere prayer and heartfelt desire to impart to men the often <u>unrealized</u> **significance** of *The Most Wonderful Words* ever bequeathed unto men! Sadly, few even **recognize** them as such. But, for those who do, the mere thought of them fills with wonder, appreciation, and joy! As the gentle Galilean Himself said, 'The words that I speak unto you [and those words spoken *through* My inspired Apostles], they are **Spirit**, and they <u>ARE</u> **Life**.' May you, dear reader, find as never before, their amazingly **True** Reality and comprehend with new insight the **Wonder** of these *Precious*, Divine Words!

Part I – Contents

(Page 1 of 3)

The Christ – Words *of*

Lord Jesus, Everything You Have Said
The Words Voiced Stunned Them
(The Most *Startling* Words)
The Most *Glorious* Words Ever Spoken

The Most *Comforting* Words Ever Spoken
The Most *Beautiful* Words Ever Spoken
The Most *Joyous* Words Ever Spoken

The Most *Wondrous* Words Ever Spoken
The Most *Profound* Words Ever Spoken
I AM In My Father, And My Father Is In Me
(The Most *Elegant* Words)

The Most *Unshakable* Words Ever Spoken
The Most *Welcoming* Words Ever Spoken
The Most *Picturesque* Words Ever Spoken

Part I – Contents
(Page 2 of 3)
The Christ – Words *of* – Con.

The Most *Gracious* Words Ever Spoken
The *Truest* Words Ever Spoken
The Most *Charming* Words Ever Spoken
The Most *Sacred* Words Ever Spoken
The Most *Calming* Words Ever Spoken
The Most *Instructive* Words Ever Spoken
The Most *Truthful* Words Ever Spoken
The Most *Triumphant* Words Ever Spoken
The Most *Reassuring* Words Ever Spoken
The Most *Humble* Words Ever Spoken
The *Greatest* Commandment I Say to Thee
Let Me Hear You Speak, Lord
Hold My Word Close to Your Breast
What More Can You Say, Lord
Many Believe Jesus' Parables Prove
What They Thought They Understood
Hear a Parable of 'The Net and the Sea'
Listen, Now, If You Would Know
Jesus, the Master Wordsmith, We'll See
Of What Kind of God Did Jesus Tell
'Dare to Love!' our Saviour 'Said'
What Other Words Might HE Have Said

Part I – Contents

The Apostles – Words *of*

The Most *Mysterious* Words Ever Spoken
The Most *Encouraging* Words Ever Spoken
The Most *Emboldening* Words Ever Spoken
The Most *Telling* Words Ever Spoken
The Most *Awe-Inspiring* Words Ever Spoken
The Most *Patient* Words Ever Spoken
The Most *Mystical* Words Ever Spoken
The Most *Revealing* Words Ever Spoken
The Most *Unbelievable* Words Ever Spoken
The Most *Thrilling* Words Ever Spoken
A Name Seldom on Men's Lips Today

Farewell Words

The Christ

Words
of

**Lord Jesus, *Everything* You Have Said
Are Like Gleaming Pearls and Gems of Bread,
To Adorn My Mind and To Satisfy My Soul
Oh, Words of Truth! I, *In Awe* – <u>*Behold!*</u>**

What is the **value**, caring friend, you place upon the words Jesus gave us? Do you realize that no other words convey truth as do *His* words? Do you grasp the amazing **fact** that *these* words are those, not of a mere man, but of God, *Himself?* Do you recognize them as ***<u>The</u> <u>MOST</u> <u>Important</u> <u>Words</u>*** ever spoken? The collective body of Jesus' sayings bequeathed to mankind through the New Testament scriptures are priceless beyond calculation. For they, as no other words, speak to ***<u>the</u> <u>deep</u> <u>soul</u> <u>needs</u>*** of a suffering, sorrowing, and sin-laden humanity. And do provide, <u>when</u> <u>properly</u> <u>understood</u>, complete assurance of God's working out a **glorious** purpose in ***<u>each</u>*** and ***<u>every</u>*** individual's life! Commit, then, as many of His words to memory, to beautify your mind; and <u>feast</u> upon His faithfully recorded **oral expressions**, often, to nourish and heal – *<u>your</u> <u>soul!</u>*

**The Words Voiced <u>*Stunned*</u> Them
<u>*None*</u> Were Expected! <u>*Nor*</u> Dreamed!
The Most <u>*Startling*</u> Words Ever Spoken
By The <u>*Most*</u> Wondrous Man – <u>*Ever Seen*</u>!**

Nothing could have prepared those people for what they were about to hear. <u>*No precedent existed*</u>. It was contrary to all human, and even *previously-thought*, **divine** wisdom. Yet, when those words flowed from His mouth, all hearts were stopped in rapt attention, amazement and surprise! Little wonder, tho, they are <u>*seldom*</u> heard today, even in religious circles, as the fallen human heart can scarcely comprehend their meaning, nor identify with what is asked of it! What **were** those <u>*nearly*</u> unbelievable, most startling words? Listen, now, **<u>anew</u>**! '**Love** *your <u>enemies</u>*, **Do good** *to them <u>who hate you</u>*, **Bless** *them that <u>curse you</u>*, *and* **Pray** *for them <u>who despitefully use you</u>*.' Who **<u>dare</u>** <u>think</u>, much less <u>*do*</u> such a thing? Yet, Christ did. And He asks those who bear His name to do – <u>*no less*</u>!

**The MOST _Glorious_ Words Ever Spoken
Humanity Has _EVER_ Longed to Hear,
The <u>Promise</u> of a <u>New</u> World Coming
And Deliverance from – _<u>Every Fear</u>!_**

Throughout the ages, since the dawn of time, men and women have shed _millions_ of tears, grieved and sorrowed over the incalculable suffering of the world. '_<u>Why</u>?_' man's heart cries out! 'How senseless!' Yet, thankfully, the most glorious words _of promise_, man could ever hope to hear, have been given! 'And God shall _wipe away_ **all** tears from their eyes; and there shall be **no more** death, _neither_ sorrow, _nor_ crying, _neither_ shall there be **any more** pain: for the former things are passed away. And He that sat upon the throne said, 'Behold, I make **ALL THINGS** _NEW!_' Yes! God has assured us of the outcome of His Master Plan. _**No** **thing**_ will be exempt from the Great Restoration back to Paradise! The New, now-**unalterable**, Creation! _Incapable_ of 'falling' from Grace! Ever again! **Gone** will be heartache, dear friend – _evermore!_

**The Most _Comforting_ Words Ever Spoken
Sent Down As On the Wings of a Dove,
'I'll _Never_ Leave, _Nor_ Forsake You'
I Have Pledged Ever More – _My Love!_**

In this life, kindly friend, there are times when the **only** thing that may calm one's heart is a Loved one's promise to remain _**near**_ us, _**with**_ us, _**by**_ us. To be recipients of their touch, and soothing presence, during times of trial, sickness, heartache, or despair, is the only consolation we crave. Yet, because humans are imperfect, we may be deprived of this. **Not so** with the Lord! He is incapable of reneging on His promise, nor can *anything* prevent Him from fulfilling it! No matter how many times _**we**_ might leave or forsake _**Him**_, as when '**All** the Disciples forsook Him and fled' on the eve of His crucifixion, He will never do so to us! The Son of Life has **willed** to remain **true** forever. And because of this unbreakable commitment, **one day**, every heart will be true – _in return!_

**The Most _Beautiful_ Words Ever Spoken
He Uttered Softly With _So Tender_ A Plea,
Are _the_ Only Words Mankind's Ever Needed
To Live in Peace, Joy – _and True Harmony!_**

During His last Communal Meal with His Beloved disciples, Jesus gave the **one** sequence of words that was at once a command and a prayerful plea. Those **four divine words**, had they been **truly** comprehended by man, *and lived*, would have ushered in a Heaven *on Earth*. For man needs _no other words_ than these to live **gloriously, happily, abundantly**! And **that** is what makes them **_SO_ beautiful**! For in four brief words of such elegant simplicity are **revealed** both **God's Nature** and man's **magnificent Purpose** – his *Reason for Being*. Those Divine words are, and will forever be, **Love Ye One Another**! Worthy of being engraved upon every marble stone, God is in the process of writing them in *every* human heart! So attests the author of Hebrews! – _God's Kingdom Come!_

**The Most _Joyous_ Words Ever Spoken
Whatever <u>Else</u> Could They Possibly Be,
Save – 'He Is Risen! He IS _<u>RISEN</u>!_' And,
Because _<u>He</u>_ Lives, So – _<u>Will</u> <u>We</u>!_**

You, beautiful heart, who are so saddened, confused or distressed about the passing of a beloved one, a parent, sibling, or child, ponder these thoughts. The Visitors from a dimension beyond our own hastened to convey to the bewildered, terrified, and heartbroken disciples a *strange*-sounding, yet hope-kindling message: '*Why* do you seek **the Living** among the dead? He is <u>not</u> here. *<u>He</u> <u>Is</u> <u>Risen</u>!*' So said the celestial beings in the tomb of rebirth! That Man Who had borne all departures from love in His very person was **alive**, and, as He had said, 'Because *<u>I</u>* live, YOU shall live ALSO.' His Victory over the grave now absolutely assures us, yes, **_<u>guarantees</u>_** us, that we will *<u>not</u>* pass into oblivion, ceasing to be as though we never were! No! We will be *<u>as</u> <u>He</u> <u>is</u>!* **Radiant** with Life! – *<u>Ever</u> <u>More</u>!*

**The <u>Most</u> Wondrous Words Ever Spoken
Did, the Galilean Speak That Day, Declaring
'I AM The Resurrection and The Life'
Our Hearts <u>*Still*</u> Hear – <u>*Him Say*</u>!**

Words, there are, my faithful friend, that inspire and thrill, but <u>***no***</u> combination of words *ever spoken* convey what those seven words do. For when one truly hears them, one stands in awe and wonder! They **transcend** understanding, challenge our conception of Life and Reality, and reach into the depths of our souls. They carry <u>***a Power***</u> and <u>***a Ring of Truth***</u> no other words from no other spokesman ever did impart. *Why is this so?* It is because intuitively we sense a meaning beyond intellectual grasp. The Lord is not only the **Resurrector** of men, but He is also the **Resurrection *ITSELF*!** What a paradox! For *<u>how</u>* could a person be a process, and *<u>simultaneously</u>* remain a person? The fullness of meaning is yet to come, but look no further than your heart. It freely **testifies**–*<u>This is so</u>!*

**The Most _Profound_ Words Ever Spoken
Fraught with Meaning, Mystery, and Might,
Unveiling THE Great Truth of The Ages
God of _Very_ God, Light of _Very_ Light!**

To be completely and totally ONE with another, yet remain an individual, is a **paradox** of the most sublime nature – A claim Jesus boldly proclaimed! Early Christian thinkers were **mesmerized** by this statement, and never ceased to contemplate its meaning. For the validity of this one statement _alone_ elevated Jesus far above any small, man-conceived definition of Him! It revealed nothing less than **His Infinite nature**, Divine origin, and latent power! Have you not guessed it? _'I and My Father are ONE'!_ The original Greek text allows for no diminishment of person in Jesus. He WAS wholly what the Father Was! _**And still is**!_ God of _**Very**_ God, Light of _**Very**_ Light! Though not the _same_ person as the Father, in all other respects – **Identical**! Look, then, no further than Jesus. In Him **All** the Fullness of the Godhead – _bodily dwells!_

**I AM _In_ My Father, And My Father Is _In_ Me
No More Elegant Words Are There, Such _Grand Simplicity!_ Save, I AM in _You_, and You Are In _Me_
Oh! Divine Consolation! Ever ONE – _Are We!_**

'At that day ye shall **know** that I am _IN_ my Father, and ye _IN_ Me, and I _IN_ you.' With these words, our Lord uttered in His unmatched style an all-comforting, all-inspiring Truth: God **IS** ever with us! _Where? In the Depths of our Very Being!_ You, and I, beloved, are inseparably united with Him! Others have tried to describe this relationship with more sophisticated words in an attempt to probe its meaning. Yet, helpful as their efforts are, they fall short. His words **cannot** be improved upon! _They capture a Mystery_ that is best said with fewer, less technical terms, as they reach the **heart**, and _not_ the mind. Let others speak of 'focal points of individualized consciousness', of a great 'Universal Mind manifesting in personalized expression,' as philosophers and modern-day scientists assert. Jesus' words still stand apart, as **Genius** – _beyond compare!_

The Most _Unshakable_ Words Ever Spoken
As Marble Pillars they Stand Unmoved,
More Solid Than Rock of Gibraltar
***Those* Words, that Jesus – _Did Choose_!**

Just prior to Jesus and His disciples crossing over the brook Cedron into a beautiful garden, He spoke the most lengthy recorded prayer of His life. Yet, four words stand out among them as the unassailable foundation and assurety of **all** that He claimed, the core Verity of every promise He ever made! He said, 'Sanctify them _through_ Thy Truth: **Thy Word Is Truth**.' Upon these four words, the universe is upheld, its perfect working and reliability! And so it is with our lives, as well. To every doubt that confronts us, we can say, _God's Word Is Truth!_ To each uncertainty, we can counter, _God's Word Is Truth!_ To all thoughts of fear or anxiety, we can declare, _God's Word Is Truth!_ There is _**no**_ unpleasant situation or disturbing occurrence this phrase is not applicable to, and to which it will _collapse_ in its power to belittle or intimidate us. Hold fast, **Beloved!** – _Truth Prevails!_

The Most <u>*Welcoming*</u> Words Ever Spoken
Extended with *Such* Longing and Plea,
To <u>All</u> Those Weary and Troubled
Liberated, at Last – <u>*To Be*</u>!

<u>*Never*</u> were there words spoken with such profound empathy and deep compassion! The listeners stood **transfixed** before the genuineness and magnetic power of His Presence. Even those who disbelieved were moved beyond their understanding. And when He said **'Come unto Me'** and *'<u>I</u> <u>will</u> <u>give</u> <u>you</u> <u>rest</u>'*, the crowds felt <u>*drawn*</u> as if by an unseen force that they could scarce resist! <u>*Never*</u> did such an **invitation** as His appear so attractive and enticing! <u>*Never*</u> were One's open arms so appealing and desirable! **'Come Unto Me'**, He repeated, as the people drew closer and CLOSER to His Person. *'<u>Ye</u> <u>shall</u> <u>find</u> <u>rest</u> <u>for</u> <u>your</u> <u>souls</u>,'* He continued. And many came. And many received Him. And **many** believed! And again, His melodic voice resounded over the hills, **'Come Unto <u>ME</u>,'** for *'<u>My</u> <u>Yoke</u> <u>is</u> <u>easy</u> <u>and</u> <u>My</u> <u>burden</u> <u>is</u> <u>light</u>.'* And many a day these folks found **comfort** in Hiswords–and <u>*smiled* *anew*</u>!

**The Most _Picturesque_ Words Ever Spoken
Painted – To <u>Adorn</u> the Altar in Our Souls,
To Ever Impart to Our _Longing_ Hearts, The
<u>True</u> Nature of the One – <u>_Who Beholds_</u>!**

There is One, beloved, Who beholds (_<u>ever views</u>_) His children in the most tender, endearing, and compassionate way, <u>_regardless as to their respective states of consciousness_</u>. He is portrayed as one Who **knows** His children intimately, and gladly and without hesitation **gives** His life for them. Who is He? **'I AM the good shepherd.'** Often pictured as carrying a fragile or weary baby lamb, and sometimes <u>followed</u> by, or <u>_walking along side_</u>, is a 'black sheep', symbolic of those individuals not <u>yet</u> **wholly** _'in the fold'_, <u>yet</u> <u>destined</u> <u>to</u> <u>be</u> <u>so</u>! For recall, Jesus said, **'Other** sheep have I, which are not of this fold, and them also <u>**I**</u> must bring. They **SHALL** hear my voice [at present, they _don't_], and there shall be one [wholly complete] fold.' Yes, the **Good Shepherd** _knows_ what He is doing, and this image of His Divine Role encompasses **all** that He is, and **all** He seeks to do, and in this–<u>_He cannot fail!_</u>

The Most *Gracious* Words Ever Spoken
Witnessed in Awe *from* His Mouth That Day,
Causing All in the Synagogue to Wonder
At His Manner, *and Chosen Way!*

The passage Jesus read from the Book of Isaiah had been read **before**: *'The Spirit of the Lord is upon me, because he hath anointed me to preach the gospel; to heal the brokenhearted, to preach deliverance and recovering of sight to the blind, to set at liberty them that are bruised. To preach the acceptable year of the Lord.'* Yet, **something** was **totally** different – *this time!* The unalterably tender **kindness** of his heart suffused those words, and the holy **Purity** and **innocent Joy** of His person made them breathe – and live! This is WHY they 'All *wondered* at **the gracious words** which proceeded out of *His* mouth.' For they had now truly heard them for *the very first time*, as their **very embodiment** stood before them! These words became vibrant, thrilling, captivating in their ears. And because His Inner Glory shone *through* those words, He was, initially, *'glorified – of ALL'!*

**The _Truest_ Words Ever Spoken
Are The Most <u>Practical</u> Words One Could Tell,
Revealing a _Fundamental_ Truth of Reality
The Path to Life Abundant – _as Well_!**

If only _certain_ words were to echo daily in the minds and hearts of all people, with **deep understanding**, we would have that _long-dreamed-of_ Peace and _long-sought-after_ Joy on earth! This, dear brother, are their **profound** significance! What are they? **'It is *more Blessed* to <u>Give</u> than to Receive.'** That comprehension grasps that to <u>give</u> is to <u>share</u> of one's **Inner Abundance**, allowing it to _flow_ and _expand_ in an ever-increasing capacity. And the greatest gifts are _one's time, one's listening, one's patience_ toward others, _one's <u>personal</u> service_ to others, _in encouragement, belief, and trust_. **Inner Joy, Fulfillment, Contentment,** and **Freedom** from a sense of emptiness results, as <u>_God is given living expression on Earth_</u>! **This IS man's very _reason_ for being!** And **the foundational spiritual LAW of the Universe.** To know and live it, provides a foretaste of all the Good, _<u>yet to come</u>_!

**The Most _Charming_ Words Ever Spoken
Have Enchanted More Hearts than Are Known,
Capturing _More_ Minds with Simplicity Rare
Leading More Souls – _To Their Home!_**

How many people have heard, or read, these *remarkably simple,* yet *unforgettable words*, and were suddenly arrested in their tracks, the world may never know. But, the number is inestimable! _Something_ about these words spoken by our Saviour will not allow one to 'turn away'! – **_Something_** will not permit one to discount them, nor dismiss them! –**Something** will not even let one forget them! They find immediate lodging within one's self, and their message continues to **reverberate** throughout one's being, often uncomfortably so. *What captivating words are these?* The Beatitudes, of course! Always beginning **'Blessed are'**, they offer Jesus' promises of **certain** liberation, empowerment, deliverance, inheritance, justice, supply, mercy, comfort, and fulfillment. So elegant and brief, yet **complete**, they are incomparable! – _As is their Mystical Charm!_

**The Most _Sacred_ Words Ever Spoken
Where Reverence and Love Do Entwine,
Not to Mention _Wonder_ and Mystery
Since the Very Dawning –_of Time_!**

Genesis records **a Great Mystery** regarding the _wondrous_ forces that interplay between male and female. The human body is a marvel of creation, yet the **miracle** of **conjugal relations** is an _Act_ of Creation at multiple levels of being, in Itself – and yes, even an _Act_ of Worship! 'A man shall leave his father and his mother, and shall cleave [be joined] unto his wife: and **They [two] shall BE one flesh**,' said the Apostle Paul. Yet, more is going on here than meets the eye, for he said, 'But I speak concerning _Christ and the Church_.' Paul cites mysterious and intriguing **parallels** between man and woman (husband and wife), and Christ and the Church (Christ and His Bride). Tantalizing images of physical and spiritual **Oneness** abound that speak to _a unity of Being_ few dare to entertain, nor can scarce conceive. Yet, clearly, **a shared Identity**, where we are **'members'** of each other–_is revealed!_

**The Most _Calming_ Words Ever Spoken
May Resound In Our Hearts Each Day,
Bringing Surcease of _Sorrowful_ Care
A <u>Trust</u> to Take Worries – <u>_Away_</u>!**

'In the midst of the uncertainties of this 'present evil world', it is our _privilege_ to maintain a **calm repose** in God.' So reminded us a fellow believer. That calm repose springs from our Saviour's promise: **'Let NOT your heart be troubled: ye [who] believe in God, [can] <u>ALSO</u> believe in Me.'** Yes, dear heart, we **CAN** place our trust in Jesus, and reap the rewards of <u>deciding</u> to do so, and experience the **release** of fear, irrespective of threatening appearance or daunting circumstance! What is the **<u>advantage</u>** of looking to a Divine **Man** as contrasted to a Divine _Spirit_, God the Father, _alone?_ – The fact that _<u>through</u>_ Jesus we can enjoy a real rest, or _peace of mind_, unobtainable any other way, because **humanly** He achieved and demonstrated <u>IT</u> <u>IS</u> <u>POSSIBLE</u>, and **assures** us **<u>we</u>** can do the same! How? By realizing our **humanity IS** our connection to Him, as is HIS humanity–<u>_ours_</u>!

**The Most _Instructive_ Words Ever Spoken
Are _Perhaps_ the <u>Most</u> Important Ones, Too,
Of Doctrine or Ritual I Ask You _Not_ Learn,
But of <u>My</u> <u>Person</u> So Near – _<u>to</u>_ _<u>You</u>!_**

As relevant and beneficial as can be the learning of church doctrine or ecclesiastical ritual, or even sacred history, Jesus _<u>never</u>_ _<u>once</u>_ asked that we study, learn, or memorize these things! Instead, He told us to **'<u>Learn</u> _of_ Me'**. This is because the whole of Salvation centers _squarely_ upon Him – **alone**! For to become intimately acquainted with Jesus, **The Man**, to receive _<u>His</u>_ Spirit into your soul, to share in His Heart-Throbs for humanity, **IS** to be converted and redeemed and saved! _<u>Nothing else</u>_ is _<u>required</u>!_ Not church attendance, denominational conformity, tithing, ritual participation, nor Holyday observance, wonderful as these are in themselves. The disciple, or _<u>student</u>_, who heeds this 'assignment' has discovered that His Master is not residing in a far-off Heaven, but **actually is present** _in His heart_, thru Spirit, to **learn _from_ Him**, _personally_ – <u>Today</u>!

**The Most <u>Truthful</u> Words Ever Spoken
Upon 'The Witness Stand' Were Heard,
Voiced <u>*So*</u> Solemn by The Humble Jesus
Though *None* Believed – <u>*Any*</u> <u>*Word*</u>*!***

As Jesus stood with hands bound, before the Judgment Seat of Pilate, the governor of Judea, He asked Jesus the most significant question of his interrogation – *and* his life: **'Art thou a king then?'** Whereupon Jesus answered, 'Thou sayest [correctly] that **I <u>AM</u> <u>a</u> <u>king</u>**. <u>*To*</u> <u>*this*</u> <u>*end*</u> <u>*was*</u> <u>*I*</u> <u>*born,*</u> <u>*and for*</u> <u>*this*</u> <u>*cause*</u> <u>*came*</u> <u>*I*</u> <u>*into*</u> <u>*the*</u> <u>*world*</u>, that <u>I</u> <u>should</u> <u>bear</u> **<u>Witness</u>** <u>unto</u> <u>the</u> <u>Truth</u>.' Yes, Jesus told the Truth, the **Whole** Truth, and *Nothing* but the Truth! And in concluding His testimony, He added, *'Every one that is of the Truth heareth* [understands, or is sympathetic to] *my Voice.'* But Pilate, troubled and doubtful of his own actions, could <u>not</u> hear [agree and appropriately respond to] **The** Truth! His involuntary **exclamation** of 'What <u>*IS*</u> Truth?' clearly evidenced his confusion, ambivalence, and uneasiness before **The One** of such 'Kingly' manner, which he **could NOT**– *deny!*

The Most _Triumphant_ Words Ever Spoken Even _Before_ the Cross Declared, Announcing His Victory Over All that Would Veer, from the Heart of the Father – _so Fair!_

Many do not realize that Jesus was the acknowledged Master and Lord of Life even _before_ His tremendous Accomplishment of enduring the Cross, though He stated it in the clearest of terms. He confidently and authoritatively asserted prior to His arrest, trial, and crucifixion, **'_I have [ALREADY] overcome the world!_'** He had fully prepared Himself to successfully meet the super-human challenge of the Cross, and most notably at the unseen _spiritual_ level where the Victory would be decided. And what of His exclamation of '_It is Accomplished_'? This, too, was a shout of Triumph, but one that was meant to '**place a seal**' of **corroboration** for those then-present witnesses upon what was **already** attained. Yes, dethronement of 'principalities and powers' **was** formally enacted, that day, the outcome of a certain and **foregone conclusion**–thru the _Unconquerable Power of Love!_

The Most _Reassuring_ Words Ever Spoken
To Address _Every_ Concern and Fear,
High in Old Galilee's Mountain
After His Rising – _Appeared!_

Beloved friend, do we have a Saviour whose power, though tremendous, is actually still _limited_ in its **ultimate** reach? Can Jesus truly 'save to the _uttermost_', as Holy Scripture assures us? – With His Love 'winning over' even the most 'incorrigible' person? Or can there come a time when even **His** great power is _insufficient_ to save a person from him- or her-self? Listen to our Saviour's reply: '**ALL Power in Heaven and in Earth is Given Unto Me!**' Brother in Christ, 'All Power' means just that – ALL Power! – _NO_ detrimental power, from ANY Realm, Source, or Being – whether emotional, mental, physical, spiritual, or even misguided, or corrupted, **WILL** power, can survive indefinitely in the Healing Balm of His Love, in the Light of His Presence, in the Transforming Energies of His Person! No, you can be sure He will **exercise _that_ Power** for **everyone's** sake! And _ultimate good!_

**The Most _Humble_ Words Ever Spoken
Did Our Saviour Quietly Speak That Day,
Revealing a Mind, _Oh!_ So 'Meek' and Mild
And a Heart 'Lowly' – _as Clay_!**

Holy Writ informs us Moses was *the most humble* man on earth up to his time. Possibly his speech impediment served to make him so. Yet, one would not naturally expect the **Master Orator**, not to mention, The **_Master of Life_**, to share such a sentiment. Yet, this is precisely what we find in examining His Life actions and pronouncement on His own importance or power. He said, **'I can of mine own self do _NOTHING_.'** – Do *'nothing'* did He say? – How can this be? Is this not the One Who performed mighty miracles, and even raised the dead? The key to grasping this enigmatic statement is to understand Jesus realized that *without* His fellow human beings, whom He called brothers, His Life, **grand and magnificent**, *as it was*, was *worthless* to Him! *And* His Outgoing Love! This is the Saviour we worship! Who puts **all others**– *first!*

**The <u>Greatest</u> Commandment I Say to Thee
Is a Two-Fold Statement of Purity, Rehearsed
by the Heart, and Practiced by the Soul, Upon
These Words, The Universe – <u>*Unfolds*</u>!**

When Jesus was asked what was the Greatest Commandment ever given to men, He promptly replied, *<u>first</u>*, in three solitary words, ***'Thou Shalt LOVE!'*** Then, after identifying the object of this love, He declared again, 'Thou Shalt <u>LOVE</u>!' Reciting this statement ***<u>twice</u>*** signified its paramount importance, and that its action is to be repeated over and <u>*over*</u> again! The unendingness of Love is thus shown in its constant <u>replication</u>, and, if you will, its ceaseless reproduction and birthing – *throughout humanity!* For you see, beloved, it was a **prophecy**, as much as a commandment. Recall that even the universe 'groans and travails', awaiting 'the **manifestation** of the Sons of God.' And *what is* this manifestation, this long-awaited outpicturing, but the Love that is *infinitely pure, holy, unalterable, and imperishable!* Yes! **All** of the law of life, of the universe, is fulfilled in this 'word' – *<u>Thou Shalt Love</u>!*

Let Me Hear You Speak, Lord,
Clear, and Strong, and Free,
As _When_ Your Voice Did _Travel_
O'er the Mountains – _and the Sea_!

An ancient seer foretold, 'He shall _**not**_ strive, _**nor**_ cry, _**nor**_ lift up His voice in the streets'. He Whose voice _rang_ with **Truth**, _echoed_ with **Love**, _resounded_ with **Beauty**, did _not_ have to shout to be heard! He spoke clearly, distinctly, even powerfully, often choosing the hills and mountains to **broadcast** His speech, and the seas to **amplify** His word. The outdoor amphitheater for His discourses allowed _thousands_ to hear Him at one time. _When_ He spoke, others fell silent, as His voice resonated with a magnificent _**dignity**_. Centuries later, nature _still_ carries **His Immortal Words** on Its breezes and over murmuring brooks. But, for those _with_ ears to hear, He **still** speaks in quiet majesty. So, **listen** for Him in reverential silence, _as did His country men and women,_ and you will be captivated, and **entranced** – _along with them_!

**Hold <u>My</u> <u>Word</u> Close to Your Breast
As You Cling To It Tenaciously, And So
Then <u>Miracles</u>, *Commonplace,* You'll Find
As Love Blossoms Forth – *<u>In Thee</u>!***

How **precious**, dear heart, are the Lord's *Words of Life* to you? Did you know He compares His Word to apples composed of **<u>solid</u> <u>gold</u>** and pictures framed in **<u>pure</u> <u>silver</u>**? – Representing untold monetary wealth! Yet, *His Word is more precious than this!* – It is *<u>more</u> <u>valuable</u>* than ALL the riches of the world! Should you lose your home, profession, belongings, friends, even your health, all you possess, *<u>IF</u>* you have His Word enshrined in your heart, you would still have cause for **Rejoicing!** – *believing* in the **Goodness** and **Sweetness** of Life, *anticipating* the **Triumph of Love!** *Expecting* the **Restoration** of any former loss – *<u>in this life</u>!* With His **Sure Word** of Promise, you can remain positive, hopeful, and growing in Love. *Miracles attend such as these!* **Remember!** Jesus **<u>IS</u>** *the* **<u>Living</u> <u>Word</u>!** No greater treasure more practical or satisfying or rewarding – *<u>than Him</u>!*

What _More_ Can You Say, Lord, _Than_ You Have Said, Your Words Have Been Our Daily Bread, Though an Army of Poets Greater Words Seek, _None_ Can Surpass Yours – _Most Meek!_

Beloved friend, though Jesus was the **Greatest Man** to have ever lived, He never sought for greatness as do men. He was 'lowly' in heart, and sought only to ***bring out*** the greatness – in others! Likewise, He did not set out to speak _the most wonderful words ever spoken_, yet His Words could not help but be so! Do you know _why?_ Those words recorded in the New Testament are **complete**, as no other words are. _There is nothing lacking_. They are **whole** and **entire**. And they are **Divine**! It is their **utter simplicity** that confounds both the skeptic and the scholar. Not to mention their **startling beauty** and incomparable **power**! They 'pierce' _directly_ to the heart and soul of man! Carrying with them a **convicting** capacity to heal! Jesus left us **all** we _need_ to hear! Though all we _want_ to hear –_is yet to come!_

**Many Believe Jesus' Parables Prove
The 'Lost' Will *Surely* Their Salvation Lose!
And That *Into* a Burning, Fiery Place Will Go,
But Similes <u>Never</u> Can Say, '*<u>This</u> Is So*'!**

A great deal of doctrinal misunderstanding would be avoided if only people would pay close attention to The Saviour's chosen manner of teaching. The stories Jesus related to the populace at large were *<u>always</u>* given as **'Parables'**, using the figure of speech known as **'Simile'**. 'The Kingdom of Heaven is *<u>like</u> <u>unto</u>*', Jesus repeatedly said, signaling to careful listeners (and readers) that what was to follow is a tale, or observation, *comparing two <u>dissimilar</u> things to each other.* <u>At</u> <u>no</u> <u>time</u> was Jesus saying that the graphic tale He was painting represented **the actual, literal thing** – only that there was a resemblance in some fashion. And, then, to re-emphasize the Parable should <u>*not*</u> be taken as literal fact, Jesus would say, in closing, '*<u>He</u> <u>that</u> <u>hath</u> [inner, spiritually discerning] <u>ears</u> <u>to</u> <u>hear</u>, <u>let</u> **<u>him</u>** <u>hear</u> [or understand]!*' – As the true meaning was not intended to be apparent – <u>*at*</u> <u>*all!*</u>

What They *Thought* They Understood, They Did Not, as the Saviour's Clear Testimony Taught, Yet, This Being True Sheds a Vast Light Anew, On the Meaning, Jesus NOW – *Would Impart!*

Once, the disciples asked Jesus, 'Why do you speak unto the people in parables?' His answer was quite illuminating, though overlooked by most. He replied, 'Because it is given unto **you** to know the mysteries [the true, *intended* meaning] of the kingdom of heaven, but to them it is not given [*yet*] . . .Therefore speak I unto them in parables: because hearing they hear not, ***neither do they understand.*** ' Now, the parables were plain enough. Jesus chose simple terminology for common working men. But, note, Jesus emphatically stated the people-at-large did ***not*** understand their meaning! This can only be so if the stories taken *at face value* – could ***not*** have been the **actual** meaning! Even today, the parables are widely misinterpreted, but thanks be to God, the Truth is being made progressively known by various authoritative, credible sources – vindicating the Supreme God *of Love* – and ***ultimate Redemptor*** – *of All!*

**Hear a Parable of 'The Net and the Sea'
In The <u>True</u> Way It Was Intended to Be, And
Answer the Lord with a 'Nay' *as You Should*, *<u>If</u>*
You Believe the Apostles Knew – *<u>All</u> <u>They</u> <u>Could</u>!*

After reciting the parable of 'The Net and the Sea', Jesus uttered a concluding statement regarding a 'furnace of fire' and 'wailing and gnashing of teeth'. Jesus then immediately asked a penetrating question (intending we, His future listeners, ask of ourselves!). In Matthew 13:51, Jesus said unto them, '*Have ye [**truly**] understood all these things?*' – With, no doubt, a quizzical and intensely curious look in his eye. Whereupon, they said unto him, 'Yea, Lord', confidently asserting they did understand, with a distinctive note of pride. **But, NOTICE!** Jesus did *<u>not</u>* say, 'Yes, I see that you do understand'! – Because He knew they *<u>didn't</u>!* Nor would they! – *<u>Until</u>* the Holy Spirit should choose to explain! They took the 'surface' meaning to be the actual, 'deeper' meaning, as most people, regretably, do to this very day! A severe **purification** period to come, for some, but *<u>not</u>* – *<u>as</u> <u>envisioned</u>!*

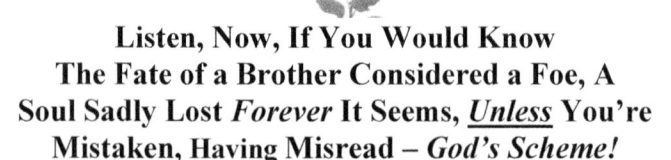

Listen, Now, If You Would Know
The Fate of a Brother Considered a Foe, A
Soul Sadly Lost *Forever* It Seems, <u>*Unless*</u> You're
Mistaken, Having <u>Misread</u> – *God's Scheme!*

Friend, many believe the Apostle Judas is *eternally lost* due to his revolting act of betrayal to the Master. They even cite scripture quoting Jesus, Himself, to uphold this position. Yet a closer examination reveals something quite different. In Christ's High Priestly prayer, He spoke to the Father these words: '<u>*Those*</u> that Thou gavest Me **I have kept**, and **NONE** OF *THEM* [<u>the twelve Apostles</u>] **is** Lost.' (John 17:12) Here, Jesus introduced the governing statement. *<u>Any</u>* comments to follow are *<u>qualified</u>* by its clear and unequivocal meaning, and must be interpreted in its light. Jesus went on to say, 'But the son of perdition [is 'lost,' *<u>temporarily</u>*].' And to what end? *'That the scripture might be fulfilled!'* – **Not** lost forever due to his horrendous action! Moreover, Jesus said He was to 'give eternal life to *<u>as many</u>* as [the Father] had given Him. And *how many* did He say the Father had given Him? See John 17:2, '**all flesh**', <u>*or everyone*</u>!

**Jesus, the Master Wordsmith, We'll See Frequently Utilized *Hyperbole*, A Figure of Speech the Learn-*ed* Did Know, and Recognize as <u>Exaggerated</u> Depictions – *of <u>Woe</u>!*

The Glorious Galilean probably was *well versed* in several languages, Hebrew, Aramaic, and Greek almost for certain. Jesus, too, was well acquainted with the principles of rhetoric, meaning specialized grammatical constructions. In particular, one such figure of speech Jesus utilized is termed 'hyperbole', or obvious and intentional <u>***exaggeration***</u> for effect, such as to evoke strong feelings or create a lasting impression, but **never meant to be taken literally!** Such statements as 'I had to *wait an eternity'*, or 'Her comments *burned me up*!' are both hyperboles. Now how does one tell when <u>*Jesus' statements*</u> are hyperbolic? Should the literal interpretation violate our God-given **<u>reason</u>, <u>sanity</u>,** or **<u>the dictates of *genuine* Love</u>**, then we can **know** it to be so. All parabolic depictions of hell clearly fall into this category. Dire consequences, yes! But, having a <u>*limited*</u> time duration & <u>*remedial outcome!*</u>

**Of What *Kind* of God Did Jesus Tell
A God of Wrath and a God of Hell, Or
A God of *Divine* Peace and of *Infinite* Grace
Extending to, the Whole – <u>*Human Race!*</u>**

Jesus made what the Jewish religious authorities of His day believed to be a wholly *incredulous* statement. In <u>*no way*</u> could it possibly be true, they reasoned. For to them, it challenged the **glaringly obvious fact** that <u>*their ancestry*</u> directly listened to the Voice of the Creator, and that they had visually witnessed <u>first-hand</u> God's physical appearance during the time of Moses. Yet, *what did Jesus say?* 'Ye have <u>*neither*</u> heard His voice at any time, <u>*nor*</u> seen His shape [that of **The Father**]!' (John 5:37) This is, of course, because the **True God** '<u>*IS*</u> Spirit' (John 4:24, the indefinite article 'a' is <u>not</u> in the original Greek), omni*present*, omni*potent*, and omni*scient*, Who dwells in 'unapproachable Light!' Invisible to human eyes and inaudible to human ears! <u>***THIS***</u> God of Love possesses ONLY '*everlasting mercy*' (Psalm 100:5), and again, 'His mercy **endureth forever**,' as Psalms repeatedly – <u>*declare!*</u>

**'Dare to Love!' our Saviour 'Said',
Yet, *Where* in Scripture is This Read,
It's In His Every Action True, And In
His Dream of Life – *For You!***

God harbors a Mighty Dream of Life in His Heart for every one of His children. And though He has very special and individual plans for each of us, His overall purpose for our lives is the same: He desires – above all else – that we **'Dare to Love!'** Did Christ, our Lord, ever actually give voice to these *exact* words? He may very well have, though they were unrecorded, but even *if* He didn't, we can be certain THAT was **the innermost meaning held in His Heart!** When Christ said, 'Love ye One Another, *as I have loved you'*, He most assuredly meant to love with the **daring of spirit** and **abandonment of self** He so profusely exhibited throughout his brief, but so brave life. For daring is a major prerequisite if we are to overcome our natural shyness and self-doubt, not to mention others' resistance to the expression of Love – *to All!*

What <u>Other</u> Words *Might* HE Have Said
***This* Life, *This* Love, This Living Bread,**
Though *Un*recorded, Voiced to Atone
Unpenned, Yet – *<u>Spirit</u> <u>Known</u>!*

'And there are also **many** other things which Jesus did [and, no doubt, *<u>said</u>*].' So recorded Apostle John. Yet, what *might* some of them have been? Utilizing the principle of extension, or extrapolation, we can be reasonably certain of the validity of some. Jesus said, 'I AM the Resurrection', and likely said, 'I AM the <u>Ascension</u>', though no scriptural record was made. He said, 'I AM the Door', yet could also have said, 'I AM the <u>Bridge</u> [*between* humanity and God]'. Jesus could also easily have said, 'I AM the *undisturbable* <u>Peace</u> of God', embodied in human form. Not to mention, 'I AM the *<u>Reconciliation</u>*' of the *created* back to The Creator. <u>**All**</u> such statements would be TRUE! Why *speculate* on such matters? Because it sheds light on what we **know** has been said, by offering insightful shades and nuances of meaning – *<u>unfolding</u> <u>still</u>!*

The Apostles

Words
of

**The MOST _Mysterious_ Words Ever Spoken
Did the Apostle Paul Recite on _That_ Day,
Causing True _Marvel_ – and _Wonder_ At
What _So Few_ Brief Words – _Can Say!_**

When Paul the Apostle to the Gentiles was in prison in Rome, he penned three simple words. That brief sentence was a **central** part of what was revealed to Him as the Revelation of 'THE **Mystery** which had been _hidden_ from Ages and _from generations._' Men have read those words repeatedly, yet there remains an indefinable, _marvel-eliciting_ **depth** and **breadth** to those words none other possess. _What words are they?_ – '**Christ in you**'! To which Paul hastens to add, 'the _hope of glory!_'. These words hearken back to what Jesus, Himself, said that 'I [AM] _in You_'. In this brief thought can be sensed the Purpose of Life and tantalizing intimations of a **Reality** of our being few dare entertain. Yet, these words ever point in that direction. A **_Communion_** _of Being_, a sharing of unparalleled Intimacy, and Unity – _Mysterious Still!_

The Most _Encouraging_ Words Ever Spoken Leaves the Heart So *Grateful* and *Relieved*, Assuring Us of Our <u>Destined</u> Success, and Of the Certainty – <u>*We Will Believe*</u>*!*

'Being **confident** of <u>*this*</u> very thing, that – **He** Who hath begun a good work in you – WILL perform [original Greek: **complete**] it – until the day of Jesus Christ.' Beloved, this one statement causes the angels in Heaven to rejoice in humanity's behalf because they know that *the Saviour <u>alone</u>* **secures** and makes **unalterably permanent** our salvation, and <u>*not*</u> we ourselves! No matter how many times we may falter, lose faith, or turn away from our Creator out of ignorance, weakness, or unwarranted fear, He **will** call us back, and we **will** unfailingly respond due to the <u>***irresistibility***</u> of His Grace! What a tremendous **relief** to know this, as it frees us from the overwhelming and presumptuous burden of thinking **we** are responsible for something we are <u>*totally*</u> <u>*incapable*</u> of accomplishing on our own. Even the so-called 'incorrigible' and 'wholly lost' will return to the fold, being **confirmed** –<u>*to the end*</u>*!*

**The Most _Emboldening_ Words Ever Spoken
Reminding of <u>What</u> We Most _Truly_ Are,
Declared with Conviction Triumphant
Sustained by – _Heaven's Day Star!_**

Irreplaceable friend, the time comes in the life of every Christ follower when he or she must face a devastating or frightening situation which appears to be unbearable or undefeatable. Yet, it is then we are reminded by the Holy Spirit that '**We are _More_ Than Conquerors _through_ <u>Him</u> Who Loved us.**' Yes, we are MORE than conquerors – *more than* the greatest Victors who have ever lived! **More than** even those great leaders of **Righteous Causes**, who in the midst of world-wide conflict, brought deliverance to millions and secured the blessings of Liberty for posterity. Though we be hindered, deterred, cast down, or battered on every side, *we **cannot** be defeated!* – As the Power of <u>HIS</u> Love will not allow it! Even if we be, *for a time*, seeming victims of mistreatment, ill health, or financial ruin, we can KNOW ours **<u>IS</u>** the Victory – _Forevermore!_

**The Most _Telling_ Words Ever Spoken
Though More <u>Brief</u> They Could Never Be,
Two Words Alone Speaking _Volumes_, Offering
Such an _<u>Intimate</u>_ Portrait – _<u>of Thee</u>!_**

The shortest sentence in all of Scripture one could <u>_so easily_</u> pass right over, without further thought. It reads simply, **'Jesus wept.'** So concise, so succinct. So _seemingly_ unimportant. **But, not so, beloved friend!** Jesus had just conversed with Mary, so distraught over her brother Lazarus' death, and observed relatives and sympathizers weeping, too. John recorded that upon seeing, and experiencing, this outpouring of grief, Jesus **groaned** in His spirit, and was _<u>troubled</u>_. The picture that emerges of Jesus reveals a Saviour-God who literally, <u>emotionally _feels_</u> the **Heart-_ache_** and **Heart-cry** of His people! He is empathically bound to their sufferings, and is **ONE** with them in the deepest, most-connected human sense! No immovable, aloof, impassioned-to-pain, Saviour, here! **<u>His</u>** grief was so profound that those Jewish people there exclaimed, **'Behold! _<u>How</u>_ He loved him!'** They knew the Truth–_<u>Do you</u>?_

The Most _Awe_-Inspiring Words Ever Spoken
'<u>**Behold**</u>**! The LAMB Who** _**Taketh Away**_**!'**
Every Departure _from_ **Love and Life**
That <u>_All_</u> _Be Redeemed –_ <u>_**One**_</u> <u>_**Day**_</u>_!_

A forerunner of the greatest person to have ever lived said he was unworthy to <u>_even_</u> unloose the shoe latchet of the **Anointed One**. Though the Latter's estimation of him, John the Baptist, was that _none_ born of women, were greater than he! How **GREAT**, then, **must** the One called the Messiah be! <u>_So_</u> great, my friend, that He had the Power to do what no man could do – '<u>_**bear**_</u> away [original Greek] the sin <u>_of_</u> <u>_the_</u> <u>_world_</u>! When John exclaimed the word, 'Behold', as a preface to this amazing statement, he was telling his audience to stand still, quietly, reverently, and be witness to what few would directly see. The sacrificial **Lamb of God** in His human Incarnation bearing, or <u>_carrying_</u>, upon His shoulders, the weight of the world's transgressions. To be dealt with **permanently**, **perfectly**, for all people, in **His** Person–<u>_on_</u> <u>_the_</u> <u>_Tree_</u>_!_

**The Most _Patient_ Words Ever Spoken
They Continue <u>On</u> and <u>_ON_</u>, to This Day,
An Unalterable Waiting for Love to be Born
In the Hearts of <u>All</u> – _Gone Astray!_**

Dear Heart, a liberating, **stupendous Truth** resides within the meaning of a much quoted, but _most often_ **grievously** misunderstood Scripture – Because it is nearly always taken to mean the _exact opposite_ of what it is intended to mean! That verse is: **'<u>Today</u> _is_ <u>THE</u> Day of Salvation!'** Most take this to mean the 'offer' of Salvation is extended for _a limited duration of time_, and that at some juncture, will be withdrawn _forever_, from any given individual, who has not repented and accepted Christ as Saviour. **Yet, beloved, nothing could be further from the Truth!** Since **EVERY** future day _becomes_ TODAY upon its arrival, the opportunity for Salvation is ongoing and continuous! – At <u>NO</u> time is _<u>the</u> <u>door</u> <u>to</u> <u>reformation</u>_ **<u>ever</u>** permanently closed to any wayward human soul! The **Patience** of God **WILL** win out, inexhaustible – _as It Is!_

**The Most _Mystical_ Words Ever Spoken
Whether by Prophet, Sage, or Seer, Can
Awaken Ourselves to _Such_ Wonder and Awe
And to _Summon_ a World of – _No Fear!_**

The most spiritual, transcendent, meaning-filled words ever spoken are: **'Be Still, and Know, I AM God.'** One could contemplate these seven words a lifetime and _never_ exhaust their profound meaning. Reciting these words regularly brings _a sense of Peace,_ not of this world. Jesus spoke of **The Great 'BE Still'**, or the _Tremendous Stillness of Being_, from whence all Divine Contentment and Unassailable Safety arises, when He said 'Peace, **Be Still**' to the tumultuous waves. And He repeatedly declared **The Great 'KNOWING'** in **The Great 'I AM' declarations**. And in the **fullness** of this knowing, fear ceases to exist! – No fear of life, death, pain, nor loss. For **here** is the Light of the Heart, _the Power of Infinite Love_, shining in the darkness of being. And as one worthy messenger so eloquently proclaimed, 'Amplifying Itself UNTIL It is Victorious!'–enveloping all–_World without End!'_

**The Most _Revealing_ Words Ever Spoken
On God's Nature We've _Longed_ to Hear,
As They Unveil the Ultimate 'Eyeglass'
On _Any_ Doubt with – _Answer Clear!_**

The perceptual 'lens' with which we view our Creator determine our understanding of His nature. Thankfully, the Holy Scripture provides, *in one verse*, the one and ONLY **perfect 'lens'** that serves as the **context** with which all other references to deity are to be evaluated and understood. Apart from an exact and correct understanding of this Scriptural *'Rosetta Stone'*, or doctrinal language 'key', many perplexing or mis-translated verses will trouble our souls relentlessly, as they would cast doubt on our Creator's ultimate intentions toward His children, gone astray or not. This perfect and **all-encompassing** description of God's Heart should serve as the 'moderator' to any other verse that would, *by itself*, seem to cast disparaging remarks on our Father's Perfect Character and True Justice toward men. Those saving words? '**God IS Love!**' **Never** hate! *Never* condemnation! – *Amen!*

**The Most _Unbelievable_ Words Ever Spoken
Which the _Few_ Believe, Now, as Then,
<u>Because</u> It Is ALL _Too_ Wondrous
Requiring a Miracle – _Within!_**

The Apostle Paul was graced with special and unique revelations, and was God's chief instrument for delivering the _Fullness_ of the Gospel of Christ to the world. His were the **mature** teachings of God which Christ had _wanted_ to give during the time of His earthly sojourn, but was unable to because His Apostles **_'could not bear them'_**, then. Even now, with this central aspect of what Paul called the 'Mystery Teaching', recorded, in _plain English_, for all time, in his epistle to the Corinthians, **few** believers comprehend the simple, natural, and unambiguous meaning those words convey. In Truth, nothing short of a _miracle of enlightenment_ from God will allow one to believe it at all. What is that teaching? – **'That God may be <u>All</u> in <u>ALL</u>!'** Or, That God may be '_everything_ in _everyone!_' No persons exempt here. The Indwelling is –_Universal!_

**The Most <u>Thrilling</u> Words Ever Spoken
Did John Hear on Patmos Isle That Day,**
The **Heart-Throbbing <u>Dream</u> of *Our* Saviour
Come True! <u>*Joined*</u> To His Beloved – <u>*Always*</u>!**

Is there *<u>anything</u>* more **thrilling**, dear heart, than to **<u>BE</u>** either the bride or the groom when a marriage ceremony *<u>begins</u>!* What greater cause for Holy thrills could there be? The Desire to give **wholly** of one's self with every thought, breath, word, and deed. One's heart beating in rapturous anticipation for a life together of love, sharing, caring, and oneness! And **<u>who</u>** is the Lord's Beloved save those ones for whom He died –**humanity,** now *awakened*, purified, and redeemed! As Holy writ says, 'arrayed in fine linen, clean and white, for the fine linen is the **righteousness** of saints [holy ones].' Yes, 'for we shall be **<u>like</u> Him**'! So, hear! 'The **<u>Marriage</u>** of the Lamb <u>IS COME</u>, and His Wife's made herself ready [for Him]!' Let the wedding processional begin! – *And* the Vows of **Eternal Love** – <u>*At Last*</u>!

A Name Seldom on Men's Lips Today
Even the 'Spiritual' Rarely Voice It, Nor Say,
Which *If* They Only Knew, Could <u>Shatter</u> Walls
of Doubt, <u>Propel</u> Deliverance – *to Them, Too!*

Frequently, dear heart, very spiritual, Godly people, solicit their Creator for healing, deliverance, supply, guidance, forgiveness, or peace. Yet, **many** today never even *once* mention the incomparable Name of **Jesus of Nazareth** in connection with their prayers. They invoke the name of the Divine Mother, the Holy Spirit, Archangel Michael, supposed cosmic beings, ascended masters, or nature spirits. They seek favors through their intercession. But, all the while not *once* acknowledging **The Divine Son of the Living God! The <u>Supreme</u> Mediator *between* God and man!** This often is due to ignorance or false teaching regarding the Role of Jesus in God's Universal Plan. And it is the *USE* of <u>His</u> Name that **unleashes Power** to mankind on earth! But, due to the Law of Free Will, It **must** be recited either mentally or orally. For without reverential **believing** *<u>in</u>* HisName, *in <u>Him</u>,* many miracles–*<u>remain</u> <u>unborn</u>!*

Farewell Words

Within the words of the Saviour are **Life** and **Healing** and **Truth**. His words are unparalleled in the history of the world for their sheer beauty, captivating elegance, and unmatched power! '*Never* man spoke like this man', the officers exclaimed, so uniquely compelling were His words! He became **The** MasterWordsmith, uttering words *impregnated* with Life, and with them calm was **born** from storms and life **arose** from death. Spoken in a whisper or out loud, His words **resonate** with Truth. And though centuries have passed, they have proven *timeless* and **deathless** as Himself! Lending solace, comfort, and courage, they bring Vibrant and **Incomparable Hope** to a despairing world! So, *drink in* of them every day! Feed upon their all-nourishing, wholly-satisfying substance. Delve **deeper** into them. And you will *no longer* be a slave to sorrow, depression, and sadness ever again!

With Every Good Wish, The Author

Part II

A Message to Empower *the* Heart!

Take Heart Beloved!

Never Doubt
Evermore
From *This* Day On,
It's True!
I AM
With You *Always!*
I Have Pledged
My Love
To YOU!

(Jesus *The* Christ)

Part II – Introduction
Victory <u>Can</u> Be Yours!

We are told, though the Power of the Gentle Galilean, we can live a **Life of Victory** and experience the **Joy of a Calm Spirit**, *in spite of our circumstances*, <u>each</u> and <u>every</u> day. How often, however, are we given a more complete explanation, the **<u>full</u>** reason *<u>how</u>* and <u>why</u> this is truly so? Genuine, living **Trust** CAN be obtained, exercised, and **proven** to be <u>**practical**</u> and event-altering in facing the ongoing challenges of life. By immersing one's self in Truths little realized or taught of **God's Power** to **uplift** our hearts, we **<u>can</u> receive** His liberating viewpoint – and become *<u>free!</u>*

Part II – Contents

Oh! Dearly Beloved Child of Mine
The Divine Message of Our God
How Beautiful the Trust God Freely Gives
Not All-Powerful God, but as 'Mere' Man
The Conquering of Fear Our Lord Did Then

Fear Not the Raging Storm
Love Believes All Things, We're Told
Never Despair, Your Cause Is Not Lost
Hear, Now, A Golden Message
Lord, My Awakened Heart Does Say

I Come to Uplift You, Inspire You Today
Into the Realm of Life I Leap
I Wonder What Wonders Could Be Done
Lord, What Would You Have Me Do Today
To Trust in the Lord

Angel of Mercy, Come to Me
'I Say Unto You, I Say Unto You'
A Special Day the Lord Has Made
I AM In You, and You In Me
Creation is a Fact, Scientists Now Declare

Part II – **Contents** – *Con.*

For God So Loved the World
His Words Can Always Be Trusted
A Truth That Must Be Told, and Should
A Message Transcendent He Brought
One Day, 'Soon', There Certainly Will Be

My Dearest Darling
Lord Jesus, Without You
Lord, Should All Else I Desire Not Come

Farewell Message

**Oh! Dearly Beloved Child of Mine
<u>*All*</u> Things Will Turn Out <u>Right</u>, You
Have Loved the Stars too Fondly
To Be Fearful of – <u>*The*</u> <u>*Night!*</u>**

So penned an unknown author, a sentiment of profound meaning. '**All things** work together for good to those who love God.' This is **equally** true for those who do not <u>*yet*</u> love God! You, who have stood in raptured awe before the wonder, mystery, and majesty of the night sky cannot help but recognize the validity of these words! You may not have done so since childhood. Yet, the memory is *<u>hidden</u> <u>away</u>* in your soul. The darkness **cannot** swallow up *the Light!* For now, it serves only as a backdrop against which the Light so brightly shines! But, one day, **all** will be Light! Scripture says, 'And the [celestial] city had *no need* of the sun; for the **glory** of God did lighten it, and the Lamb <u>**IS**</u> the Light of it.' This is <u>*why*</u> the hosts of Heaven **always** proclaim 'Fear not!' They know the outcome of our Creator's plan. And – *<u>it</u> <u>is</u> <u>certain!</u>*

The Divine Message of Our God Evermore, My Dear, Sweet Friend, *IS* – 'The LIGHT Was For *All* Time, *AND*, The LOVE Was For – <u>*All*</u> <u>*Men!*</u>'

John wrote, '***That*** was the **True Light** which lighteth **every** man that cometh into the world.' Time is the dimension in which men dwell; Eternity, the dimension God inhabits. Yet, till time ceases to be, and the consciousness of <u>*its*</u> <u>*passing*</u> departs, God's Light will **illumine** it, having broken through its confines, infiltrating its every moment! This is what Jesus did when He 'passed *through* the heavens'. His <u>*Bright*</u> <u>*Presence*</u> is within the longest minute and the slowest moving hour. And <u>*The*</u> <u>*Love?*</u> 'For God so loved ***the world*** [the world of ***All*** men], that He gave [<u>*to*</u> ***All*** men] His Only Begotten Son.' How could he do otherwise, exempting **none**, as 'God IS Love'! That Love will **never** be withdrawn! Nor can it ever be rendered powerless. ***Every*** human heart is destined with all certainty to be utterly **transformed** by It – <u>*one*</u> <u>*day!*</u>

**How _Beautiful_ the Trust God Freely Gives
To Those Open, Receptive Hearts Still,
Imparting Courage to the Soul, And
Strength To Do – _God's_ _Will!_**

Once, a wise and insightful poet wrote, '**Say** what you believe, if you believe it's true, and _never_ be afraid. **Do** what you believe, believe in what you do, and _never_ be afraid. Always **_BE YOURSELF_**, and what you choose to be, and once your choice is made – _hold your head up high, look the world in the eye, and NEVER be afraid!_' Thousands heard these words sung to a melody which found its way into their hearts, never to be forgotten. It is fundamentally the same message of Jesus Who said, 'Let _not_ your heart be troubled,' and 'It is I, be _not_ afraid.' We are our **_true selves_** when we _receive_ **God's Trust** _as our own,_ and become completely convinced God will see us through every difficulty. Then, we can experience **_quiet_ confidence**, truly REST, and _how_ beautiful, dear friend – _is this Rest!_

Not* All-Powerful God, but as 'Mere' Man Jesus Once *Dreamed* 'I Surely <u>Can</u>', Then With <u>Great</u> Effort, He Set Out to Do, Those Works that demanded His Dream–*<u>Come</u> <u>True</u>!

When Jesus was on earth, He had **<u>A</u> <u>Dream</u>**. Though He were God, He had emptied Himself of His Divine Powers, even *<u>part</u>* of His Divine Knowledge, to rely *<u>solely</u>* upon God The Father, as would any other human, to live a life of perfection. And what <u>WAS</u> *His* **Dream**? It was to live a life of **total** obedience to The Father. It was to <u>always</u> return **Good** for evil, no matter how weary He was, or how horrendous any provocation. *His* **Dream** was to endure the unendurable, to love the unlovable, and to be fearless in the face of the most fearsome foes. And He **Dreamed** *<u>He</u>* could accomplish this *solely* <u>**as a man**</u>, though it had never been done before! And His Success redeemed a World! What is *<u>your</u>* **Dream**, my friend? You have the **<u>same</u>** <u>human</u> <u>capacities</u> to draw upon *as did Jesus*, though you often mistakenly believe yourself to be weak, incapable, and mentally lacking. You <u>have</u> what it takes! **Dream!** – *<u>and</u> Act!*

The <u>Conquering</u> of Fear Our Lord Did Then, Which Has Troubled the Souls of *So Many* Men, <u>*No* *Longer*</u> Tossed To and Fro, All Threatenings Vanquished, as All Lies of – <u>*the* *Foe!*</u>

Beloved, people have been told that one can be **wholly sincere**, and *yet* <u>lose</u> their salvation because of being deceived into believing false doctrine or teachings. We are told it is of paramount importance to be '**Right**', *far moreso* than to be **sincere**. But what does scripture say? 'And ye shall seek me, and FIND Me [come to know Me, and have union with Me], when you shall search for Me with **ALL YOUR HEART**' [complete and total **sincerity!**] (Jer. 29:13) <u>*Never*</u> will God 'forsake' any son or daughter who embraces false doctrine, believing it true, but who is sincere, or **genuine** in their understanding. **Correctness** of doctrine is *<u>not</u>* the issue, as **no** Christian's theology is perfect in every point! No, to believe otherwise is to be 'tossed to and fro, and carried about with every wind of doctrine' (Eph. 4:14) One need **never** fear <u>mistakes</u> in doctrine, as Christ WILL correct – <u>*ALL!*</u>

**Fear _Not_ the Raging Storm,
My Love, Beating Against You So,
I Ride _Its_ Crest, and Walk _Its_ Waves
And, My Arms Around You – _Throw!_**

Gentle heart of the Lord, when fear overtakes you, and you feel as though you are being overwhelmed by life, recall this **mighty** truth! _No_ storm ever comes crashing _your_ way apart from the Saviour making **His** way _through it_ to your soul! Christ, our Lord, demonstrated this reality when a tremendous gale arose upon the Sea of Galilee threatening to engulf His followers. Supposing they had seen a 'ghost', they became _all the more_ terrified. The situation is no different today. When facing **life's storms,** we often only perceive a _'ghost'_ of His memory, believing God far distant, nebulous, and unreal. To disprove this notion, Jesus embarked the boat and proceeded to calm the storm with the command **'Peace! Be Still!'** No doubt, He **embraced** His disciples, and assured them He was truly there! As He is there, with you **now** – _too!_

**LOVE *Believes* <u>All</u> Things, We're Told
Yet, Precisely *What* Does This Mean,
But, the <u>Good</u>, the <u>Best</u>, the <u>Bold</u>
Of Any Outcome – <u>*Hidden*</u> or <u>*Seen*</u>!**

What so few people realize, my hopeful friend, is our God is a **Daring** God, always believing the impossible *should* it be the best! God is One of Supreme Excellence, accepting *nothing less* than the **Attainment** of the *most* beautiful, desirable, lofty goals of which the human, and divine heart, are capable of conceiving! And there are *<u>no</u>* limits! So, be assured then, **God's Dream**, cradled in His Heart for man, for *your* individual life, *<u>will</u>*, with all certainty, one day, come to pass. Yet, it is within your power to *<u>hasten</u>* its arrival should you so choose! Men would shy away from the grandest, *most* glorious possibilities due to unbelief and lack of spiritual vision. But, God has no such misgivings. Align yourself with the Vision of the Almighty. For what **God** *<u>believes</u>*, **God** *<u>achieves</u>!* Determine, **now** then, to believe – *and <u>so</u> <u>can</u> <u>you</u>!*

**Never Despair, Your Cause Is <u>Not</u> Lost
To Find <u>Healing</u>, Before My Throne, As
My Sacrifice is More than Ample – Still
For *<u>Every</u>* Trouble – *<u>to</u> <u>Atone</u>!*ns**

If we could but hear Him, surely, our Lord is saying: 'Though you have **asked** for years or **decades**, for a certain physical ailment to be removed, all things, *<u>your</u> <u>healing</u>*, are possible, **still!** Though you have **sought** bodily rest and renewal for endless days and countless nights, without its arrival, all things, *<u>your</u> <u>refreshment</u>*, are possible, **still!** And though you have **knocked** steadily and repeatedly upon the door of good health most of your life, without your entrance being granted, all things, *<u>your</u> <u>restoration</u>*, are possible, **still!** ***Beloved!*** When *your* time of healing does come, and I <u>assure</u> you ***come* it will**, <u>*all*</u> pain of your past will utterly dissolve within your soul! Your deliverance is a foregone conclusion. Be comforted by this certainty! I AM the Lord – *<u>Who</u> <u>heals</u> <u>you</u>!*

**Hear, *Now*, A Golden Message
Clinging Close, Tho Seeming Far,
Telling of <u>*Your*</u> Importance in God's Plan
And *of* The Glory – <u>*Where You Are*</u>!**

Do you feel, at times, your life holds no real significance? That your absence here on this planet would be of no lasting consequence? Many sadly do. Yet, <u>right where you are</u>, God IS! The trouble is you do not **feel** nor truly **know** this. Paul prayed, 'That the eyes of your understanding being enlightened; ye may know what the riches of the **<u>Glory</u>** of His Inheritance [is] <u>***IN***</u> the saints.' Your magnificent life purpose, this **glorious** reason for being is *<u>within</u>* you, placed there by God Himself! You, dear friend, are an intrinsic and essential part of God's Plan, 'being ***predestinated*** according to the **Purpose** of Him . . . that [you] should be to the **Praise** of His Glory'! Your life is a praiseworthy one! And *<u>uniquely</u>* capable of bringing praise and honor to Him! In turn, bestowing praise – *<u>on you</u>!*

**Lord, My Awakened Heart Does Say
I AM the <u>Great</u> <u>Possibility</u> of God *<u>Today</u>!*
With Powers Untapped, I Do Now Shod, My Feet
With *<u>Those</u>* Sandals That Lead Me – *to God!***

Beautiful daughter (or son) of the Lord, never doubt for one moment that which is **potential** within you can and *WILL* become **actual**! For this is the very **Purpose** of your life! – To awaken to your Life Mission, and to LIVE It! **You ARE God's great possibility!** The passing of years cannot diminish It, nor can the disbelief of others. Continue to pray, seek, search, and above all, **believe**, you WILL have disclosed to you the TRUTH of your being! It will be that which makes you <u>COME</u> <u>ALIVE</u> and offers you the Greatest Fulfillment! **Cast away** the belief that it is *too* late, or you are *too* old, or you've *too* many weaknesses or limitations! With OUR God, 'ALL things <u>*Are*</u> – POSSIBLE!' And those 'All things' **most assuredly** refer to your deepest heart yearnings and dreams! So, don those sandals whose **inscription** is THIS glorious *<u>personal</u>* Truth! (Eph. 6:15) They will carry you forward –*<u>to your Destiny</u>!*

I Come to <u>Uplift</u> You, Inspire You Today
Elevate Your Thoughts to *Where* I Do Stay
I AM *Not* Far from You, Before Me Do Bow
I <u>*Will*</u> Bring Peace to Your Weary Heart – <u>*Now!*</u>

Beloved friend, how the wide world so desperately is in need of **Peace**! Worry, anxiety, and preoccupation fill the minds of countless individuals who are in turmoil and great distress. Perhaps you are one. Yet, *if* you turn your attention to Whom Isaiah revealed as the <u>***Prince of Peace***</u>, you will find the relief and solace you seek! For it is only in your <u>**now**</u> **moment** where you can experience this rare quality – where the Author of peace resides! True, your troubles may persist, but you will be raised above them. 'Of the <u>***increase***</u> of His government [Lordship] and Peace [Inner Calm] *there will be no end.*' How so? **By the extending of His Peace – into men's hearts!** <u>THIS</u> is how Peace will increase, blossom, and flourish. Wait no longer for It, **Turn to <u>*Him*</u>** and experience It – <u>*Right Now!*</u>

**Into the Realm of Life I Leap
With Arms <u>Flung</u> Back, and Head *<u>Bowed</u>*
Down, Into the Blue Ocean of God's Deep
Where Truth and Love – *<u>Are</u> <u>Found</u>!***

My hesitant friend, if you knew what <u>true</u> faith could do for you, you would seek her above all else! Many feel one has to ***<u>struggle</u>*** to achieve faith, in effect, do **battle** with faithlessness. Yet, this more often than not depletes one's strength, *<u>not</u>* establishes it! Simply stated, faith is a **decision** to *believe* God will see you through every situation – regardless of its threatening appearance. Faith is a **choice** to believe that a *<u>greater</u>* Good will arise out of any seeming negative circumstance. Faith is an **attitude** we adopt that realizes we, as Children of God, already possess the ***<u>Power</u>*** to remain peaceful, joyous, and free in the face of disappointment and undesirable outcomes. For when we ***<u>once</u>*** decide to abandon ourselves to this mindset, the **Truth** of our being *<u>Victors</u>* over circumstance, and of **Love** of Life being our *<u>daily</u> <u>inheritance</u>* – *<u>will</u> <u>emerge</u>!*

I Wonder *What* Wonders Could Be Done By *Me!* As Jesus Said 'Greater You'll Do', Don't You See, I *Wonder* What Wonders Are Mine to Express! I've the Word of My Saviour, How Can I – *Do Less?*

Our Lord and Saviour Jesus Christ very plainly stated: 'He that believeth in Me, the works that I do *shall he do also*; and **greater works** than *these* shall he do; because I go unto My Father.' You and I, beloved, have come *no where near* to tapping our human, **much less** our divine, **potential**! Whenever the lower human self would tell you that you have nothing of any real value to offer, recall Christ's words! It is *these* words of **Truth** that accurately describe your reality. *If* you do not know precisely **what** works you CAN perform, ask God to reveal them to you. Be willing to attempt new things, undertake bold ventures, launch out into fresh waters. Those 'greater works' are to be found *THERE!* Jesus performed *increasingly greater works* over the course of His ministry. YOU are fully equipped to do the same! Explore and discover your abilities, **then** go build upon them – *as did He!*

**Lord, _What_ Would You Have Me <u>Do</u> Today
What Would You Have Me Think and Say,
I _<u>Needn't</u>_ Be Troubled Nor Doubt Anew
'Tis to <u>Love</u> With a Heart – _<u>Ever</u> <u>True</u>!_**

What, beloved friend, _really_, is your **sole** purpose on earth? _Do you know?_ When you feel discouraged, unclear, lost, or bewildered as to the **<u>Reason</u>** for your being here, remind yourself of this: **<u>You</u> <u>Are</u> <u>Here</u> <u>to</u> <u>LIVE</u> <u>Love</u>!** And what does it mean, precisely, to _'Live Love'?_ It means to leave the isolation, self-involvement, worry-proneness of the little self behind, and to become self-_<u>forgetful</u>_ – **in service to others!** To cultivate '_<u>other</u>_ consciousness'. To bring Joy to _<u>their</u>_ lives. This **alone** will make of your life something **<u>Magnificent</u>** and **<u>Whole</u>**! And You will become Free and Fulfilled! Though abandonment to your Reason for being, God's **<u>True</u> <u>Desire</u>** for you, painful _<u>self</u>_-consciousness will depart! The **<u>Romance</u>** _<u>of</u>_ **<u>Life</u>** will have become a Living Reality – _<u>at</u> <u>long</u> <u>last</u>!_

To <u>Trust</u> in the Lord Is To *<u>Rest</u>* In His Love, Believing *<u>This</u>* More Important Than Answered Prayer – *<u>from</u> <u>Above</u>!*</br>

What is of **greater value**, my friend – A quiet, calm, undisturbed **Trust** in God regarding any important prayer request in your life, or having that petition answered the way *<u>you</u> believe it should be?* You might feel – dependent upon the seriousness of the request, its pressing need, or dire concern – it would definitely be having the prayer **answered**, *<u>as desired</u>*. This is logical, but it is also mistaken! For to live in trust, is to **truly live!** And it is **THIS**, my dear friend, your **heart** <u>most</u> longs for and prays to have! – *<u>Not</u>* the prayer, in itself, coming true! Why is this so? Because though our analytical mind would deny it, **Peace of Mind** is the *<u>only</u>* goal worth having and desiring! Therefore, anything that detracts from this **IS** detrimental to our highest good. Ponder this, and know its Truth –*<u>for</u> <u>yourself</u>!*

Angel of Mercy, Come to Me
<u>Deliver</u> the Pure Christed Energies,
***Strengthen* My Resolve, *Empower* My Soul**
Fill* Me With <u>Daring</u>, A Heart Now – *<u>Made</u> <u>Bold</u>!

As you know, beloved, angels are emissaries sent by God to minister unto the heirs of Salvation. They 'transmit' to those traveling 'The Way' special dispensations of Grace required in time of great need. During Jesus' earthly walk, it was no different. While praying earnestly upon the Mount of Olives, in the garden of Gethsemane, just prior to His betrayal and arrest, such a being came to Him to reinforce the balance of His Soul. 'And there appeared an Angel unto Him from Heaven, *strengthening* Him.' No doubt, this was a mighty Archangel, perhaps even Michael himself, bearing relief to the Saviour of the World! Due to his **direct** intervention, Jesus was able to move ahead with an unmatched composure and resolve. You, too, have the angelic host available to you for your protection and deliverance. Christed winged beings –*<u>are</u> <u>there</u>!*

'I Say Unto You, *I* Say Unto You'
With These Words My Authority Declare,
That *Whatever* Follows Is Wholly True
Tho Difficult to Believe – *or to Bear!*

Dear heart, our Saviour occasionally introduced new teaching with these precise quoted words. He did this because He knew *full well* what He was about to say would frequently **appear** to be untrue, and doubts could easily arise. By lending the **full weight** of *His personal divine authority,* He was saying His words *could* be ***trusted***, and that God *would* **honor** His words at the time of *His* choosing. When Jesus said, 'Ask [in prayer] and it **shall** be given unto you,' He knew perplexities would arise, as many prayers are not speedily answered. Our drawn out waiting is often discouraging and even painful. But, His **prefacing** words, nevertheless, in effect, **assure** us: 'Don't lose heart, beloved, I will yet make good on my Word!' So, keep on asking! Keep on believing! *Never* doubt! His Word–*IS true!*

**A *Special* Day the Lord Has Made
And, YET, It Is <u>Hidden</u> From Most,
Only Through Eyes of Joy Is It Seen
It's *<u>This</u>* Day – In Which *<u>Heaven Boasts</u>!***

Countless people, caring friend, have regrettably failed to develop an appreciation for Living, an awareness of the **Miracle** of Life, and of the incalculable value of each new day! For many, each day is drab, routine, unexciting, and boring. But, 'the Day the Lord has made' – *is not!* If the day you find yourself in is uninteresting and gloomy, then, be sure, it is a day **you** have made – *<u>not</u>* the Lord! – **Made** by the <u>direction</u> and <u>focus</u> of your consciousness! **Called forth** by your <u>intention</u> and deliberate <u>will</u>! The Day God makes, by contrast, is so wonderful, the psalmist excitedly proclaimed, 'This is the Day the Lord has made, Let us **Rejoice** *in It* and be **Glad**!' So, choose to focus on the Good. Look for, dwell upon, Joyful things! ***<u>Be</u>*** Joyful! Use your imagination, if need be, to conjure up glorious sights! A Day*of*Joy, ***<u>invisible</u> <u>before</u>***, will**welcomeyou** to a HiddenDay–*<u>Hidden</u> <u>No</u> <u>More</u>!*

**I AM _In_ You, and You _In_ Me
Far _More_ Close than Imagined to Be,
_My_ Thoughts Rise Up to _Become_ Thine,
Yours, Then <u>Glow</u> – _<u>With</u> <u>Love</u> <u>Divine</u>!_**

How **near**, dear one, in proximity, is the Precious Saviour, _<u>to</u> <u>you</u>?_ While it is true Jesus bodily ascended into Heaven, far more took place than met the eye. He was _**translated**_ into a wholly different state of being. A state wherein the very _**essence**_ of His thought processes and heart feelings now **indwell** the human soul. He, in a very mystical, yet profoundly real way, literally _**lives**_ His Life <u>through</u> us! This means He is _**Aware**_ of us, and our surroundings – _<u>from</u> <u>within</u>!_ When **you** gaze upon a sparrow, _<u>so</u> <u>does</u> <u>He</u>_ – _**through**_ your eyes! When **you** hear distant rumblings of thunder at eventide, _<u>so</u> <u>does</u> <u>He</u>_ – _**through**_ your ears! When you feel the gentle pitter-patter of rain across your face, _<u>so</u> <u>does</u> <u>He</u>_ – _**through**_ your sense of touch! To what purpose? So total ONENESS, in the **Intimacy**, and in the **Unity** of Divine Spirit – _<u>might</u> <u>prevail</u>!_

Creation is a <u>Fact</u>, Scientists Now Declare <u>Vindicating</u> the Holy Scriptures Everywhere, Proof Long Sought For, NOW Readily Obtained Exalting and Honoring – *<u>God's Holy Name</u>!*

'In the Beginning, God **created** the Heaven and the earth.' (Gen. 1:1) and 'God **created** man in his own image; male and female **created** He them.' (Gen. 1:27) 'And God **made**...*everything* that creepeth [moves] upon the earth after his kind.' (Gen. 1:25) Most scientists have long taught that all life forms came into existence through *blind, undirected, natural forces* over millions of years through a supposed process called 'evolution'. Yet, **hundreds** of scientists now KNOW that evolution is **a failed, disproven theory**! And declare 'special creation' is **a scientific, *demonstrable* FACT**! They do this in virtually every branch of the life sciences and paleontology: such as, anthropology, biology, micro-biology, and genetics (information coding). Further, there are **no** 'intermediate' species as erroneously taught, ***<u>nor</u>*** any rational mechanism of generating coding in our genes. As God alone–*<u>did so</u>!*

For God So _Loved_ the World
So Very Long Ago It Was True,
Yet, What of Those Who Live <u>Today</u>
The Likes of Me – _and You_!

'For God so <u>LOVES</u> the world, that He <u>GIVES</u> His Only-Begotten Son.' These words are crafted in the *continuously present tense* and are every bit as true as the original verse upon which they were fashioned. Every day, every hour, every minute, God the Father is **giving** His Son to each and every individual as a result of His ever-present, continuously active **Love** for them HERE and NOW! Most are unaware of this happening, yet at any moment an individual can turn within to *the Infinite Presence of God,* and say, 'Father, I **receive** the gift of your Son! I **acknowledge** His existence within me! I will henceforth **submit** myself to His Will, and **bow** before His inner majesty! He loves me **_SO MUCH_** that He would **never** choose to be apart from me, **so He is not**. Now, I in return, <u>by your Grace</u>, choose to never be apart, again – *from Him!*

**His Words Can _Always_ Be Trusted
BECAUSE _Trust Worthy_ and Faithful Is _He_,
To Preserve Them Down Through the Ages
As _He_ _Said_ They Would – _Evermore_ _Be_!**

Beautiful, yet uncertain heart, can you take the Lord at His Word, or have the scribes or translators altered them _for their own purposes?_ Knowing such doubts would naturally arise, Jesus declared with Authority, 'Heaven and earth **shall** pass away, but **_My_ _Words_ shall _NEVER_ pass away!**' This was the solemn oath assuring His followers the **Integrity** of His Words would _continue_, and no human, nor magistrate, nor ecumenical council could change them. Recall, He said, 'The _**Words**_ that I speak unto you, they ARE **SPIRIT**, and they are **LIFE**.' And True Life, _God_ Life, cannot meet with 'corruption', or human alteration! God the Father and Jesus Christ His Son have decreed it so! Yes, _translations_ may be deficient, but original language texts, multiple thousands, remain – _divinely_ _unchanged!_

**A Truth That *Must* Be Told, and Should
Though <u>Forbidden</u> by A Misguided Good,
Could Jesus Have Been The Saviour Fair
If He <u>Were</u> An Avenging Angel – *<u>There!</u>***

You who seek **the *deeper* Truths of God** may have been told that the Old Testament God was none other than Jesus Himself *prior* to His earthly incarnation. Many believe He was the One who freed the Israelites from Egypt, and who gave the Ten Commandments to Moses. Further, who ordered the *merciless killing* of thousands, including elderly, cripples, women, helpless children, and even infants, in order that the Israelites should gain the Promised Land. **But, *No*, beloved!** *This being was <u>NOT</u> Jesus our Lord!* – The eternally pure and All-forgiving Son of 'The ONLY **True God**'! Tho known by few Christians, the being who appeared in the burning bush clearly identified himself as an '*<u>Angel</u>*', and functioned in the *role* of God, as the then-permitted *temporarily 'supreme'* authority over men! (Exodus 3:2) Vengeance **was** a dominant characteristic of <u>this</u> '*god*', but **never** – *<u>of the Lord!</u>*

A Message *Transcendent* He Brought from Above, Knowing the World Was Devoid of Love, Seeds of TRUTH He Would Carefully Sow, So *That* The World Would, One Day – *Know!*

What is it, dear heart, that Jesus wanted people to **know** more than *anything else?* He told us so, plainly, in John 17:3: 'And this IS life eternal, that they might KNOW THEE, the only **True** God, and Jesus Christ, Whom Thou hast sent.' To know God, the *True* God, that is, His true attributes, characteristics, traits, and **intents** were what Jesus wanted his brothers and sisters to know **more than any other thing!** For He knew that the common conceptions of God, a God of judgment and punishment, a God of rigid adherence to law, a God of anger and wrath, particularly those taught by the religious authorities, were flawed, and often outright error. Jesus came to reveal **a God of Love**, which the Jews had little real understanding of. *This* God that Jesus revealed had not been seen, indeed, *could not* be seen, as He is 'The **Invisible** God'! Only 'The **Visible** Son' – could make Him– *known!*

One Day, 'Soon', There Certainly Will Be <u>*Another*</u> Grand Declaration of 'Let There Be!' As Voiced in the Beginning, A Divine Fiat Proclaimed, Ushering in a *New* World -- <u>*Ordained!*</u>

In the beginning, God said, 'Let there be Light!' And instantaneously there was Light. But, 'the darkness *comprehended* it <u>not</u>.' For the Light only served to scatter the darkness, not to convict it nor convert it. But, one day, the Lord will declare 'Let there be **comprehension** *of* The Light!' And, Lo!, **All**, **everywhere**, who were once residing in darkness, or had darkness residing in them, will understand everything The Light is meant to convey! No more suspicion of the Light, nor distrust of the Light, nor doubts regarding the Light! Only complete and full comprehension and appreciation of and agreement with the Light! This will be ***the Second Great Act of Creation*** extant throughout a cosmos! And God will then declare, 'And I see (witness) the comprehension of My Light, and It <u>*IS*</u> the Ultimate Good!' No more un-comprehending darkness! Only **knowing** – <u>*in Light!*</u>

My Dearest Darling
Oh, My *Most* Beautiful One!
Arise Up <u>Into</u> My *Yearning* Arms
By the <u>Resurrection</u> Power – *<u>of</u> <u>God's</u> <u>Son</u>!*

Beloved friend, the person you have held **most dear**, perhaps a sweetheart, a child, or your mother, *<u>your</u> <u>most</u> <u>beautiful</u> <u>one</u>,* will one day embrace you again, and the **Joy** you will know will seem to fill the world! Though lost to you by accident or infirmity or misunderstanding or old age, that *<u>special</u> <u>someone</u>* will **greet** you again, and **hold** you, and **kiss** you with a Love grown more powerful still – by absence and longing and desire unleashed! That **all-glorious reunion** is a *<u>certainty</u>!* You will *<u>not</u>* be deprived of their presence and preciousness ever again! He Who said, **'I AM the Resurrection and the Life'**, will call to him or her, and send them to your side in the *twinkling* of an eye, on that unforgettable day. As you witness and experience the twinkling of shafts of **Joy** streaming out from the windows of their – *<u>newly</u> <u>born</u> <u>souls</u>!*

Lord Jesus, Without _You_ Where Would I Be Save _Adrift_ Upon Life's Restless Sea, You Are My Anchor, My Morning Star, My Tether to God's Love – _You Are!_

Can you possibly imagine, dear heart, what your life would be like had not the Son of God revealed Himself to your mind and soul? For Jesus, as no other, is the **perfect Guide** and **Life-line** to no less than the Heart of the Creator! He illustrated and provides purpose, as no other – the **True Reason** for living – _the giving of Love every day!_ As the Light of the World, He has saved you _from_ a life of darkness and doubt! The ever-growing awareness of His very **real Presence** continues to relieve any loneliness you may feel in a world oblivious to His Central Role in Creation. So many are lost and confused about Life, its **Glorious Meaning** and **_Certain_ Promise**. Yet, you have been chosen to understand **The Truth**, _now!_ Knowing your identity as a **brother** to the Lord and a **co-heir** of **God-Life** – _makes all the difference!_

Lord, Should ALL Else I Desire _Not_ Come
Should All my Dreams Become Undone
If All My Hopes and Longings Fail
Your Light and Love _Will_ – _Still Prevail!_

'For *other* foundation can **no** man [or woman] lay than that is laid, which is *Jesus Christ*.' What, my friend, serves as the **anchor** of your life? Your underlying **stability**? Upon what can you cling to that is **immovable** – and *unfailing?* Is it a Loved one? A great Dream? A Goal or secret Longing? If it is not God's will that such things be, to naught they will come. Can you _let them go_ when God makes clear to you they are not in your **Life Plan**? Can you _relinquish_ them to the Father even though your heart aches for them still, and you weep inside because they didn't materialize? If you cannot, humbly ask the Lord to illumine your soul to see the **larger picture**, wherein the reason for 'denial' is made plain. **God IS With YOU – Still!** His 'withholding' is really your '_unfolding_' into greater awareness of Him and Blessing – _to Come!_

Farewell Words

Never become convinced, beloved, that simply because your prayer requests have not been granted to date, God has declined them. ***Continue*** to reach for the trailing hem of the Lord's garment! ***Persist*** in believing an answer will yet be given. ***Never cease*** to draw close to the Lord's perfumed, invigorating Presence! ***Anticipate*** seeing that dawning, incomparable smile on His face as He bestows **His** long-desired blessing – upon you! ***Persevere*** in your alert listening to hear Him respond to your question, '*If* Thou wilt!' – with **'I WILL!'** You, see, precious one, you **must *not*** look to what length of time has transpired since your asking. Time, ultimately, is an illusion, and ONCE the change you seek has come, it will **vanish** in the presence of God's **newly-created** Reality! So, I encourage you. ***Press on!*** Love will YET– *respond!*

With Every Good Wish, The Author

Part III

A Message to Heal the Body!

A Healing Mercy Rose!

Velvety Rose
On Darkened Wood,
The **Herald** of
Healing! New Birth!
Love's *Glorious*
Promise, and Legacy
To All, Who Seek
for such **Healing**,
– *On Earth!*

Part III – Introduction
God Desires You Whole!

Tell me friend, is there a **need** for healing in your life? Have you sought remedy for your impaired health only to find disappointment, and to see your faith falter and wane? Do you no longer anticipate being well again, as you feel this is a forlorn hope? **Let me encourage you**, then, **to believe anew** that *'All things [truly] are possible'*, still, *for you!* No matter how long you have been ill, you can **begin** to experience healing where it is most needed, first, in your mind and heart! **Jesus of Nazareth** is still very much in the business of restoring health! And the *new concepts* and *insights* in this book may be precisely what you need to believe *again!* – **Not only** for your *own* healing, but for the deliverance and healing of those you love and cherish, *as well!*

Part III – Contents

Oh! See It Swaying Gently
I Had to Wait, to Yearn, to Ache
Into the Wilds I Went That Day
Oh, Beautiful Pool of Bethesda
Beautiful Healer! Robe of Crimson Hue
To Be Delivered of Your Sickness
'So Great Faith!' He Exclaimed, Beloved
Love's Shadow, Cast on Me
Joy of Healing Will My Companion Be
A Touch of Garment
I AM the Eternally Unfolding Rose
Lord, My Greatest Need Today
Lord Jesus, My Best and Noblest Thought
One Sign Alone the Master Declared
You Are the Lord's Anointed
Unspeakable Joy to God Will Be
Father, 'I Thank Thee'

Farewell Message

**Oh! _See_ It Swaying Gently
By a Holy Breeze That Blows,
In the Tranquil Part of Your Heart
Feel – The Peace of – _The Mercy Rose!_**

Deep in your heart, dear friend, is a spiritual symbol, one of the most revealing and endearing ever given unto men. A picture of a _thornless_, **Eternal Rose**! This imagery is representative of the One Who was the True Thornless flower on earth! Known as the **'Rose of Sharon'** in former days, and as 'He Who would have _Mercy_' in latter times, _the_ **Mercy Rose** breathed out **Peace** wherever He went. His Peace was so profound, that depending upon their own inclination, men marveled, fell silent, were amazed, healed, or in awe of His Being. That same _**Invincible**_ Peace is in you, today, as God is in you. Ask that you might _**feel**_ that Peace in an ongoing basis, and become a reservoir from which Peace might then overflow. The **Peace** of God's Mercy, and Its attendant **Healing power**, is available for you, who **believe** it's true – _budding anew!_

I Had to *Wait*, to *Yearn*, to <u>Ache</u>
Through Those <u>Many</u> Decades Long,
As I Heard the Spirit Say, '*Not* Yet'
To My Heartfelt – *<u>Pleading Song</u>!*

Even as a boy, the Lord Jesus possessed an almost <u>*overwhelming*</u> desire to **heal** the sick and the hurting about Him. How He must have *longed* to extend the hand of healing to the pitiful and the hopeless there. Mature beyond His years, <u>even</u> at ten years of age, He acutely **felt** their pain, *<u>entered into the suffering</u>* of those heartbroken, **chronically ill.** <u>*Another*</u> decade, He witnessed this, repeatedly asking His Father to allow Him to intervene. Still, the Spirit said, *'No'*. This, even though He was '*filled* with Compassion' toward them! *<u>Ten more years</u>* would pass with Jesus <u>earnestly</u> asking His Father, '***<u>When</u>*** will You allow me to Heal? ***<u>How much longer</u>*** can I go on this way?' You see, dear friend, He possessed the Power, but *not* the Permission! Then, one bright day, He heard a long-awaited-for reply, **'Yes!'** His cries were over! His healing ministry had begun! And it **continues** to this very day, for such –***<u>as you</u>!***

**Into the Wilds I Went That Day
Where Vast Fatigue and Burning Ray
Did Meet Me – Day After *Daunting* Day
To Give <u>YOU</u> Hope, as Spirit Sustained,
God Will Do, For *<u>You</u> – <u>The Same</u>!*

Just prior to His call to active ministry, our Lord and Saviour Jesus Christ was led by Spirit into the wilderness. The hills of Judea and her barren deserts could be quite dangerous; particularly should one be without nourishment for any length of time. And without water, one would quickly suffer the **searing** pangs of thirst, and night would **chill** one's bones to a painful numbness. Most would perish within a week. Yet, Jesus chose to endure *<u>six</u> <u>weeks</u>* of torment, and *tempting*, by the Dark Prince, upheld only by His ***<u>Spirit-Inspired</u> <u>determination</u>*** to press on and **survive!** With virtually all human strength gone, He was literally starving to death! Yet, after *<u>40</u> <u>days</u>*, helpless and dying, angels ministered to Him, nursing Him back to health. God will **sustain** you, *as well*, dear one – *<u>till</u> <u>your</u> <u>healing</u> <u>arrives</u>!*

**Oh, Beautiful Pool of Bethesda,
What Message In You Might There Be,
No *Length* of Illness, Nor *Degree* of Pain
Can Stay God's Healing Hand – *From Me!***

Long-suffering friend of God, you who have been ill for what seems like ages, will *one day* be ill no more. Your Day of Healing is closer, now, than you might imagine! There was a man who had been severely ill for *thirty-eight* years, nearly **four decades**. He was lying upon a pallet beside the Pool, *as he had done so many times before,* hoping to be the first to enter after its waters mysteriously rippled. The person who did was miraculously healed! Scripture tells us Jesus '***knew*** he had been thus now – *a long time*.' **How did Jesus know?** Through supernatural means? *No!* He had seen this man *scores* of times, if not hundreds, yet, He **chose** not to heal him! **Why?** Because God has an ***appointed time*** to deliver each of us. You, too, can rest assured; your incurable illness **will be cured**, one day, **completely**, permanently – *by Him!*

**Beautiful Healer! Robe of Crimson Hue
Eyes of Blue-Violet, Presence Fresh as Dew,
Come! _Oh_, Come! Embrace Me! Let Your Touch
Your Health – _Pour Through_!**

Perhaps more than any other activity, whether teaching, preaching, instructing, or encouraging, the Lord engaged in physical and psychological healing most of all. He knew that those who were of '_little_ faith' needed a **tangible validation** to their physical senses of His power to correct any ailment, whether rooted in the body or the mind. His glorious Presence **alone** was often enough to reverse the downward spirals of degeneration, and arrest the crippling momentums of negative thinking. Yet, those of us, now, who have the benefit of the Gospel records, can **know** and _be certain of_ our own **personal** healing _prior to_ any outward manifestation. For when we align ourselves with The Word, 'By His [Atonement] we _ARE_ **Healed**', we discount evidence _of_ our senses, believe, instead, **His Truth!** Rejoicing! Till our bodies–_do the same!_

To Be Delivered of Your Sickness You Must First Come to See, 'Men *Like* Trees Walking' Before the Master – *Heals Thee!*

The blind man allowed himself *to be led, anointed,* and *have hands laid* upon him in prayer. But, he had to answer the question, *'What do you see?'* To which, after looking heavenward, he strangely replied, *'Men like trees walking.'* Jesus then proceeded to restore to him full, normal sight. A brief time later, the Lord declared, 'Whosoever will come after me, let him deny himself, take up his cross, and *follow* me.' The blind man came after Jesus, as he was led; denied himself by surrendering his skepticism; symbolically *took up a cross* carved from **a tree**, and carried it aloft, upright, **walking** with it – The **very picture** Jesus had *caused* him to **see** prior to his healing! God wants you, sweet-hearted friend, to understand, or *to see*, the **agency** of your much desired healing: the All-Delivering **Power** of the Cross – *made one's own!*

'So <u>Great</u> Faith!' He Exclaimed, Beloved Brought GREAT Marvel To Him, While 'So *Grand* Joy' Came – *<u>To</u> <u>The</u> <u>Centurion</u>!*

Once, Jesus remarked to a Roman soldier, 'Verily I say unto you, I have not found ***so <u>great</u> faith***, no, not in Israel' (the chosen people of faith!). This officer had beseeched Jesus to heal his beloved, dying servant, but asked ***only*** that Jesus 'speak the Word' of healing, *<u>without</u>* going to his servant. The centurion had no doubts about His authority and power to restore life. **'As thou hast believed, so be it done unto thee'** was the reply. Now, **<u>how much Joy</u>** do you think arose in the Roman's heart at that time? Recall, this man had built a synagogue expressly for the Jews; no doubt, one of *<u>many</u>* acts of faith in God's promise to reward the faithful. His reward was both his servant's healing, and most surely, an ***<u>immense Joy</u>***, a **'so *<u>grand</u>* Joy!'** A <u>further</u> healing of his downcast, sorrowful spirit! So, continue to believe. Such Joy – *<u>can be yours, too</u>!*

**Love's Shadow, Cast on Me,
With Soothing Calmness Passes By
Outpicturing the Shadow of His Cross
Healing All – <u>*Who*</u> <u>*Vow*</u> <u>*to*</u> <u>*Die*</u>*!*

Did you know, dear friend, that even **so little** as a ***dim*** shadow imbued with the Master's Love passing over a person restored their health? Unlike earth's **dark** shadows, and those of men's fear-tormented minds, His shadow casts a Twi-<u>*light*</u> of renewal, restoration, and Redemption. A glowing Twilighted shadow of a *beginning* dawn! – ***Not*** of a life's *end!* No different with the Cross! Its shadow is flung clear round the globe from which none will *ultimately* be able to 'escape'. Its shadow carries deliverance *from* darkness, <u>*not*</u> envelopment by! Even Love's Chief Apostle, Paul, embodied **so much** of *the Saviour's Love* that the **Hallowed Shadow** associated with His person healed many! The lesson, then? Fear NOT shadows! Even they remind us of Love's Redemptive Power – <u>*over*</u> <u>*all*</u>*!*

**Joy *Of* Healing Will My Companion Be
As I Hear It Singing In My Heart,
You Are *Whole!* You Are Free!
And Evermore – *Will Be!*__**

My sincere friend, the quality we know as Joy, arises from a variety of related God-Realizations. Regardless as to our circumstances, if we can but realize they are **temporary**, with *no* permanent reality, then, and only then, can we experience a sense of freedom. With this awareness of freedom comes that all-desirable quality, or experience of being, called **Joy!** The Prince of Joy once declared to a crippled woman of eighteen years, 'You are loosed [now *free*]!' And 'all the people **rejoiced**' as she stood up delivered and whole! You, too, should echo the Master's words whenever you feel restricted, hindered, or imprisoned by health issues, and declare the Truth, 'I AM Free!' In time, you will begin to **feel** their Reality and know a Joy undiminished, as you invite healing – *to appear!*

A Touch of Garment
The Slightest *Feel* of His Robe,
<u>Beyond</u> Finger Brushing on Sabled Cloth
Did the Master Make Countless Souls – *<u>Whole</u>!*

As many as touched the mere hem of His garment were healed. What the Scripture does not record is many seekers were healed after ***HE*** touched the hem *of <u>their</u> souls!* All required for one, was a look of compassion. For another, a word of power. And for another still, an unspoken prayer. Far greater than all His physical healings combined, which **could** be seen, were the emotional/psychological healings – *<u>not</u>* seen, but later *known!* ***Those*** healings of people's **inner** thought-feeling worlds were actually incredibly more complex, thereby *<u>far</u>* more amazing than healings of the human form, alone. The Love that resided in His Heart *reached out* as would *<u>invisible</u> hands* to the multitudes, and untold numbers *knew* their hearts were touched by **fingers *of*** **Merc**y, and **instantly healed!** – *<u>as</u> <u>will</u> <u>you</u>!*

**I AM the Eternally *Unfolding* Rose
In The Depths of The Hearts of Men,
Though Dormant I Remain – For Centuries
But then, I *Will* Blossom Forth – *and All Win!***

Deep in the heart of every man dwells the *germ* of Righteousness! This germ is the **perfect** pattern of the divine image in which every man is made. The Apostle Paul stated that he sought 'by **all** means to save *some*', whereas our Lord and Saviour's position is that by **ONE** means [**The Cross**] he will save ALL. That one means is the infiltrating of His Irresistible Love through *every* barrier of the heart! That germ, or seed, indestructible – **will** flower when the right conditions and needed learning situations have been presented. Potential, hidden, but destined to manifest, the **Rose of Mercy** will unfold Its petals – and the Mind of Christ will have established yet another outpost in the world! The **gentlest** petals of such soft texture will have **proven stronger** than – *the hardest hate!*

**Lord, My Greatest Need Today
Is That I Might _Feel_ Thy Presence Sure,
So Much a Part of Me, That I, Sense Me
AS You – _Oh! Wondrous Cure!_**

What, beloved friend, is the one thing most in need of healing? Is it mental distress? Bodily pain? Financial 'ill health'? Or broken relationships? _**The Greatest Need is for an Ongoing Sense of Oneness with Him!**_ A sense of union, of joining, a sense of shared identity! A feeling of identification with Him. Apart from this, we feel lost and adrift in Life. Recall that Jesus' **central concern** in His final, most lengthy, recorded prayer made a brief time prior to His Passion, was for this ONENESS. This **Realization**, _a **healing** of the SENSE of separation!_ This prayer came before any other as it was the key to _every_ other prayer! He IS in us, and _one times one times one,_ is becoming us! As we yield ourselves to Him! **Multiplying** His Presence throughout the _entire_ Universe – _through us!_

**Lord Jesus, My _Best_ and <u>Noblest</u> Thought
By Thee Eternal Salvation Is Wrought,
Within My Soul to Extend to Men
An <u>Outward</u> Picture of
The Christ – _<u>Within</u>!_**

How well, dear friend, do you _reflect_ the Light of Eternal Love – _on earth?_ A great mystic once said, 'God, You are the sun, I AM your reflection.' How often do you meditate and dwell upon Jesus, Life's Lord, Who _alone_ can infuse your being with **Virtue** and **Power**? Who <u>alone</u> can cause your Life to be a Noble thing of **Imperishable Beauty**, that shines like the Sun – _<u>in unending influence for Good</u>?_ Malachi speaks of 'a book of remembrance' recording names of those who speak _often_ 'one to another' about the Lord, who reverence the Lord, and _**think** '<u>upon His Name</u>'_. Are you one of **those** whom God accounts as making 'up [His] **jewels**', who <u>sparkle</u> with His radiance? If so, the sun [_Son_] of Righteousness will arise with **healing**, light-emanating wings, forever to – _<u>illumine you</u>!_

**<u>One</u> Sign *Alone* the Master Declared
Distinguished His Own from <u>*All*</u> Anywhere,
<u>One</u> Mark Whereby Others Might Behold, The
One <u>Telling</u> Truth of the Sheep – *<u>of</u> <u>His</u> <u>Fold</u>!***

What is it, dear friend, that **sets apart** a follower of Jesus Christ from others? What is the singularly identifying, most prominent characteristic of the **authentic** Christian? Many profess to be believers, yet how is one to truly know? *By one means only!* Jesus said, 'By this [one thing <u>alone</u>] shall all men know [with certainty] you *<u>ARE</u>* my disciples, that you *<u>Love</u> <u>One</u> <u>Another</u>!*' To which He added, '*<u>AS</u>* – I have loved you.' Oh! Now we see! *<u>Demonstrated</u>* Love! *<u>Expressed</u> Love!* Love *<u>made</u> <u>manifest</u>!* Love in every aspect of one's living: Love in speech, action, motive, will, service, even sacrifice – all reflecting Love in *<u>thought</u>!* Love <u>indiscriminately</u> given to all people, irrespective of others' actions! Meaning **respect** for and **thoughtfulness** to others always! All else is paled – *<u>into</u> <u>insignificance</u>!*

You Are the Lord's Anointed
His **Light Through You Doth Shine,**
Sent into the _World_ – to Turn, Men's Hearts
_To_ Him, and to Triumph – _Over Time!_

With every **good** thought, intention, deed, _and_ hope, wish, and dream, you beloved, are elevating the consciousness of Mankind! Even as a single drop of water into the ocean elevates _its entirety_, though imperceptible to most, **you** do the same! As a **child** of the Most High God, _you_ possess this **all**-reaching power of **influence** and **blessing**! Through the realm of Spirit, you touch every individual who draws breath at some level of their being. Never, _ever_, believe your life does not have **great significance!** _If_ the Spirit of the Lord **be** upon you, then **you**, have been sent, _as was Jesus_, to 'preach [or _live_] the glorious news and to **heal** the brokenhearted.' **You** are God's ambassador of goodwill and the fragrance of _His Presence_ is about you! **Holy** are you in His sight! Your 'ministry' will help bring triumph – _to all!_

**Unspeakable Joy to God Will Be
When Love's Work Is Done!
Every Soul Redeemed
All Hearts – *One!*

The <u>greatest</u> Rejoicing ever to occur in a Universe whose sole desire is Perfection and Completeness and Harmony, will be when *every last single solitary soul* has been reclaimed from error and imperfection, and brought into the Fullness of Being, which is the Kingdom of God! Thus will ***God's* Dream** of **Heaven** – throughout the visible and invisible universes – be made an Eternal, Unalterable Reality! This is the **true** meaning of the Parable of the Lost Sheep. That sheep was *<u>not</u>* one of a few, or even the first, to be 'lost' – and then 'found', but rather the *<u>very</u> <u>last</u>* to be redeemed! This explains why there was *<u>such</u> **<u>unparalleled</u>** <u>Joy</u>* in Heaven! Such had *never* been accomplished *before!* The family of God was now whole! *<u>All</u>* hearts reunited! *<u>All</u>* home safe! Love's declared Vow to save *the World*, in its *entirety* – *<u>was</u> <u>kept</u>!*

**Father, 'I _THANK_ Thee,' Our Lord Did Say
When He Did Rejoice, or Sorrow Display,
Afore Dining with Friends, or in Prayer
Immersed, <u>Always</u> A Heart Filled
With Gratitude – _First!_**

In that hour Jesus **rejoiced** in spirit, and said, '**I thank Thee**, O Father, Lord of Heaven and Earth, that Thou hast revealed unto babes.' At the tomb of His beloved Lazarus, where Jesus wept and 'groaned' in Himself, He lifted up His **tear-shedding** eyes, and said, 'Father, **I thank Thee**, that Thou hast heard Me' before crying 'Lazarus, Come forth!' Before feeding the multitudes, He '**gave thanks**.' Prior to the last supper, He broke bread and '**gave thanks**.' <u>Always</u>, Jesus was giving thanks, expressing Gratitude to God, and showing **appreciation** thru unceasing, **demonstrated** love. His prayers were those of **thanksgiving**, _coupled with praise_. Kind heart, our Saviour left us repeated examples so we might realize the <u>POWER</u> of this attitude. As Apostle Paul said, '**Thanks be to God**, Who gives **Victory**, through Jesus Christ–_our Lord!_'

Farewell Words

Those whom God chooses to become His emissaries, beloved, very often undergo extensive life training, involving a gradual, yet steady **transformation**. This training not infrequently involves hardship, **suffering**, **illness**, and sorrow. The **experiencing** of broken dreams and unmet desires. The recognition that 'things of the earth', including *other people*, are incapable of providing the fulfillment one's heart craves. And, finally, the realization that <u>Divine</u> <u>Love</u> **alone** can satisfy the hungry soul of man! God often 'calls' such individuals in night seasons. Decades may pass, yet God is working in their hearts *unceasingly*. While in the very depths of the valley of despair, their empathic ability develops and their **compassion** for others flourishes. Then, Lo! God's Love *for others*, **Inner Healing**, and later <u>outer</u>, becomes–*<u>their</u> <u>own</u>!*

With Every Good Wish, The Author

Part IV

A Message to Liberate *the* Spirit!

In Jesus' Presence!

Oh!
Lovely Saviour!
Who Welcomes Me,
With **Peace**
Beyond
The World I See,
Cause My Heart
To Evermore
Be
– *Thine Own!*

Part IV – Introduction
You <u>*CAN*</u> Know Him–*Today!*

The *Presence* of Jesus! How many <u>*long*</u> to know It! Yet, most have felt such to be reserved for the few, the saintly, the chosen. Yet, if we are to experience a life of Peace and Victory, in the midst of our oh! *so* uncertain a world, we **must** have conscious, heart-*felt* contact with Him! We must, in fact, we able to emotionally *sense* His Reality! – To <u>*feel*</u> His Love flowing into us! This book reveals specific ways to establish such a relationship, and enable one to receive the many *life-freeing* and *mental health saving* benefits that only His sacred heart can provide. The Power of **His Person**, as you seek Him, will make it so!

Preface

The messages in Part IV have been written in the first person *as though* the Lord Jesus, Himself, spoke these words directly. The author does **not** claim to have received these words verbatim from the Lord of Love, but rather has received their *essence* from Him into his spirit by prayerful listening and reverential meditation. May you, dear heart, receive them into *your* spirit as they are intended – to convey His *Unfailing* **Love** and *Ongoing* **Concern** for you, and to open a portal in your consciousness to allow His **All-Conquering Peace** and ever available Deliverance to become firmly established in your Soul!–*Right* now and *always!* **Shalom!**

Dear Reader,

This Part IV is the result of one person's compelled response to an incredibly trying situation. In order to survive emotionally and spiritually, he was moved to press **nearer to Jesus** to a degree he had never done before. With his peace being assaulted and eroded on a daily basis, his ability to carry on was greatly jeopardized, and deliverance, *in the midst of such challenging circumstances*, would be his only salvation. To his precious Saviour, then, he turned, and cried out for the help needed to rise above the dark despair and unrelenting fear besetting him. Not surprisingly, *to the believer*, relief was speedily forthcoming, and new insights and modes of thinking *and being* were disclosed that **restored** his peace! May you, dear friend, have any peace restored that *you* may have lost through the years due to great personal trials, as you read this book; where practical, yet *supernatural* help, is available. Peace-and *Joy*-filled, living faith, is there!

A brother in Christ

Part IV – Contents

The Peace of God Your Heart Will Know
The Peace of God I Can Know Today
Oh! Peace of God! You I Must Know
Oh! Saviour Divine! Thou Love's Pure Light!

In My Presence, There Peace You'll Find
In My Presence, Tranquility Is There
In My Presence, Restoring Silence Does Reign
In My Presence, You Will Serene Be

In My Presence, Great Relief You Will Find
In My Presence, Your Deepest Needs Are Met
In My Presence, My Light Will Bestow
In My Presence, A Stillness Is Known

In My Presence, You'll Know 'All Is Well'
In My Presence, My Person Do Seek
In My Presence, True Relief Can Be Found
In My Presence, Joy Awaits You There

Part IV – Contents – *Con.*

In My Presence, True Trust Abides
In My Presence, Love Is Showered On Thee
In My Presence, Optimism Is Born

In My Presence, Your Child Within
In My Presence, The Light of Love
In My Presence, Is A Promise of Mine

In My Presence, I Offer the Key
In My Presence, Victory Is Known

Farewell Message

**The Peace of God Your Heart *Will* Know
As the <u>Calm</u> of My Spirit Over You doth Flow,
Like a Sweet, Gentle Breeze in a Meadow Fair
You Can Release Every – *<u>Burdensome Care</u>!***

Beloved friend, are you *lacking* in Peace today? Is there an uneasiness in your soul, a sense that 'all is <u>not</u> well' in your spirit? Is your mind weighed down with burdensome thoughts and troubling apprehensions – *fear* of what might be coming? This is NOT the will of your Heavenly Father who, as the Apostle Peter said, desires that 'peace be ***multiplied*** unto you'! To find deliverance from this unnatural state of being, one thing alone you need do as the old, sweet, heaven-inspired song admonishes: '**Turn** your eyes upon Jesus, Look <u>full</u> in His wonderful face, and the things of earth will grow strangely dim, in the **Light** of His Glory and Grace!' Here, you are <u>not</u> ignoring your difficulties, nor minimizing challenges, *rather*, you are receiving the <u>full</u> assurance that Peace, ***true*** Peace, can be yours in the midst of any storm. Only the Light of *His Countenance* can impart this–*<u>my Love</u>!*

**The Peace of God I Can Know <u>Today</u>
As This Is the Gift My Saviour Would Say,
Is the <u>One</u> True Need My Heart Would Find
If I Am to Experience – *<u>Peace</u> of <u>Mind</u>!***

The mentality of the world, dear heart, is one of being uneasy, restless, troubled, living in an unnamed, relentless, often indefinable fear and sense of dread. It is part of *'the spirit of the world'*. Yet, when we **invoke** the Spirit of God, we enter into the 'Mystery of Godliness'. I Tim 3:16 says 'God was manifest in the flesh, justified in the Spirit, seen of angels, preached unto the Gentiles, believed on in the world, and received up into Glory.' And while this verse applies directly unto Jesus our Lord, it has application to us, as well. In **surrendering** to God's Peace as a conscious act of the will, **refusing** to worry, **declaring** God's *present triumph* in our lives, we, too, experience 'God in the flesh'; we, too, are 'justified in the Spirit'; we, too, are 'seen (observed and in the presence) of angels'; we, too, are 'believed on in the world'; and we, too, are 'received up *into* Glory.' The Glory of Heavenly, **heart-assuring** Peace, right here *and <u>right</u> <u>now</u>!*

Oh! Peace of God! *You* I Must Know
If Heaven's Light I Would <u>Experience</u> Below,
Come Forth from My Heart Whence You Reside,
Make *Manifest* Thy Self to Thy – *Willing Bride!*

There is, beloved, an unrecorded declaration of Jesus which reads, 'I AM the Peace of God!' Yes, He *was*, and still **IS**, the Peace of the Living God – made manifest unto men! And it is to His Beloved, humanity, you and I, He will one day be formally **wed**! – Joined in indivisible union! Yet, in the interim, the **betrothal period**, the Peace He harbors in His Heart is meant for you and for me! *How might we, then, best access It?* By repeatedly turning to Him in our minds and hearts throughout the day, by saying, 'Lord, I *look* to Thee!' 'Lord, I *trust* in Thee!', and 'Lord, I *rest* in Thee!' By entering into this dialogue, these three 'faith statements' will serve to quiet our minds, and calm our hearts. We can, you and I, relinquish our distressing thoughts over to Him, Who will in return, **replace them** with thoughts of certitude and true life-freeing reliance. **Only** God's Peace, the heart-**felt**, given *Awareness* of His Presence – *can do this!*

Oh! Saviour Divine! Thou Love's Pure Light!
Awaken **My Soul to the <u>Dawn</u> That Might,**
Purify and Cleanse *Every* **Thought Today,**
Sweeping <u>All</u> that Is *Unlike* **You –** *<u>Away</u>!*

My Light, dear heart, is given you to **Illumine** those thoughts of yours that are not in accord with mine. Recall that I said, 'I AM the Light of the World. He who followeth Me shall not walk in darkness, but shall have the Light of Life!' I become the Light of *<u>Your</u>* World – your *<u>Inner</u>* World – where the Gracious Work of Redemption takes place, as you welcome Me into the Chamber of your Heart. Until my Light makes plain, **much** of the true nature of your thoughts, and resulting actions, eludes you and remains unknown, even though you are a true devotee of Mine. By directing the SearchLight of My Love over the stream of your consciousness, I make you aware, by evident exposure, which thoughts constitute the 'seedlings' of sin – tiny *departures from Love*. Come to My Light! Let those thoughts be transformed by – *My <u>Radiant</u> <u>Presence</u>!*

**In My Presence, There Peace You'll Find
To Settle Your Heart, and Quiet Your Mind,
A Peace the World Can Never Give,
Bought By My Blood So You May Live!**

My Child, when anxiety becomes your constant companion, when fear makes you its unwilling captive, when dread touches your very soul, turn to Me, and Me alone! Within the citadel of your mind, begin to recite slowly and calmly, *'Lord Jesus, I receive Thy Peace'*. No matter how you feel at this moment, even if you are near panic stricken, continue to say these words. Say them twenty, forty, fifty, a *hundred* times, just keep reciting them with deliberation and feeling *until* my calmness descends upon you, as It most surely will! Actually, It is there all the time, but you are simply unaware. By saying these words, you'll be attuning your consciousness to mine, and my Peace will be felt by your whole being! *Receive My Peace!* It is meant for you today! Your worries, cares, and heartaches will subside, as My Victorious Peace – manifests – *through you!*

**In My Presence, Tranquility Is There
Awaiting the *Asking* It Might Be Shared,
A Nobleman I Am Called By Many a Man,
Tho Not of Love, Yet of Something As Grand!**

Peace, my Child, is **the One Great Need** of your heart! My Peace! Some know this now. Others will yet find It to be the only true healing balm in an environment of the challenges and trials of this world. Though I am the God of Love, I was ***not*** called *the Prince of Love*, but rather *the Prince of Peace!* The reason being? – From a foundation of peace, I can clearly see all things! There is no distraction. I see straight through to the center of all hearts and know their workings. My Magnificent Peace affords Me this capability. Totally at One with Myself, with no discord within, I am in a position to extend my Peace to whomever I choose. Recall that after my resurrection, my initial greeting was always,'Peace Be Unto You!'**The Peace of My Presence!** Yet, my Peace would be valueless if you could not experience it first-hand. I died that you might partake of it – do not *ever*believe you cannot!

**In My Presence, Restoring *Silence* Does Reign
Where Emanation of Roses Perfumes the Same,
I AM the Holy Fragrance of God Above,
Calming Hearts & Bequeathing Love!**

How, beloved, *does one come into my Presence?* You must first learn how to have your mind quieted **by Me**. You must begin to consciously allow Me to slow your thoughts, and dwell upon a single beautiful concept or idea, promise or ideal. At first, this will be most difficult. You will feel anxious, even rushed. You will feel uncomfortable and will struggle to continue. When this happens, you must affirm, *'Jesus! You are my Greatest Reality!'* You must **know** that I AM your Saviour and Deliverer in THIS life, *here and now*, not just in the future! But, I assure you, as you persevere, this process will become easier and eventually enjoyable. You ***will*** be strengthened, become calm, and free! Here attunement of your being to My own will take place. You will be able to say, *'I can rest now'*, setting aside worries in my sheltering Presence! I AM the Rose of Sharon! My Love is *ForeverYours!*

**In My Presence, You Will Serene Be
As You Respond to My Pleading *Come* Unto Me,
A Gentle Carpenter, I Carved with Such Care,
To Shape *Hidden* Beauty – Awaiting There!**

My precious Child, respond to my call, and I will take away your life-crushing fears, your seemingly inescapable anxieties, your life-mocking worries, and your Christ-denying concerns. In their place, I will fill you with calm and tranquil thoughts, soothing and comforting thoughts. You recall my great Invitation to 'Come unto ME, all ye who are heavy laden, and I will **GIVE** you rest (Deep *Soul-Satisfying* Peace). This, beloved, was my greatest gift! It **shone** *through* my Love. It was That which caused so many to stand in awe of Me as they witnessed a Peace that could not be *disturbed!* – Or *afrightened!* – Or *destroyed!* My Presence proclaimed It! My voice exclaimed It! My touch conveyed It! Even as My Father and I are One, so My **Peace** and My **Presence** are **ONE!** They cannot be disunited. As you bask in my Peace, Its surpassing beauty will call forth beauties – *within you!*

**In My Presence, Great *Relief* You Will Find
As I Fashion your Thinking, *Remold* Your Mind,
No Longer Troubled About So <u>Much</u> to Do,
I Release You So Dreams May Come True!**

There is no need to do *anything*, my Child, in My Presence. Nor, is there any *sense* of any supposed need. Instead, just an awareness of **Joyous Being**! Recall that 'ye are **<u>complete</u>** *in* [*Me*]'. There is no goal to frantically strive for, nor any dream to restlessly pursue. I <u>AM</u> <u>the</u> <u>fulfillment</u> <u>of</u> <u>all</u> <u>things</u>! Does this mean you are to abandon your goals and dreams? No. But, you are to realize that It is *<u>I</u> who will perform them <u>in you</u> with **My** strength, <u>not</u> your own!* This takes the heavy burden of accomplishment off of your shoulders and places it squarely upon My own. You can then experience **true contentment**, perhaps for the first time in your life. A restless, worrisome, nervous, agitated spirit is not from Me. A calm, composed, patient, trusting, restful spirit IS! So, relinquish your ambitions to Me. Do not be prisoner to them any longer. Make of <u>Me</u> your *Chief desire* and *aim*. Peace will be yours!

**In My Presence, Your *Deepest* Needs Are Met
Soul Needs of Knowing My Plans *For* You Yet,
I AM the God of <u>Certainties,</u> Of This You Can
Be Sure, and *Rest* in This Knowledge Secure!**

On several occasions, my child, in my earthly walk, I sought to reassure and calm many a distressed and terribly upset brother by declaring: 'With God **ALL THINGS** are *<u>POSSIBLE</u>!*' This Glorious Truth, spoken with conviction and power, broke the encircling pale of fear about their hearts, and opened the door to allowing <u>*greater*</u> **possibilities** (miracles) to occur. But, there is far more to this statement than most realize. The '*all things*' cited <u>always</u> means the Good, the Best, the Most God-Glorifying things – possible, *or that could even be conceived of! Not <u>only</u> by man, but <u>even by God, Himself</u>!* It must then necessarily follow, that the underlying Truth is: 'With God all things that <u>*ARE*</u> the MOST **Love**-exalting are <u>CERTAIN</u> to one day <u>BE</u>!' – in God's *perfectly appointed time periods*. So, when you come into My Presence, know with **certainty** your greatest good I will achieve, *for you!*

**In My Presence, My Light Will Bestow
A Holy *Boldness* Destined to Grow, Into
A <u>*Confidence*</u> You Have *Never* Known,
Springing *from* My Heart – Alone!**

My Child, my servant declared, 'God has not given us a spirit of fear, but [a Spirit] of **POWER**, and of **LOVE**, and of a **SOUND [<u>*undisturbable*</u>] MIND**.' When you come unto Me in your powerlessness, with your feelings of lovelessness, and unsound-mindedness, I welcome you with open arms, and surround you with and immerse you in my stabilizing Spirit. As you faithfully keep your daily tryst with Me, you will find yourself maintaining greater and longer-lasting **composure** as you face the ongoing challenges of life. Situations that greatly upset you before, will be handled with grace and dignity. It is the superimposing of **My Heart Presence** that affords you this inner strength, and brings an *ever-increasing* sense of Peace to your Heart! Not a brashness nor arrogance, but a quiet, holy boldness will emerge, a rarity the world seldom sees, but one which it will never – *forget!*

In My Presence, A Stillness Is Known
Where *few* Precious Words Speak Volumes
Alone, Where Words of Endearment My Spirit
Rushes to, Troubled Hearts Find Peace – *Anew!*

My dearly beloved child, the words that move my Spirit to rush to your aid are words such as these: '*Precious Saviour!*' If all you ever say to Me in your prayers are these words, I will draw you ever closer to My Heart! For in these two words reside *all* your asking, *all* your wishes, *all* your believing! However imperfect or incomplete. So never feel when you are burdened with unceasing worries and intruding faithless thoughts that you need to pray with eloquence or in carefully constructed sentences. **I know your heart**, and even one word alone, be it only '*Lord!*' will magnetize to your being the Peace you long for, and **must** have to live a *Victorious Life* in my Name. And should you find you cannot utter one word due to your troubled state, no matter! Simply rest in my Presence, with bowed head and humble heart, and I will cause Peace to *flow* into your being – surely, *without fail!*

In My Presence, You'll *Know* 'All Is Well' The Eternal Verity to Dispel Thoughts of Hell, Whether In This World or That to Come, You've Nothing to Fear, *Nor Cower From!*

Beloved Child, it is my deepest heart's desire that you cease to live in such damaging fear of a supposed place of *eternal* torment known as 'hell.' It is true that I cautioned many a soul of *dire consequences* they would surely reap, should they continue in their departures from the Royal Law of Love. The Great Law of Cause and Effect is operative throughout My Universe, and no person is exempt. Yet, what the majority of My followers have misunderstood is that **all** such drastic measures, should they be deemed necessary for some *few*, are *remedial* in nature, and *saving* in outcome. All scriptural references to the needed correction of *this* magnitude were *mistranslated*, having *limited duration*, and always serve to **wholly purify** the wayward soul. My Redemptive Love's **Power**, reaches even *beyond* such severe penalties, as My Cross, ALL-conquering, has MADE **Peace** – available now, and **evermore** – *for all!*

**In My Presence, My *Person* Do Seek
Revealing Myself To Those Who Are Meek,
Your Jesus of Nazareth I'll Always Be,
Those With Inner Eyes – *Shall See!***

Beloved, know you not that I AM a living **Person**! I possess the form and likeness of a man, as I AM the *perfect Man!* I delight in revealing Myself as the **Divine Human** that I AM! One true follower of mine described my appearance as One with 'a quiet gaze, whose eyes are *soft and friendly as hearth embers burning low.*' Others describe a radiance about Me, a glorious Light on My face, and an **all-pervading** Peace! This beloved son also perceived my voice *'compassionate as a brooding dove'*, yet *'clear and triumphant as a nightingale!'* – extending gracious words to his soul! You, too, may behold my face with Inner Vision and hear my Voice with Inner Ears! Though my precise features may appear different to various ones, depending upon their need, you may still behold my Person! Come unto Me, then! Enter the *Presence of My Person* and you needn't be bowed down with heaviness–*ever again!*

**In My Presence, True Relief Can Be Found
Though Pain Has Beset You All Around,
Such _Shall_ Pass that You Might Know,
My Love, Alone, In You – _to Grow!_**

Beloved, Come to Me! And in my sovereign Grace, should I not immediately remove your pain, whether physical or emotional, I will at once *lesson it* that you may bear it **till** I remove it from your person altogether. I will share your pain and diminish its hold over you. Remember, you do *not* have a High Priest Who cannot be touched by the feeling of your infirmities! I AM your compassionate and empathetic God! And *my Grace will prove stronger than your temporary pain!* You may rest assured as I have your best interest at heart, always! Your suffering will 'whither' and discomfort 'die away', but my Love for you, my Love IN you, will expand and grow and flourish! I ask only that you TRUST me in this matter. **I cannot fail you, beloved!** Take comfort in these words! I AM Emmanuel! God *with* YOU! Receive the balm of my Spirit,and become increasingly free!

**In My Presence, Joy Awaits You There
Tho Your Heart Is Burdened With Many a Care,
Sadness and Sorrow Will Have to Flee, as
Wellsprings Rush Upward, *in Praise*, of Me!**

A timeless and liberating refrain echoes in the hearts of those who enter My Presence: 'No storm can shake my **inmost** calm, when to that Rock I'm clinging. Since Love is Lord of Heaven and earth, *how can I keep from singing?*' Yes, beloved! Singing songs of praise and adoration of Me! Making melody in your heart! As my Holy Word says, 'In [My] Presence is fullness of Joy.' When you lay down your burdens at my feet, and redirect your attention to My Divine Reality, surely, as I have said, 'Out of your [**innermost** being] shall flow rivers of Living Water.' Sadness and sorrow increasingly are <u>*washed*</u> <u>*away*</u> in this miraculous flood as you contemplate my **Great Love** for you! Such 'diminishing' feelings may return, but always with lessoned power to depress your spirit. Make it a practice, then, to *sing* songs of praise to Me each day, *hum* tunes of gaiety. Joy will lighten your heart!

In My Presence, True Trust Abides
Doubt That Has Plagued You Must Fall Aside,
A Sense of Assurance As You've Never Known,
Reserved For Those I Call My Own!

Nestled in the folds of your Being, My precious Child, is a Divine Plan. It is a permanent and indestructible part of you. It is upon *this* plan that *complete* and *total* Trust in Me may legitimately rest. As you continue to come into My Presence, during quiet hours of reflection, or during recurring moments of called-forth stillness, the Trust you have in Me will grow as stages of this Plan are unfolded to your awareness. Remember your earthly childhood when you lay yourself down to sleep, you felt a security that *enveloped* your Being, that arose from your knowing your guardian parents had provided for your every need and were there keeping watch still. *This Trust you may know again, Dear Heart!* My Divine parental Care, along with your majestic Life Plan, will 'conspire' to eradicate your doubts that you could ever experience the assurance your adult heart craves, and must have, to live aTriumphantLife! Believe!All is well,My Love!

**In My Presence, Love is Showered On Thee,
Any Self-Hatred Can _Not_ Withstand Me,
My Tender Affection Unaltered Will Stand,
As Disdain Melts Away and Departs
from Your Hands!**

My dearest child, I speak to you who due to past negative occurrences, hurtful situations, or seeming failures on your part, you have developed a self-image which belies the Supreme Truth of My appraisal of you. By coming into My Presence, thoughts and feelings about your unworthiness, valuelessness, undesirability, and unimportance to Me, are shown in the revealing Light of My Presence to be *wholly false and without foundation*. You cannot, dear heart, remain in My Presence for long, without the shower of My Love upon you washing away such mistaken ideas and falsehoods! *Never* do you have cause for disdain about yourself! At no time do you have reason for even the slightest dislike! Though you have made mistakes and acted in ways unbecoming of a child of God, My **Forgiveness** cleanses you completely *the very moment* you ask for it.So, hold your head up high! My Love!

**In My Presence, Optimism Is Born,
The Soul's True Stance in Calmness or Storm,
Believing All Outcomes will *Yet* Turn Out Right,
Through the Most Trying Day, or
the Darkest of Night!**

'Be of **Good Cheer**! I have OVERCOME the world!' With these words I set forth the attitude that is near all-conquering – *in itself!* Such a positive attitude will empower you to approach any undertaking with an optimistic spirit that will energize your body temple and strengthen your sensitive heart! While it is true you cannot *always* be happy in this present world, due to the many hardships and tragedies many experience, you can learn to remain consistently **cheerful**. For this, beloved, is one of the *greatest gifts* you can bestow upon your fellow woman and man! You'll never know, this side of Heaven, how often a sincere, genuinely offered, smile has saved a troubled soul from utter despair, or delivered a sorrowing person from mental anguish. Such is the Power of **YOUR** cheerful smile, facial expression, and voice tone. Therefore, Believe for theBest!The Son will break thru *for you!*

In My Presence, Your Child Within
Is Set Free to Wonder and Marvel Again,
The World Opens Up Before Your Wide Eyes,
As Your Heart Discards All Needless 'Whys'!

Child of My Heart's longing, continue to come into my Presence, trusting as a little child, and you will find the nagging doubts and whys that plague your soul vanishing away! One of my names is '**Wonderful**' because I AM a God of Wonder, and my works are termed '**Marvelous**' in sacred writ. Meditate on what I have done for *you* in my earth walk, and I will awaken your sense of marvelously-new Wonder, and ponder what I AM doing for you **now** in my present Mission as your Great High Priest. No longer torture yourself with repeated 'whys' – *Why* did this happen? *Why* did this not happen? In Me, these questions cease to have relevance. I, your Great I AM, your Lord and Redeemer, will <u>**hush**</u> 'the whispering voice of the infinite why!' And I will free you from its debilitating power. I live to serve you, **now**, and intercede for your spiritual welfare and growth. Let, then, '***Whys***', be replaced by, '***Wonder***' *– of Me!*

**In My Presence, The Light of Love,
Brightly Shines, as a Million Stars, Above,
Darkness is Banished, Fear Falls Away,
As Upon My Breast Your Head May Lay!**

My dearly beloved child, an inspired poet once wrote: 'Look up! *Look up!* Fear nothing! For in the darkest night – a million, *million* stars crown you with their light!' No truer words were ever spoken! When you enter into my Presence, 'looking up' unto Me, though veiled from your earthly sight, the Light of My Being is poured out upon you! My radiance envelopes your form and at inner levels nourishes and heals your soul. Continue in your trysts with Me, and there will come times when you will *tangibly feel* this energy of my radiant Love for you! Some have experienced it as a shower of Light, others an immersion into Light. But, happen to you, one day, it will! In my *Living Light* you may find repose and rest, as did my beloved disciple who laid his head so trustingly upon my breast. I am here for you, beloved! The spiritual realm I inhabit is so close to you, you will be amazed when once you realize its proximity. Lo! I AM with you – *Always!*

**In My Presence, Is A Promise of Mine
Tho One *Not* Welcome by the Natural Mind,
Its Fruit the *More* Sweet to Evermore Be,
As Life Openly Triumphs In Thee!**

Beloved Child of Mine, pay heed to these words of a fellow brother: '*All* that will live Godly in Christ Jesus shall suffer persecution.' Never pleasant when one encounters it, nor while one endures it, yet **Peace** shall be its *outcome*, as your faith is strengthened in my Power to deliver you – *and bring good out of evil!* I have told you this before, that you be not taken unawares and feel as though you have done some wrong, bringing punishment upon yourself. No, as a bearer of My Light, the darkness in others is *offended* by your Presence, and would seek, at the very least, to drive you away by ridicule, looks of ill-will, or belittling tone. When such happens, remember My Words! '***Blessed are ye***, when men shall revile you, and persecute you, and shall say all manner of evil against you falsely, for my sake.' *My* Life in you, will sustain you, and enable you to remain *mentally and emotionally above* your detractors–a sweet Triumph of the Soul!

**In My Presence, I Offer the Key
To Find Possibilities, You *Before* Couldn't See,
It is *Never* Too Late to Begin Life Anew,
Where Your Most Cherished Dreams
May Come True!**

My Beloved child, to you who feel much of life has passed you by, to you who regret your lack of accomplishment in achieving your Oh! *So-Wondrous* dreams of youth, to you who grieve over lost opportunities and pine over mistaken steps, **I Say Unto You:** As you enter my Presence with regularity, *your life will be reborn!* I will resurrect those discarded dreams, and breath new life into your lost hopes and ideals! I will even **cause** you to recognize the limitless possibilities all about you, to which you were blind before! No matter what past circumstances, people, or outcomes have 'said' unto you, speaking falsely of your supposed unworthiness or inability to achieve, **I Now Say Unto You**: *It is never too late* to fulfill your Destiny, to experience Joy and tremendous Interest and Enthusiasm for Life! For By My Heavenly Authority I declare: Your dreams are truly–*My own!*

**In My Presence, Victory Is Known
The Trophy For Which My Life Did Atone,
I AM Your Saviour! The Master of Men,
In Me You Will Triumph – *Again!***

Beloved Child, The Atonement (effected by My crucifixion at Calvary) for you, and all mankind, secured an eternal Victory, the conquering of death, in *all* its dreaded forms. Know, too, that when you come into My Presence, you encounter a Risen, *Glorified* Saviour! Thru this wholly unique, supreme, <u>*Sacramental*</u> *Act* of My Life, I won the Trophy for which I did willingly suffer – the **certain** Redemption of your Soul! I *WILL* have your salvation become reality! No power can nor will deprive Me of YOU, beloved, my precious child for whom I gladly died, and now LIVE! Let this Truth ring throughout your being and bring irrepressible Peace to your heart! So, when you experience feelings of failure or loss, remind yourself **IN ME** you are '*MORE* than a Conqueror'. Let your mind entertain thoughts of **Triumph**, which is now your birthright in Me, who have given you <u>*new*</u> *birth!* I, Jesus, verily declare it so! *Amen!*

Farewell Words

Dear friend, an awareness of **The Presence** of the **Gentle Carpenter** is needed today more so than at any other time in human history. This is because a great *seldom-acknowledged* loneliness and hidden dread is extent in the world today as never before. It resides within the souls of nearly all men and women. Many try to escape it through continuous activity of various sorts, yet when night falls and they are alone, <u>they become as lost and crying children in the night</u>! – Feeling as though orphaned and abandoned! Christ, the Lord, however, stands ready and able to **reveal** Himself to you in a humanly *intimate* and heartfelt way, allowing you to feel, to *emotionally sense*, His Presence about you, and derive Its sustaining influences of Peace, Safety, Trust and Care. Enter His Presence daily. The *Power* of His **Victorious Peace** –<u>*will be yours!*</u>

With Every Good Wish, The Author

Part V

A Message to Secure *One's* Well-Being!

The Blessings of Wealth!

Beloved,
I *Wish*
Above <u>All</u> Things,
That Thou
Mayest **Prosper**
And
<u>Be</u> In **Health**

III John 1:2

Part V – Introduction
'According to The Riches of His Glory!' (Eph. 3:16)

The most giving man who ever lived, contrary to popular belief, is likely to have possessed a *measure* of **real** wealth. At birth, He was given pure gold and costly ointments, by **kings** giving their **finest** and **best**! Jesus apprenticed to a skilled and well-respected profession, amounting to that of a general contractor and master stonemason. He, also, established a base of operations in Capernaum, referred to in scripture as '*THE* house', probably His <u>own</u> personal property. Further, Jesus was supported by a contingent of female followers, a number possessing considerable financial means. Not to mention, His clothing was of such **exquisite craftsmanship** that *well-paid* soldiers vied over their ownership while He was dying. Come and learn, no pauper was He, our <u>King</u> – *of Kings!*

Part V – Contents

The *Master* Key to Greatness
Lord, *Many* Believe You Were Stranger To
I Wish *For* You to Prosper
Trust <u>*Not*</u> in Uncertain Riches
A Sower Went Out to Sow Seed
God Shall <u>Supply</u> All Your Need
The *Time* of Your <u>Visitation</u>
The Eight Manifestations of Abundance *from*
The Super Abundant One
Well Springs of Wealth
Fortune's Golden Keys
A Rosary for Riches

**The *Master* Key to Greatness
Whether Influence, Power, or <u>Gold</u>
The Gentle Teacher of Galilee Taught
Is To *<u>Serve</u>* the <u>All</u>, To *<u>Assist</u>* the <u>Whole</u>!**

Friend, is there a Master Precept of *universal application* to one's life? In other words, is there a rule built into life itself that, *if* followed consistently, would produce the quality of **greatness** in <u>ANY</u> endeavor of one's choosing? The Master Teacher said there was: 'Whosoever would be **Great** among you, shall be your minister; and whosoever of you would be the chiefest, *shall be servant of <u>all</u>.*' Whether that greatness be in one's sphere of influence, quality of character, power to persuade, or **one's capability to acquire monetary might!** Jesus placed **<u>no</u>** qualification **<u>nor</u>** restriction upon this **<u>magnifying</u> principal**. So seek out an arena where you can serve the **<u>most</u>** people. The ***<u>more</u>*** people you serve, educate, empower, inspire, uplift, *<u>in humility</u>*, the higher you will be exalted and the **greater** blessed, to bless **more** – *<u>in return</u>!*

Lord, *Many* Believe You Were Stranger to Wealth of the Earth, Lived in Poverty, Too, Yet, a *Different* Picture Begins to Unfold, When We Listen to *What* Holy Writ – *Has Told!*

The most giving man who ever lived, contrary to popular belief, is likely to have possessed a measure of *real* wealth. Recall, at birth, He was given **pure gold** and **costly ointments**, probably kept for adulthood needs. Tradition holds the Magi were also *kings*, who brought their *finest* and *best* offerings to the **King** *of* **Kings!** No token gifts were these! Even His clothing was of such *exquisite craftsmanship* that **well-paid** soldiers vied over its ownership. Further, He apprenticed to a skilled profession of **general contractor/stonemason**, a more accurate rendering of 'carpenter'! No doubt, He was highly sought after for His expertise by officials of the government's vast building campaign, recent scholarship reveals. Jesus, then, utilized *considerable* resources – *as our example!*

I Wish *For* You to Prosper
As Did <u>*I*</u>, Child, Way Back When,
<u>*Not*</u> as a Pauper, But as a <u>Prince</u> of Life,
Who <u>*Received*</u> God's Blessings – <u>*Then*</u>!

Perhaps you have heard, dear friend, the scriptural verse stating, 'According to <u>HIS</u> *<u>riches</u>*,' (Phil. 4:19) referring to the <u>royal</u> 'Prince of Life' (Acts 3:15). These verses traditionally have nearly always been understood to mean the Lord's *spiritual* wealth. Yet, there may be more **literality** to these verses than ever suspected. Jesus' outreach was supported by a **multitude** of female followers, including Mary of Magdala, a woman many scholars believe to have been of considerable financial means. Another influential benefactor, named Nicodemus, was a wealthy religious ruler. Further, there is a strong possibility Jesus even owned ***<u>His own house!</u>*** As He apparently acquired a 'base of operations' in the city of Capernaum, referred to often in scripture as '*<u>THE</u>* house'. His <u>personal</u> needs? Amply provided for – *<u>to be sure</u>!*

**Trust _Not_ in Uncertain Riches
My Servant Did Plainly Say, Yet
Rather Trust In The Living God, Who
Gives You <u>Power</u> to Gain Wealth – _Always!_**

Many do not realize, beloved friend, that God, Himself, is the _Source_ of all wealth. Moreover, He is the One Who **gives** freely the _Power_ to acquire wealth! (Deut. 8:18) And apart from _this_ Power, one's attempts to attain it will ultimately prove impotent, and devoid of meaning. But, with it, wealth will prove a blessing of great measure. **What _IS_ this Power?** In I Tim. 17-18 we are told wealth's **purpose** is to be 'ready to _distribute,_ willing to _share_ [with those less fortunate]'. With this end in mind, wealth is a **noble aim** worthy of one's efforts and attention. Further, this Power involves the bestowal of the **Vision** to _believe_ wealth is our **birthright** should we prove worthy of it, and ours to <u>claim</u> to elevate our life's circumstances above monetary struggle and bondage – to freedom to do those _greater_ works of **charity** –_and_ _to_ _bless_ _others!_

**A Sower Went Out to Sow Seed
But, Much Fell on Fruit_less_ Ground,
It Wasn't Until He Found <u>Good</u> Soil
His _Hundred-Fold_ Was Found!**

You recall, dear friend, the parable told by Jesus of _'The Sower and the Seed'_. This true-to-life story depicted a farmer who scattered seed over the land. Some fell by the wayside and were eaten by birds, others upon stony places and withered away, while others fell among thorns and were choked. But, some seeds fell into good ground, and brought forth **thirty**, **sixty**, and **one-hundred fold!** Now, few have ever taken this as a _literal possibility_ when it comes to **one's finances**. But, consider. Jesus identified the seed as 'the Word of God', also called elsewhere 'the Word of Faith'. And when we exercise our God-inspired **Faith** _through_ **action**, <u>**and**</u> find an environment conducive to <u>multiplied</u> growth, Jesus plainly indicates as much as a hundred-fold **increase** can be expected! _Find_ that good soil, should you choose, believe – _and act!_

'God Shall <u>Supply</u> All Your Need'
Was *The* Promise Given On That Day,
Yet, One's *<u>Need</u>* Reaches Out *<u>Far</u>* <u>Beyond</u>
The Barest Necessities – *<u>I</u> <u>Dare</u> <u>Say</u>!*

Many, dear heart, believe, and correctly so, that God will provide for their every need as they exercise their faith. Their *'<u>need</u>'*, however, is nearly always interpreted to mean the meeting of those *essentials* required to sustain life; such as food, water, shelter, and clothing, even medicine. *<u>Yet,</u> **<u>Is</u> <u>this</u> <u>the</u> <u>entire</u> <u>Truth</u>?*** The verse concludes with, 'according to *<u>His</u>* **Riches** in Glory, in Christ Jesus.' The word 'Riches', encompasses **far more** than the *'basic'* requirements of Life. The Apostle Paul had in mind the entire range of 'commodities', including the '*<u>higher</u>* needs' of man–<u>those which **nourish** and **sustain** the <u>Soul</u>! Such as high purpose, meaningful work, interesting vocation, personal mission, creativity, beauty, and abundance. *Nothing less* can do justice to the word, **'Riches'**! Our God's storehouse is **full** to Overflowing! Why not <u>claim</u> *yours–<u>today</u>!*

'The *Time* of Your <u>Visitation</u>',
You Ask, What Could *<u>That</u>* Mean to Me,
Save, the Entrance to a Whole New World
Where, <u>Your</u> Dreams Become – *<u>Reality!</u>*

If fortunate enough on a few **rare** occasions, we encounter an extraordinary occurrence. Through <u>*seemingly*</u> pure happenstance, we are presented with an **opportunity** that sounds entirely 'too good to be true.' We are told our lives can be **immeasurably** better should we embrace it, and are assured we will never again be the same! Yet, most of us discount it as an impossibility or a false hope. Our lives are what they are and will never be much more! – Whether in the arenas of relationships, health, **wealth**, career, or even spirituality. The Master of Life wept over Jerusalem, saying, 'because you did <u>*not*</u> **recognize** the time of <u>*your*</u> visitation.' You, too, friend, have had 'visitations.' Have you recognized them? Or did they slip through your fingers, ungrasped? Should a **new** life be offered you, pay heed. It may have been sent – *<u>from above!</u>*

The Eight Manifestations
Of
Abundance

Not only was the raging sea stilled and the dark storm abated – but the sun was made to *burst forth*, and the blue sky to *speedily propagate* – from horizon to horizon!

Not only were the hungering multitudes fed – but their portion was made to *overflow* into twelve large baskets *full* of *hundreds* of fish *above* and *beyond* their immediate needs!

Not only did He offer the fullness of Life to others – but He *showered* Life around and about Him, *continuously*, upon whomsoever would receive it!

Not only did He provide a single cup of water to quench one's present thirst – but He also made available a mighty fountain where '*torrents* of Living water' gush forth from within!

Not only did He speak of the beauties of one single flower – but He spoke of beholding the lilies of the field, their *profusion*, and how they were *clothed* in such *rich variety!*

Not only when ministering to a person did He heal only one of their ailments – but He also mended *however many other* disorders which kept their lives limited and constricted!

Not only did He offer a single encouraging word needed here and there – but also illustrated His teachings with *one example after another*, *parable* upon *parable* – seemingly without end!

Not only did He tell us to occasionally share with the needy – but to *generously give, continuously,* out of the *abundance* which He has placed within our hearts!

'And of the *INCREASE* of His government [His provision, His blessings, His supply], there shall be *NO END!*'

from **The Super Abundant One!**

Well Springs Of Wealth

Seek wealth only for the beneficent possibilities it offers
– therefore you already have compelling reasons to do so

Value the resultant opportunities for increased personal growth and maturity
– as you are exposed to new learning situations

Thrill to the prospect of doing good for deserving individuals
– and mankind – as a whole

Live daily the principles of caring, compassionate service
– knowing that such service is the whole aim of wealth to begin with

Well Springs Of Wealth - Con.

Yearn to bring more beauty, goodness, and sweetness into the world
– through your diligent and honest efforts

Desire to give with far greater passion than to receive
– for it is in giving that you will find your greatest joy

Trust continually in the perfect workings of our perfect God
– to supply your every need – and all your heart's desires

Realize that you are wholly deserving of achieving financial abundance
– as you bring yourself in alignment with God's intended, consecrated purposes

Well Springs Of Wealth - Con.

Recognize that acquiring wealth is a blessing and noble aim
– and attracting wealth is the Creative Principle in action

Know that wealth is the Principle of Love given manifold material expression
– though wealth will not be thrust upon you

Ask rightly, then prepare to receive unceasing giving from God, the Great Giver
– the choice is solely yours

Remember always that wealth proceeds from inner spiritual resources
– and is a natural outgrowth of Inspired, God-Given Vision

Fortune's Golden Keys

In the Depths of my Being, I invoke the Spirit of Victory – *and it is this spirit that will draw fortune to me*

I know that true earthly Fortune consists of an Abundance of monetary and physical resources – *wherein my every need is met, whether that need be for one dollar, or ten-thousand*

I recognize the time has come for my tremendous – and long-maturing – potential, to acquire Fortune, be unleashed in the world – *for the good of myself – and <u>all</u> <u>others</u>*

<u>Fortune's Golden Keys</u> – *Con.*

I acknowledge my duty to myself – and Mankind – to now fulfill my Destiny of self-realized monetary Freedom – *cognizant of the fact that the time period involved is governed solely by advanced or outmoded beliefs, and subsequent actions*

The joy set before me bids me go 'Onward and Upward' in my chosen endeavor – *whether it be in assisting the downcast in spirit – or the uprooted, dispossessed, to new dwellings*

Benevolent Forces assist me and afford me their Sponsorship – *I am never alone in my quest to attract greater abundance for others – <u>and</u> <u>myself</u>*

<u>Fortune's Golden Keys</u> – *Con.*

So Aligned am I with GOOD that I decree with absolute Conviction and perfect Certainty – Success is Mine! – *It is not possible that I could fail!*

I now Activate, Set in Motion, continually, the <u>*flow*</u> of Fortune – *because I know its purpose, and the devotion necessary to others for its appearance – and permanent stay*

Fortune is Mine to Command! – *provided I keep my heart (attitude) <u>right</u> for its receiving – and <u>pure</u> for its most favorable disposition*

A Rosary For Riches

Seek riches only if a genuine desire awakens in your heart
– if missing, you are unready for it

Recognize that true earthly riches comprise wealth and resources
– but only those necessary to successfully realize the highly individualistic purpose for which you were born

Claim all those riches intended for you as your birthright
– for you, along with your enlightened brothers, are co-heir to all things

Vow to use riches to glorify the Creator and to bless the Creation
– to do one apart from the other is an Impossibility

A Rosary For Riches
- Con.

Offer yourself as a channel through which riches may flow
— your selfless and altruistic thoughts alone can ensure this outcome

View riches solely as a tool to bless, liberate, and heal
— otherwise, it is valueless

Reverence all you benefit and recognize their special gift to you
— the privilege of serving — through giving — to them

Be content with all that belongs to you today
— but be eager for all you can give — to others — tomorrow

A Rosary For Riches
- Con.

Show gratitude unceasingly for all granted, and yet-to-be granted
– to the One Who provides for your every need

Exercise faith in your growing capacity to give with pure motive
– expecting nothing – nor wanting anything, in return

Nurture humility for being accounted worthy to receive abundant blessings
– and vow perpetual commitment to responsible and wise stewardship

Resolve to acquire riches as a powerful mark of high ethical attainment
– and demonstration of a Noble Ideal

Special

Till

True
Love
Comes!

Your Heart – *Fulfilled!*

Love, Alone,
IS –
The **Greatest**
Of All
Miracles

May *<u>You</u>*,
Dear Heart,
Know
The **Ecstasy**
Of –
True Love!

True Love – Introduction

What, my precious friend, is your **heart's deepest longing**? Is it not the finding of *True Love?* You intuitively know that Love is Life's greatest treasure. For with the Presence of <u>such</u> Love, Life becomes a glorious adventure, a wondrous sharing, a union of the utmost fulfillment! **Genuine Romance** is your *<u>birthright</u>* and <u>destiny</u>, ordained by God Who loves you so. But, to <u>hasten</u> Its arrival, you must **<u>first</u>** begin to live daily a greater Life of Faith, hope, and expectancy, until the time a deeply **personal** and **wholly-mature** Love enters your world! Your life will take on an **enchanted quality**, and even before will do so, in anticipation of **True Love**, as promised by the Heart of Life, becoming your very *special* own!

Contents

Love Is At the Door
I Enfold You by My Love
Sweet One Who Completes My Soul
Lord, Let Not My Soul Mate Stand
Your Desire For True Love
True Love Goes On and On
My Friendship I Extend to You
Your Soul Mate Will Come
I Walk the Path of Love
Hear This Missive from My Heart
True Love Waits, The 'Old' Saying
I Voice A 'Marriage Vow' Today
My True Love Is Coming
My Life Blossoms Forth
Romantic Attraction If It Is To Be
Set Me Free to Love, Dear Lord
God Keeps Her Promises
I Give to You, and You Give to Me
Oh! The Sweet Refrain I Most Adore
When You Find Your True Beloved
To the Altar of My Heart I Go
The One Divine Message of The One
Desire of My Longing, Destined Love
Farewell Words
Beatitudes of the Romantic Heart
Contemplation

Love Is At The Door
Knocking Gently Once Again,
Tell Me Now, Oh! Dear, Sweet Life!
Shall I – <u>*Let Him In*</u>*!*

Do you, dear friend, believe Love, like opportunity is *said* to be, knocks only once (or perhaps twice!) but rarely ever more frequently? If you do, you not only *keep* the door closed, but you bar it with chains and bolt locks, thinking you are ensuring your safety from the many other <u>*non*</u>-Love bearers! A **True** *Heart*-**Love** of your own may well be *continuously* knocking, seeking entrance to your world. But, you've already judged that person to be of *no* romantic interest. View **<u>not</u>** each knock as *possibility* of receiving Love, but rather the **certainty** of your **giving** It! Open to friendship **first**. Ask yourself '*How* may I be of service to this person? *How* may I be a blessing to them? Seek to give the special gifts you have to share with the sole intention of enhancing another's life. To the delightful surprise of more than one, Love's been known – <u>*to follow*</u>*!*

**I *Enfold* You by My Love
You *Enfold* Me – by Thine,
Two Hearts Enfolded *by* GOD's Love
<u>Our</u> Hearts, and <u>His</u> – *<u>Entwined</u>!***

Even as the first woman was *especially* made for the first man, suited in every way for each other, so it is for every pair of 'soul mates'. There *<u>is</u>* a partner, 'out there', for you, dear heart, whom God will *<u>one</u> <u>day</u>* steer your way. Initially, that suitability may not be evident. In fact, it may be seemingly absent, until such time as God **ordains** it emerge! In some ways, you will be found to **balance** each other out, supplying to the other that which one ***<u>most</u>*** needs. And, there will be **Joy** in these 'findings out', I promise you, and surprise and delight! The two of you will, as *<u>king</u>* and *<u>queen</u>*, lavish your adoration and love upon each other! The Word of Life tells us, 'The *<u>King</u>*dom [or *<u>Queen</u>*dom] of God *<u>IS</u>* Joy'! God inhabits, lives within, this royal union. And it is *<u>His</u> <u>Embrace</u>* upon both of you, making you, as you have so long desired – *<u>Joyfully</u> <u>One</u>!*

**Sweet One Who <u>Completes</u> My Soul
I *<u>Rejoice</u>* at Thought of Thee,
One Day We'll Find Each Other Out
Then, *<u>ONE</u>*, Forever More – *<u>We'll</u> <u>Be</u>!***

Did you know, my **romance** desirous friend, that out there, *<u>somewhere</u>*, beyond the blue horizon, a person is living and breathing solely to find you, to love you, to live for you! And this is **not** idolatry, but enlightened *<u>Self</u>*-interest. For God has made you a **perfect** half – of a <u>perfect</u> whole! And when you are brought together *by Him*, the joining of your hearts will give birth to a Love transcending all you have known! A new awareness will cause you both to **want** to love and serve God *<u>as</u> <u>never</u> <u>before</u>!* For the Heaven on earth you *will* experience together is **intended** by God to open your hearts to the Highest Love possible for the Divine. And God knows your giving Love *selflessly*, to just *one other*, is giving Love *totally* to Him – the Greatest *<u>Self</u>!* So RE-JOICE! God's Best *<u>Self</u>*-Interest – *<u>is</u> <u>Wholly</u> <u>served</u>!*

Lord, Let _Not_ My Soul Mate Stand Right Before Me – _Un_known, _Un_heard, _Un_felt, _Un_seen, Open My HEART to Behold Him (or Her) There Reaching Out With _Your_ Love – _and Care!_

An ancient wisdom text reads, 'Looked for, **can_not_** be seen; listened for, **can_not_** be heard; touched, **can_not_** be felt.' This, very often, beloved, accurately pictures the case with many a True Love-desirous person. Many have preconceived ideas in their minds as to _how_ their beloved's features _should_ **appear**, how their voice _should_ **sound**, even what **feelings** such a one _should_ immediately and _continuously_ generate in one's heart. And because such selective and restrictive 'filters' are used to evaluate every prospective life companion, mostly unconsciously, a genuine match may be easily and quickly discounted! The remedy? **Pray** for God to open your **heart** to 'see' what you, _of yourself,_ cannot see! Only in this way can you **recognize** whom God has chosen for you. A perfect match will appear, now clearly visible, by **true** vision – _at last!_

**Your Desire For True Love
I <u>Won't</u> For Long Deny, Your Darling
Will *Surely* Come, Though Ever
Softly – *<u>By and By</u>!*ьте**

Gentle-hearted friend, I want you to **KNOW** something with all the **certainty** of your being! You must *<u>never</u>* doubt it! For to do so is to bring unnecessary pain to yourself. He Who is orchestrating and **will** bring to fruition the Divine <u>Romance</u> of the Mighty **Cosmos**, will do *<u>no less</u>* for you, His beloved child, in the *equally* important ***Cosmos*** – of your life! Our Creator has clearly said, 'I WILL give unto you the **<u>Desire</u>** of *<u>your</u>* Heart!' The Master added, 'What things soever ye **desire**, believe ye [***<u>have</u>*** received] them, and ye ***<u>shall</u>*** have them.' This is a key, beloved! Begin to act as though the longing of your heart is a <u>present possession</u>. Live each day with joy and genuine gladness. Thank God **daily** He ***<u>has</u>*** given a Love to you! Then, watch as your Dream – *<u>comes True</u>!*

**True Love Goes *On and On*
Our Love Will Be <u>*Ever*</u> New,
Only True Love Goes On and On
My Darling, I'll *Always* – <u>*Love You*</u>!**

The above stanza is one taken from a forgotten song of days gone by. Yet, its Message is as **alive** and **vibrant** and **heart-thrilling** as when *first* sung by a beloved folk minstrel who made it famous. For THIS is the Promise of **True Love**! *Ever* young! *Ever* vital! *Ever* new! The song speaks of the white snows of Christmas melting away, the darkness of evening ending the day, and tells that time will wither the strongest tree, but that NOTHING can change – *you and me!* – The couple who **Know** (experience in their hearts) the **Oneness** and **Ecstasy** of True Love! Inseparably united, they live ONLY to serve each other, and the Greater Good of mankind! Such a love is an **eternal melody** between two souls whose indestructible devotion to each other elevates their consciousness to planes of being *few* realize. Yet, their love, as a heavenly anchored beacon, **holds the balance** –<u>*for the world*</u>!

My Friendship I Extend to You
***Until* God's Love Comes Bursting Thru,**
Tho the Passion of Youth Doth Quickly Fade
The Love that Fulfills Is – *Eternally* *Made!*

One bright day, at God's appointed time, you **most surely** will know the beauty, the rapture, and the exaltation of Life's greatest Gift – *True Love!* And once it is yours in Its fullness, you will know it is **Indestructible** and **Eternal!** This is because it springs from the *imperishable* Soul! – and *not* the transient, physical human senses. Physical excitement will fade, beloved, as will bodily passion, but the Joy you will experience from Love True will **never cease** to fill *full* your heart! Ever dependable, always trustworthy, and wholly devoted, True Love will steel into your Heart providing you the *deepest* security, comfort, and fulfillment. So, remember the foregoing, beautiful friend. It may **well prove** to be the **key** to your finding and experiencing the ecstasy of your heart's – *Deepest and Tenderest Longing!*

**Your Soul Mate Will Come
You Needn't Doubt This Is True,
As the Purest, Most Wonderful, Holy
Gift,** *of* **God Your Saviour –** *to You!*

Wonderful friend, *your beloved is there!* Remove all doubt you are destined to meet, and no power on earth can keep you apart! For you both are embodied to **unite** and manifest your lives *together* as ONE! – *furthering the purposes of God's Kingdom!* Your lives will serve as a chalice into which God eagerly can pour His greatest earthly gift. And in so doing, establish **a shining witness** as to what **True Love** – *can be!* And it can be *all* you have **imagined** it to be – with two hearts *dedicated to Him!* So, until then, simply live as balanced a life as possible, with unshakable faith in God, with dedication to a spiritual calling or vocation, and God **WILL** bring you both together! It will be so natural and such healing will occur, your hearts will joyously sing what **had** to be true – *has come true!*

I Walk the Path of Love
And Every Day I Find, Blessings
For My Heart, and Sweet Memories
– for My Mind!

Did you know, my valued friend, the *first* Law of the Universe has *always* been the same – ***To Give Love!*** And, do not concern yourself with whether It will be returned. If It is, *wonderful!* But, if not, It will be **multiplied** – within you, *instead!* Either way, you are blessed! But, you must **choose** The Path of Love each day. And precisely how *does* one do this? Determine in yourself *not* to take offense, *not* to take things personally, *not* to respond negatively to ***any*** provocation. Resist *not* any display of lack of Love, but rather recognize that '**to yield'** up to God any reactive feelings '**is to prevail!'** Also, when you do, you'll find your capacity to Love growing, and far more pleasant memories resulting. So, continue to walk Love's Path! It leads to a ***World*** of Love – and Wonder – whose *second* Law is invariably – *to Receive!*

**Hear This Missive from My Heart
<u>Evermore</u> to be of You a Part, I Know
WHO You Are – *<u>My</u> <u>Sweet</u> <u>Life's</u> <u>Breath</u>!*
And With *Your* Love, I'll <u>Never</u> Know Death!**

Yes, my Beloved! I KNOW **Who** you are! *You ARE my Sweet Life's Breath!* You are the invigorating, life-giving, spirit of my Soul! Together, we were formed as One, of the same heart flame. And it is our **Destiny** to find each other, again! Yet, in the depths of our beings, we know we are, even *now*, inseparable, for **True Love** *IS* Inseparable! And Indivisible! And Unconquerable! The essence of our Beings is, was, and ever will be **ONE**. Joined in the Great Mystery of Spiritual Love that can *never* become less than whole, nor can, by virtue of Its Divine Origin, *<u>ever</u> <u>die</u>!* Know I have committed my most **loving**, **tenderest**, and **reverential** thoughts and feelings *toward you* to the hidden, <u>secret</u> <u>chamber</u> of my heart. Where they are safe, protected, and kept **wholly alive** for the day of our re-uniting! When they come rushing out as a bridegroom to greet his bride – *<u>in</u> <u>rapturous</u> <u>delight</u>!*

**True Love Waits, The 'Old' Saying Goes
Upon _Chivalrous_ Values God's Heaven Knows,
A Love That Is Pure and Chaste Far _or_ Near
Offering Honor, Respect to – _One's Dear!_**

In the rush of the world to find happiness and freedom, my precious friend, it has forgotten, abandoned a vital Truth. A Truth that tells how Love is meant to unfold within our lives. How It is nurtured, protected, and sheltered, so It may grow unhurriedly and safely and at a natural pace. True Love _always_ waits because True Love **cannot** be rushed or hurried or be held captive to **situational ethics** and **misguided values**. Indeed, the very heart of True Love IS patience, a virtue the world no longer seeks. When two souls refrain from the sharing of their bodies in complete union prior to marriage, they fulfill **Heaven's sacred and holy law of Love**. They manifest noble Character and _proof_ of their Love through commitment to selfless restraint. For patience, _early on_, will bring the most fulfillment, contentment, and joy – **_later on!_** As God bestows His Highest – _and His Very Best!_

**I Voice A 'Marriage Vow' Today
To Be <u>True</u> to Life in A Special Way,
Promising Love, Cheer, and *Living* Faith, Too
On My Way Back to God – <u>*and*</u> <u>*You*</u>!**

Precious friend, an *ongoing* <u>conscious</u> realization of God's **Unity** with your Soul is a **major** goal of your earthly, human life. Marriage is a 'joining', a *'wedding together'* of two lives, hearts, and beings. You have a **special** someone ordained by God as your complement. <u>EVERY</u> day is a wedding day for those who recognize this, and renew their vows with fresh, ever-youthful, **Inner** Spiritual Vision. They voice their promise to be true to their Saviour, the Lord of their Heart. *And*, <u>thereby</u> espouse faithfulness to their destined life partner, chosen for them before the world began! You have a <u>*very real connection*</u>, though invisible, to your **Soul mate**, the embodiment of your deepest heart's ideals. This tie can<u>*not*</u> be severed, and allows for communication at **Inner Levels** between you. By speaking directly to him or her, <u>daily,</u> you **strengthen** your **awareness** of each other, and <u>*speed the day*</u> Reunion is – <u>*thine*</u>!

**My True Love Is Coming
Sure as the Dawn at Break of Day,
More Certain Than Stars Appearing Each
Night, My Beloved Is Traveling – <u>*My Way*</u>*!*

Do not despair, beautiful friend, that no gentle hand is there for you to reach for – no soft voice, there, for you to drink in – no visage of loveliness, there to behold – *up till now!* Because your true love IS coming! And He is **heralded** by each day's dawn, and **spoken of** tenderly by every soft, summer night sky embedded with stars, to her (or him) who listens carefully, and prayerfully! Once arrived, drawn to you by <u>your</u> <u>belief</u> in the **goodness** and **sweetness** and **faithfulness** of **Life**, your readiness, and out-picturing of the Divine Plan, *<u>longing</u> <u>and</u> <u>heartache</u> <u>will</u> <u>cease</u>!* Your complement is as a stream rushing to the sea –in eager anticipation of *joining* with you, as you are so desirous of joining with him! ***<u>Destined to meet</u>*****!** A divine *union* of mind, heart, soul, and body temple. So, take heart! – *<u>Such</u> <u>will</u> <u>surely</u> <u>be</u>!*

**My Life Blossoms Forth
More and _More_ Each Day,
As Love Comes to My Rescue,
And _Drives_ The Shadows – _Away!_**

Your sunniest day, sweet friend, will be the day you realize the _Power_ of Love to transform your life! The Love you **seek** from another _special_ someone, you must **first** learn to give out – _from yourself._ In so doing, you will manifest the **very same kind of love** your heart so earnestly desires! You will **reveal** your true Self to he (or she) who seeks _you!_ Many do not know the shadows that weigh them down most are found in their minds, _not_ the world. These dark shafts must be dispersed by Light Above! Ask **the Heart of Life**, your Creator, to take all your dissatisfied, unhappy, fearful or impatient thoughts pertaining to a future mate, and flood them with the Light of **Love's True Vision!** You'll see differently and shadows will retreat not only _within_ you – but _all about you_, soon – _as well!_

**Romantic Attraction *If* It Is To Be
Can *Never* Results of My Own Efforts *Be*,
My Own Designs to Bring Such Sweet Wooing
Won't Bear Fruit Unless It's – _God's_ _Doing!_**

God *alone* is responsible for the **attraction** felt between a man and a woman. Whether mental, psychological, spiritual, or physical, no matter. **This *IS* truly cause for rejoicing!** – *Because* when you, beloved, fully realize and believe this, you will **no longer** feel your heart *'sink'* when a *thought-to-be* desired one feels no attraction – toward you! Gone, now, is disappointment! Gone heartache and despair! Gone, too, are sorrow and any sense of deficiency or unworthiness, on your part. Instead, you can affirm **the Truth**: _God has not sent Cupid's arrow into their heart for me._ For He knows, far better than you, just who _will_ make the best match. You can, therefore, **bless** him – and *release* him (or her) in **good will** and **joyousness**. For who can truly say? Cupid may *just* be running – _a bit late!_

**Set Me Free to Love, Dear Lord!
This I Desire Truly, and Hope To Be,
That <u>Your</u> Great Love and Love Alone
Might, *Through* Me, Set My Brothers – <u>*Free!*</u>**

A Great Truth is you *should* pray to be 'set free to love!' – To have your heart capacity to love **expanded!** This prayer, far from being selfish or self-centered, is actually an <u>exalted, **_selfless_** prayer!</u> For it encompasses the highest ideal to which you can aspire! All dimensions of celestial – and earthly – Love are included: universal, parental, brotherly, neighborly, **even *romantic!*** Love in <u>*all*</u> Its <u>Fullness</u> and <u>Beauty</u> and <u>Strength</u>! For when you, kind friend, petition God to set **you** free to love, you are aligning yourself with the *<u>deepest</u> <u>longing</u>* of **His Heart!** – *The dispersal, reception, and regiving of His Divine, Wholly-Freeing, All-Fulfilling Love throughout humanity!* So, pray *to be* made free to Love! **Especially** your sweetheart! A world will be, thereby, one person – one *heart*-at-a-time – <u>*set free!*</u>

God Keeps _Her_ Promises
What a Beautiful Thought to Hold,
That by _A Love_ That Birthed the World
A Mother's Love – _Is Told_!

God will, my friend, never fail you! The *feminine aspect* of Deity, **God the Mother**, has many names. A modern-day visionary once said of Her: 'Fate is kind. She brings to those who love, the sweet fulfillment of their secret longing. Like a bolt out of the blue, Fate steps in and sees you through. When you wish upon a star, your dreams come true.' If **your dream** is to hold in your arms, one day, your one, meant-to-be, **True Love**, then *remember* – Fate _IS_ kind. She would bestow upon you this Love, when you are made *ready*, and accounted *worthy*, to receive It! Yes, the promise is given to those who sincerely strive to bless all, to help all, to Love *All!* – spiritually, truly! **Fate will intervene** and _give YOU_– your heart's dream! Only seek to Love every day of your life, morning and evening –_as does She_!

**I Give to You, and You Give to Me
True Love, My Darling, True Love –** *Only*,
**And 'On and On', It Will Always Be
Beloved! I** *<u>Live</u>* **–** *<u>For</u>* *<u>Thee</u>!*

There is a song, beautiful one, that epitomizes the perfect, ongoing **interchange** between two hearts joined as One. Popular and appreciated in a former generation, it was simply called 'True Love.' It speaks of giving and <u>re</u>-giving one to the other, <u>over</u> and <u>over</u> again, growing ever-the-more wondrous and dear as every day unfolds. The song speaks of the **Source** of this Love as coming from 'on High', whose delivery is ministered by an Angel. And, therein, lies Its secret! **True Love** is nothing less than **God's Love** given human expression in the world of form and dimensionality. And once 'tasted', It becomes the *<u>sole</u>* purpose for which one lives! Yet, this Love must be explicitly asked for, yearned for, and earnestly sought from the Divine *if* one hopes to experience It and **Become** It! Invoke this Love, the **giving** for *<u>the</u> <u>sake</u>* of giving, and the <u>re</u>-giving, from a beloved one, will one day–*follow!*

Oh!* The Sweet Refrain I <u>Most</u> Adore!
To Hear from <u>Your</u> Lips I *Ever* Implore,
'I Give to You, You Give to Me,
True Love – *Ever More*'!

Beloved friend, you whose heart *yearns* for your **true** counterpart to appear! The *other half* of **your** Soul! Hear, now, this **vital** closing message I share! Though you have lived the first half of a century, or you are in your sixties or seventies, True Love can *still* be yours! Is surely **meant** to be yours, *if* a genuine irrepressible desire lives in your heart! Many believe Romantic Love is intended **only** for the young. <u>Untrue</u>! The <u>Height</u> of Romance, ***Spiritually*** mature Love, is the most wondrously affectionate, enticingly exciting as imaginable. **Passion** of *<u>Spirit</u>!* And of *<u>Soul</u>!* And of *<u>Heart</u>!* Where even **a <u>mere</u> glance** can bring a celestial thrill, or holding hands can send one *<u>soaring</u>* into the Heavens! So, sing Love's song till Love True arrives, with **promise** for you – *<u>in</u> <u>his</u> <u>(or</u> <u>her)</u> <u>eyes</u>!*

**When You Find Your <u>True</u> Beloved,
Your Days Will *End* of Living Apart, Though
Bodies May Be Separated For A Time,
<u>Never</u> Will Be – *<u>the</u> <u>Heart</u>!*stagg**

Most beautiful friend, <u>nothing</u> can compare to being *wholeheartedly* loved by another, by a member of the 'opposite' (actually, **complementary**) sex! The love expressed between a man and woman of *this* quality and nature, the angels themselves are enthralled by! For wherever two such people are, *if* they are together, ***they are home!*** – Home in each other's arms! Home in a totally selfless, outgoing Love *poured* each into the other! **Yet**, even if not *physically* together, there is an **unmistakable connection** felt by both at inner levels providing a deepest sense of belongingness and security. The tenderness, gentleness, yes, even *reverence* shared between them serves as a golden key opening the gates of Heaven, Itself! **One kiss**, *<u>alone</u>*, shared by such as these transmutes the heartache and sorrow of *ten thousand* lonely nights into Joy unspeakable – as God's <u>*All*</u>-Fulfilling Love arrives – *<u>at</u> <u>last</u>!*

**To The Alter of My Heart I Go
Where Flowers I Lay So You Might Know,
With My _Every_ Breath I Think of You, And *By
Reverent* Love, Pledge a Heart – _That's_ _True!_**

Deep within the secret chambers of my heart stands an altar. This is the Innermost Compartment, the Holy of Holies, of my soul! And it is THERE where memories of **you**, my Beloved, reside. It is a simple, yet, elegant altar, made of rosewood and marble. To either side is a lush bouquet of multi-hued roses of the most glorious fragrance, housed in ribbon-bedecked vessels. And behind and just above it upon a pedestal stands a **snow-white** statue of *God's Divine Messenger of Love*, the **Christed-One**, offering up prayers for unbroken ONENESS between us, and _**all**_ soul-entwined mates! And I see, around and about Him is a diffused, emanating radiance. As I gently lay flowers upon the alter, I bow my head, close my eyes, and envision your smiling eyes radiant with gratitude and *the Light of Love* being shed upon me! And I am reminded, once again, **every** prayer Christ prays –_will_ _be_ _answered!_

**The *One* Divine Message of The One
Resonated With Power Through The Son,
Heard from the Beginning, Our Hearts to Mend
Such *Utter* Simplicity! – *Worlds Without End!***

'This, then, is **THE Message** which we have heard *of Him* [God's Supreme Messenger of Love], and declare unto you, that God is Light [The Light *of Love*], and in Him is no darkness [*no absence* of *Love*] at all' (I John 1:5). And, again, 'For this is **THE Message** that ye heard from the beginning, that we should *Love One Another*' (I John 3:11). And 'that which we had from the beginning, that we *Love One Another*. And this IS Love that we walk after…**THE Commandment**…heard from the Beginning' (II John 1:5-6). And 'this is **MY** [*sole*] **Commandment**, That ye *Love One Another*, as I have loved you (John 15:12). Beloved, could anything be more clear? It is one of childlike simplicity. Its observance creates Oneness, Unity, Profound Belongingness, and Joyous Security! God speed the Day Mankind enshrines this –*in the heart!*

***Desire* of my Longing, *Destined Love* of my Heart
Tho We're <u>Not</u> Together, *Nor* Are We Apart,
I *Sense* Your Coming in a Time <u>Yet</u> To Be
A Springtime *when* God – <u>*Sets Us Free*</u>*!***

Who is there among us who has not been transfixed by the *hauntingly* beautiful, even <u>mystical</u>, musical masterpiece of 'Lara's Theme' – of years gone by. The simple words evoke such hope and expectancy: '**Somewhere** my Love, there will be songs to sing, although the snow covers the hope of Spring, somewhere a hill blossoms in green and gold, and there are dreams, all that your heart can hold. **Someday**, <u>*we'll meet again, my Love*</u>. **Someday**, whenever the Spring breaks through! **You'll come to me**, out of the long ago, warm as the wind, soft as the kiss of snow. Till then, my Sweet, think of me now and then. God speed, my Love! Till you are mine again!' Mine – *<u>Again!</u>* Why is this? Because upon finding our beloved, we will feel a '**<u>returning home</u>**', a sense of **belonging together**! As tho you <u>were</u> together, at *another* place or time, tho quite forgotten! Perhaps at creation, itself!*<u>Heaven knows!</u>*

Farewell Words

Ponder, beloved, these lyrics of an inspired song, and then ask yourself the resultant question: 'Some day, my prince will come, some day we'll meet again. And away to His castle we'll go, to ***be happy forever***, I know. *Some* day, when Spring breaks through, we'll find our Love anew. **And the birds will sing, and wedding bells will ring. Some day when my Dream comes true!'** Now, ask yourself, honestly, sincerely, *Do you really believe this?* Are those few words merely a childhood sentiment of wishful, naïve thinking? Thoughts of unknowing innocence? I tell you **NO!** These words convey nothing less than **Universal Spiritual Law**, the **aim** and **goal** of *your* life, the destiny to which you will one day arrive! God does not mock His children. He ever honors **faithfulness** in *belief*, and desires above all to bestow this blessing upon you! Hold fast to your heart's Dream! God **WILL** *cause* it to come True!

With Every Good Wish, The Author

Beatitudes *of* the Romantic Heart

Blessed are the **Genuine romantic**, for they shall experience an enchanted life

Blessed are the **True lovers**, for they shall know the ecstasy of triumphant Life

Blessed are the **Exuberant dancers**, for they shall be lifted up above the resigned, *trudging* crowds

Blessed are the **Joyful singers**, for They shall have the energy of heavenly choirs *rush* into their souls

Beatitudes *of* the Romantic Heart – Con.

Blessed are the **Optimistic Smilers** for they shall *irresistibly draw* unto themselves their soul Mate, though from the far ends of the earth

Blessed are the **Praying believers**, for they shall have their destined Life-Partner and Completion of their soul – *come* unto them

Blessed are the **Cheerful Whistlers** for they shall *attract* their beloved one, through an atmosphere of encouragement and trust

Beatitudes *of* the Romantic Heart – *Con.*

Blessed are the **Beauty scatterers**, for the seeds they sow shall blossom into bouquets, and be brought to, and laid at their feet

Blessed are the **Undying dreamers**, for their vision will uphold and comfort them, when seemingly alone, and nurture their spirits

Blessed are the **Irrepressible Celebrators**, for they shall know The celestial thrill of the *truly* Romance-filled Life

Beatitudes *of* the Romantic Heart – *Con.*

Blessed are the **Quiet servants** of Humanity, for they shall know the *fulfillment* of a much-desired Requited Love

Blessed are the **Chivalrous earts**, for they shall remain *undaunted* in their quest for a personal True Love;
and will, with all certainty, *one glorious day*, be granted by our ever-faithful and unfailing Universe

– THEIR DEEPEST HEART'S DESIRE! And It Will Be, and *Is* Forever So. ***Amen!***

Contemplation

To derive the optimal benefit from the foregoing divine declarations, periodically envision **the Supreme Messenger of Love** standing on the verdant hills of ancient Palestine, on a clear Spring day, with azure blue sky overhead, and the sloping hills and valleys awash with color-drenched wildflowers. Now see **Him** raise His compassionate hands in benediction over the multitudes of people who have come to **Him** to receive His Blessing and God-Inspired, Truth-Filled words. Witness His seamless robe flowing in the fragrance-filled, cool morning breeze – in rhythmic waves, as he gives such masterful verbal expression to these great **Universal Laws of Life**, which if *truly* believed (according to your faith) will bring the fulfillment of one's deepest heart's longing for a True Love all one's own! Then, **rest** fully assured of their destined fulfillment – in *your* life! – Beloved!

So It has been give, so It shall be done!
Amen!

About The Author

A devotee of Jesus and student of scripture since childhood, Mack seeks to teach others about *'the Deep Things of God.'* Writing with poetic majesty, yet with elegant simplicity, he **'paints'** ***word-pictures*** that captivate the heart, and awaken the soul. His mission is to reveal aspects of **the Fullness of the Gospel of Christ** *few* know of, with special emphasis on the Lord's singularly unique Life-Purpose and the **All-Redeeming Nature** of His Love. Mack has authored numerous books, facilitated classes on spirituality, and gives talks on living a Radiant Life. He has been called to unveil to others – *nothing less* – than the uttermost **'Depths** *– of **The Heart** of **Love!'*** He presently resides in Central Virginia, and graciously welcomes comments.

An
Out-Reach of

Mercy Rose Ministries

Proclaiming

The
Depths
of

The **Heart** *Of* **Love!**

Mercy Rose Ministries

Its Unique *Calling* and *Mission*

The Unveiling
Of
God's Mercy Rose!

Within the writings of Mack Ethridge are *Revelatory* Insights and *New* Understanding about the heart, nature, and mission of the Gentle Carpenter from Galilee, *given the author during periods of prayer and contemplation*. Allowing one to fathom, as never before, the **Depths** of the **Deepest** Heart. And to grasp more fully precisely **why** this Teacher of Forgiveness and Compassion was – **then**, **now**, and ***always*** – The *Dawn of Redeeming Grace!* And the *Chalice of Love's Pure Light!*

Mercy Rose Ministries – *Con.*

Mercy Rose Ministries – *Is <u>Born</u>!*

The purpose of this outreach is to set forth in compelling, heart-capturing, readily understandable, even unforgettable language, *The **<u>Most Startlingly Beautiful</u> <u>Love</u>*** the world has ever known; and to reveal aspects, glories, and divine truths about His person, and teachings, which are either unknown, seldom taught, little understood, or misunderstood by His children. And, thereby, to illumine the Way to an **authentic**, direct, personal *life-transforming* encounter, and ongoing **miraculous** relationship with, to a surprisingly large degree, The <u>*Unknown*</u> Saviour of the World!

And, further, to present the startlingly joyous, heart-thrilling, and irresistibly worship-inspiring implications to the **Universe** of <u>***SO GREAT***</u> a Love given unto men.

Mercy Rose Ministries – *Con.*

It is no secret, few people are startled by 'His' teachings, anymore, and there is a **profound** reason for this. In Jesus' day, His hearers were repeatedly '*astonished* at His doctrine' (Matt. 7:28, 22:33, Mark 11:18). Yet, what is taught about this most wondrous of all men, today, that astonishes hardly anyone? The answer is clear as crystal: very little.

The Mission, and Calling, therefore, of this outreach is to **bring** to men's awareness Truths and Teachings long lost sight of by the world, allowing the *Startling Message* of God's Divine Son, His *Only* Fully-Begotten Son, to shine forth, once again, in Its Pristine, All-Illuminating, Mankind-Freeing **Brilliance**, to the world!

Mercy Rose Ministries – *Con.*

Non-sectarian in nature, this outreach is dedicated to presenting This Great and Glorious and Central Truth:

The **LIGHT** – was for ***All Time!***

And *The* **LOVE** – was for ***All Men!***

It is the sincere desire of the author that you will be greatly blessed by your contact with this ministry. Your comments and suggestions are wholly welcome, and appreciated!

Author Profile

A _Messenger_ Whose Time Has Come!

Mack, by his own definition, is a '**Word Painter**', who seeks to teach others through his writing, about _'the Deep Things of God'_ (I Cor. 2:10). At once you will perceive an unusual and rare beauty in his style, and profound insight and striking imagery in his words. Writing with poetic majesty, yet with _elegant simplicity_, he **paints word pictures** about the Lord of Life and related topics that captivate one's heart, draw in one's mind, and awaken a sense of awe and wonder in one's soul. He does all this, not only by his truly-original, thought-provoking, and compelling observations and insights, but also by the **deep feeling of Love** he imparts to his readers regarding their inestimable value, worth, and importance in God's Plan.

Author Profile – *Con.*

Though most have heard the traditional 'Gospel Message' in Its simplicity, His writings are meant to *unveil* aspects of **the Fullness of the gospel of Christ**, with special emphasis upon man's Oneness with God, and each other, the humanity of Jesus, His singularly unique Life Mission, and the **All-Redeeming nature** of His Divine Love, as revealed in the plain, yet mostly unrecognized, teachings of the Gospel records, and in the *original* languages in which they were recorded.

In a spiritual arena all their own, however, Mack's writings defy classification – falling neither solely into the confines of historic Christianity, religious orthodoxy, metaphysics, mysticism, or New Thought. Interestingly enough, a thorough, careful, and unbiased examination of Jesus' life and teachings reveal a 'profile' totally consistent with the above characterization. Mack prefers, however, to view them as:

Author Profile – *Con.*

'<u>Pristine</u>, first-century, *Illumined*, New Testament – <u>Christ</u>-<u>Truth</u>'

Told by Spirit as a small child, through **Inner Knowing**, that he would *one day* teach people the <u>Deep</u> <u>Truths</u> about God, he was **led** to *<u>begin</u>* writing at the start of the **new** millennium, symbolic of **new Teaching** (new, stylistic presentation) being given to mankind at a crucial period in mankind's pilgrimage on earth. May the inherent **beauty** of the words given him, open your heart to **<u>Truths Sublime</u>!**

Author Profile – *Con.*

Ideal for reflective, meditative, and inspirational purposes, his writings provide **<u>vitally</u> *interesting*, rich spiritual nourishment**, and facilitate a renewed sense of wonder towards, and **<u>closeness</u> to, our Creator!** And they are always hopeful, optimistic, God-Glorifying and **Christ-Exalting!**

I trust you, friend, have found, and will continue to find, them so, too!

The Magnificent Obsession!

Be thou, my Messenger of Light

to a darkened world

Promise thou, to be ever *Mindful*

of thy Life Mission

Speak thou, always,

in elevated language

to uplift the masses,

if only by their

wonderment of thee

The Magnificent Obsession! - Con.

Remember thou, thy *Identity* in Me

Listen for and Hear thou,

My Voice

Whispering to thee

every hour,

Whether by night

or by day

The Magnificent Obsession! - Con.

Rejoice thou, without ceasing,

in *seeming* darkness, or in full

Awareness of my

Ever-present Light

Live thou, to serve thy fellow-woman

and -man with *gladness,* a quality

to insulate thy heart from fear

The Magnificent Obsession! - Con.

Rest thou, in My *restorative* Presence,

between the moments of thy day

Open thou, wide, the Door to

thy Tomorrow, by Bravely *walking*

through the Door of thy Today

Receive thou, into the depths of

thy being, my Magnificent Obsession,

and henceforth become free

with clear direction

and Liberating Purpose

The Magnificent Obsession! - Con.

Make thou, the Magnificent Obsession thy reason for being, for in Truth, It and It *alone*, verily, IS!

Know thou, in every circumstance, I AM with thee, to *quicken* thy consciousness of Me, and thereby to incarnate *in* thee, *as Thee*

– my Self, my very *Own*

M.W.E.

For More Information:

Go to

Authentic Life Publications

through

www.themercyrose.com

or

Facebook page:

Teachings of The Mercy Rose

or

contact

mackethridge@hotmail.com

Book 3

Love's Supreme Act *Unveiled!*

The **Valiant *Victory***
 Of **Life's Heart**
  Over the World!

Proclaiming
Love's
Old, Sweet Story,
I <u>Witness</u>
Holy One,
To
Thine
Imperishable
Glory!

Copyright © 2010
by Mack W. Ethridge

Published by **Authentic Life Publications**

All rights reserved. Printed in the United States of America. Permission granted to quote brief portions of this book provided due credit is afforded the author.

Cover design selected by Mack Ethridge

Library of Congress Cataloging-in-Publications Data, Ethridge, Mack W.

Love's Supreme Act *Unveiled!*
– Complete edition

1st Complete Amazon Softback Edition
June 2013

Honor Due

This book, as the previous two published before it, wholeheartedly acknowledges the *inestimable* and *profound* influence of my beloved father, Floyd L. R. Ethridge, in its inception and birth. For without his Christ-like example and efforts to reach for the higher calling to God's Deep Knowledge and service to one's fellowman, I could <u>not</u> have come to know the **Depths** of the Heart of Love made manifest by Jesus – through him!

Salutation to the Saviour

He chose to give _every_ part of Himself,
Rather than lose the tiniest, _single_ part of humanity!

For He would rather 'lose' His own soul, _temporarily_, so that He might gain the whole world, **permanently!**

Yet, He would have willingly 'lost' His own soul, **permanently**, if He could have only gained the whole world, _temporarily!_

Salutation to the Saviour – *Con.*

He chose to **ascend** the Cross of crucifixion, and endure unimagined agony, rather than have humanity continue to **descend** into the horrors of insanity!

No other human would have believed as did He, that the full-gathered momentum of all departures from Love could be overcome by one man!

Divine, though He was, this had **never** been accomplished by *anyone*, much less even imagined!

Salutation to the Saviour – *Con.*

Yet, *He* did believe this, and **overcame** it He did!

He Declared and Proclaimed that Truth, and Love, and Faith, and Hope, Defenselessness, and Forgiveness could **undo** all mistakes, wrong, and evil. And proved it so!

Not only that Love was stronger than hate, but rather that there was **no contest!**

Salutation to the Saviour – *Con.*

His Life secured salvation for **all** his brothers and sisters, **His life redeemed a world**. His life will bring Peace to the Universe, and Goodwill to all!

His Message will be recognized for precisely what He said It was – the Message from the ONE God of Love, to the ONE humanity – of the Father of Love!

His Life will one day be extolled by **every** man who has ever lived. And His Words will be engraved within the hearts of all men that ever beat!

Salutation to the Saviour – *Con.*

His glorious, divine **human** person will be reverenced, adored, and worshipped in every land, by every culture, by every inhabitant, <u>within</u> and <u>on</u> – *<u>every world</u>!*

He was Sent by the Source of ALL Holiness as The *Heart* of Life! The *Heart* of Love! The *Heart* of all men – YET TO BE!

He *IS* Humanity's Beacon! Humanity's LIGHT!

Contents of Book

Essay I
Day Break
– The Dawn That *Illumined* the World!

Essay II
Astonishing Love
– Beyond Your Most *Cherished* Dreams!

Essay III
Prism
– The *Window* to the *Invisible* God!

Essay IV
Life's Victory
– The Redemption of All – *Secured!*

Contents of Book – *Con.*

Essay V
Power
– The Faith *of* Jesus Given You!

Essay VI
Prayer
– To *Open* the Heart to Life and Love!

Essay VII
The Divine Message
– The *Sole* Message Given by God – to Mankind!

Essay VIII
A Mirror Reflecting Life's Heart
– A *Human* Face on the Divine Power!

Contents of Book – *Con.*

Essay IX
With All Certainty – All Is Well
– The *Eternal* Verity of Life!

Essay X
The Magnificent Obsession
– The Wellspring of *Thrilling* Life!

Essay XI
The One Sole Explanation of All
– The Answer to All Life's Questions!

Essay XII
A Wish the World Will Make
– The Ultimate Request!

Contents of Book – *Con.*

Essay XIII
The Hush that Fell O'er the Earth
– A Silence Untold!

Essay XIV
A Visionary View to Embrace
– An Overview of God and Man!

Essay XV
A Tale Most Beautifully Told
– The *UnHidden*, Secret Truth!

Essay XVI
The Whispered Words of Wonder
– Revealed *to All!*

Contents of Book – *Con.*

Essay XVII
Concluding Poem

A Cosmic Wave *Overtaking* the World
– God's Dream!

The Final Disclosure

I AM The Bread And Water Of Life

Jesus, The Christ

Essay I

The **Dawn** that Illumined *the* World!

Day Break!

I
AM
The Way

Day Break – The Dawn That _Illumined_ the World!

Once, long ago, a new day was beginning to break. But, some*how*, some*way*, this morning seemed *different* than other spring mornings. Could it be that the sun actually **shone brighter** that day than on any other day before, or since? Was the excitement evidenced in the ritualistic unfolding of the flowers' petals somehow more pronounced and vibrant? Did the shrubbery and trees 'betray' a far greater **'gladness'** at the coming of this new dawn? – This Dawn that seemed more, *far more*, **Illumined** than others? To what could this be attributed?

How is it that as the Dawn raced over the earth, dispersing the darkness in its path, each succeeding locality or region experienced _something_**beyond** the ordinary?

I
AM
The Truth

Day Break – The Dawn That *Illumined* the World! – *Con.*

Something touched the very souls of its inhabitants, and left there a **Joyous**, though *indefinable*, sense – of an incomparable **Wonder** – unknown, and even *less* understood.

Little did the vast majority of mankind know, but on that *one*, singular day, that **Incomparable Day**, a *New* Day, did indeed, dawn upon the world! A day such as had never been seen before or since! A dawn that truly *Illumined the world* – for the very first time!

For even as the celestial body known as the sun 'rose up' out of the earth to rise far up above it, even so did another 'SON',

I
AM
The Life

Day Break – The Dawn That *Illumined* the World! – *Con.*

another **Celestial body**, rise up out of the earth with great Power and Majesty and Glory to bear witness to:

> **The Unconquerableness of Divine Life!**

And the rays of **this Great SON**, the Dawning Rays brought forth on that distant morn, are *shining still* – to this very day! That Dawn never ceasing! Never overtaken by any encroaching darkness of night! Which darkness has been forever banished from the Presence of Life – evermore! But is there no 'face' to this Presence of Life? **This *SON* of transcendent Power?** Is It *only* an

I
AM
The Resurrection

Day Break – The Dawn That *Illumined* the World! – *Con.*

Impersonal being that is of so vastly different 'an order of existence' that men and women can only stand in awe of, but never have any sense of joining or union with so Great a Being? *So Great a Life?* Are there no *human features* that can be ascribed to **this *Presence*** – to which mankind can relate?

Yes, my friend, Yes! There ARE! In an ancient book preserved down through the millennia, we are told that this **Personage** is still, even to this very day, described as *'Anthropos'!* Even though this **Divine Presence** is said to have 'Ascended' into a higher realm, a vaster Reality, this Being is

I
AM
The Son of God

Day Break – The Dawn That _Illumined_ the World! – *Con.*

STILL described as – of all imaginable things – a MAN! But, now, the difference is, an ***IMMORTAL* Man!** Yes. This is the exact meaning of the word 'Anthropos'! This Being is said to still be <u>MAN</u>! With HUMAN features! With human likeness! With the milk of human **Compassion** multiplied a thousand times! With a sense of empathy raised to the 'Nth' power! With the All-Embracingness of **the highest Human Love** – such as that expressed from mother or parent to child, _sacrificial_ – transformed into a LOVE that excels all human love, and is _infinitely_ greater than the sum total of their parts!

I
AM
With You

Day Break – The Dawn That *Illumined* the World! – *Con.*

And ever since that **Day of Resurrection** to Immortal, Victorious, Divine Life, *'Amor Omnia Vincit'* has rung down through the Ages and proclaimed:

> # LOVE CONQUERS ALL!

– *Even* that which man calls death! Yes, even eventually to the conquering **(winning over)** of all enemies of the Light – whether past, present, or future. Yes, *The Light of the World* had been Born on that fateful day! Turn to and face those Rays, my friend, and experience the perpetual Dawn of *your* New Life – in *your **now**-*Illumined Soul! For He, dear friend, *IS* indeed Risen – *for you!*

I Will Love Thee Oh Lord,
My Strength

Essay II

Beyond Your Most Cherished Dreams!

Astonishing Love!

I
AM
The Light
Of the World

Astonishing Love – Beyond Your Most Cherished Dreams!

There are those who believe that in a far distant land, some two millennia ago, something **wholly wonderful**, yet *equally mysterious*, transpired on the earth that will affect every man, woman, and child who has ever lived. It is said there occurred *an act of amazing proportions*, **a Supreme Act** of a sacrificial nature of an Astonishing human being, unlike any recorded in the annals of history. This took place on a lonely hill just outside the gates of a city whose name means 'city of peace'. And this man is said to have *borne* **within His very body**, the consequences that we, the rest of the human race, were bringing upon ourselves – consequences of dire significance and eternal import. And that by this free will

I
AM
From Above

Astonishing Love – Beyond Your Most Cherished Dreams! – *Con.*

offering of Himself to the Justice of the Universe, He is said to have secured something for every human that none other could have secured. What, dear friend, actually took place there? Is it possible that the **fullness** of what this man did – has escaped us? For:

> He was not *only* a substitute, He was humanity's **Representative**. There being a sharp, clear distinction between the words 'substitute' and 'representative'.

As a substitute, He *'filled in'* for each of us. But as a representative, He stood **'in behalf of'** each of us. Is this not saying the same identical thing? No. As a representative, He

I AM Before Abraham Was

Astonishing Love – Beyond Your Most Cherished Dreams! – *Con.*

identified with each person so closely, He could accurately be called their legal agent, ambassador if you will, acting in their behalf. And that <u>*what was done to Him*</u>, even to the point of being 'drawn up into the heart of divinity', called historically, **the Ascension**, <u>*was done to us*</u>!

If this view is true, then in some unfathomable, mysterious way, humanity, too, was drawn up into divinity, and **a union** has taken place unbeknownst to mankind. A Union <u>*yet*</u> to make Its Self known. A Union that being performed by **an Astonishing Love**, will thoroughly astonish <u>*us*</u>, when we come to realize what it all means! There are those who say we are slow to learn the greatest truths. Even **the Great Teacher** said, 'I have yet **many things** to say unto you, *but you cannot bear them now.*'

I
AM
The Door

Astonishing Love – Beyond Your Most Cherished Dreams! – *Con.*

> Perhaps the Mind that rules the Universe views us, in a *far* different way than we have **dared** expect. Perhaps we are viewed, **right now**, as something far more wonderful than we ever would have **dared** to imagine.

Perhaps the **ultimate** negative consequences of all departures from Love really have been **obliterated**, as we have been told, but have been slow to believe, and can no more touch us, nor even threaten us, ever again. Perhaps we are now *more* than mere humankind. Perhaps we are something of a different kind – a **nobler** kind, a **Godly** kind – *within*, in the Spirit, in our heart of Hearts. Who can

I AM Come That You Might Have Life

Astonishing Love – Beyond Your Most Cherished Dreams! – *Con.*

say? What can be said is that **a Supreme Act of Astonishing Love** *did* take place, committed by a man whose words have outlived kings, prophecies, and empires. A man whose teachings are unsurpassed in the history of the world. A man whose life outshines all other lives for its **brilliancy**, **authenticity**, and **masterliness**. And a man whose sheer strength of Love transcended anything the world has ever seen or known.

He said He gave His life for the world. He taught by living example that sacrificial, daring, fearless love was the **ideal** to which we should aspire. He admonished His followers to *learn* of Him, and to take on themselves the great privilege and opportunity of extending *His* Love to others,

I AM The Good Shepherd

Astonishing Love – Beyond Your Most Cherished Dreams! – *Con.*

however difficult, at times, it may be. He made love **attractive** as no other man has ever done. He made it **desirable** beyond our most cherished desires. And He assured us that we would *not* be left alone to accomplish our tasks. If we have *already* been 'taken up' into divinity, dear friend, how could we ever be – alone? *We are not!*

Oh!
How I Love
Thy Law

Essay III

The

Window to The *Invisible* God!

Prism!

I AM In The Father

Prism – The Window to the Invisible God

A *Real* Human Being

We have all seen paintings of this man who was born some 2,000 years ago. And we all recognize Him irrespective of which artist rendered His thought-to-be likeness. He was clearly a man, a human male, though depicted with shoulder-length hair, usually a beard and mustache, in a long flowing robe with a look of such sweet accord upon His face. *Clearly*, a human being, of a specific gender, but with a faint emanation of light about His head. People view this artist's conception and immediately think – Here is God! – And they are right!

Yet, why do they *never* say, **Here is Jesus, the *Man!*** They (and perhaps even you, my friend) never say this because their focus

I
AM
The True Vine

Prism – The Window to the Invisible God – *Con.*

is so much upon the Divinity of this Person, that they fail to recognize or acknowledge the Humanity of this Person! And, that, my friend, is a big mistake! Because:

> To fail to see Jesus' **Humanity**
> is sure to *obscure* His *Divinity*
> – to make It distant, removed from us, unapproachable! For His *Divinity* was revealed, made **understandable**, *through* His **Humanity!**

And, further,

I
AM
Glorified

Prism – The Window to the Invisible God – *Con.*

> Jesus' Humanity was the **'<u>looking glass</u>'** which permitted His Divinity to be *seen,* And *felt*, and *heard*. His Humanity served as the **'*<u>magnifying</u>* glass'** through which we struggling humans could view with enhanced **crystal clarity** the workings of *the <u>Divine Presence</u>* – in our midst!

Jesus' actual physical person was, in fact, the '*<u>mirror image</u>*' of the Invisible God! (Col. 1:15) And, It was His Humanity which served as the vehicle wherein the Divine could demonstrate once and for all that It was desirous of meeting man at man's level of need, which level was that of the physical existence man presently shares.

I
AM
A King

Prism – The Window to the Invisible God – *Con.*

We would do well, my friend, to seek out all of the many evidences of His Humanity from the Sacred Writings, and come to see what **surprising emphasis**, and *importance*, the eyewitnesses of Jesus placed upon His Humanity. Apparently, they knew something that many, more likely – most, do *not* know today! And then, once having seen for yourself the **many references** to His *wholly* Human attributes and traits, you will be in a much better position to appreciate and comprehend *Who* He was, *What* He did for us, and *Why* He came and dwelt as 'flesh' among us! Continue reading. You are in for some wonderful, exciting, and heart-thrilling surprises!

Who Will Have All Men To Be Saved

Essay IV

The Redemption of All *Secured!*

Life's Victory!

I
AM
Jesus

Life's Victory – The Redemption Of All – *Secured!*

A long-distant day ago, perhaps on a chilly April morn, did Life, Its **Very Heart**, <u>*win*</u> a stunningly valiant, permanently secure Victory over anything and everything that was anti-Life or anti-Love or anti-Good! **<u>All</u>** that <u>*was*</u>, <u>*is*</u> or <u>*ever*</u> <u>*will*</u> <u>*be*</u> beautiful, praiseworthy, uplifting, exalting, purposeful, empowering, life-giving, life-enhancing, or life-reverencing, was **secured** for all time by '**The Light** that was for <u>all</u> time', and by '**The Love** that was for <u>all</u> men'!

This Great Life, by Its Coming into the world, by Its consecration of (or the **blessing** and **hallowing** *of*) the human condition, or state of existence as physical, created beings, though prone to decay and corruption and moral failings at this present time, has **freed** those subject to its downward spiralings.

I
AM
Holy

Life's Victory – The Redemption Of All – *Secured!* – *Con.*

> ***All*** danger, ***all*** possibility of loss,
> of *any kind*, is now past, forevermore!
> Due to His Accomplishment, *alone!*

And it was **you**, my friend, YOU, personally, who were in View, who were clearly and distinctly held in Mind of this Great Life, when this Victory was secured! Because it was secured directly and purposefully – *for you!*

Though we would not have planned it so, nor dare entertain **the Remedy** that was designed, and effectively put in place on a lonely hill in a distant Roman outpost, **the Remedy** was *executed* (carried out), as was

I
AM
Alpha
And Omega

Life's Victory – The Redemption Of All – *Secured!* – *Con.*

the unrecognized Healer *executed* (crucified), who brought the cure – **the Cure** that resided within His very Soul! The Cure that was His *very* Person! Being 'poured out' – for all!

Now, how strong IS Life, some philosophically ask. How strong was Life, *then?* Strong enough to redeem a whole world of people? *Every single, last, solitary soul, of every person who has ever lived?* Was this Life THAT strong? Was that Love <u>THAT</u> strong? Was Life's Victory this **All-Encompassing?**

Listen, now, my friend, to inspired words preserved for posterity: 'And we know that this is indeed the Anointed, the Saviour *of*

I
AM
The First
And the Last

Life's Victory – The Redemption Of All – *Secured! – Con.*

the World'! And again, 'We have seen and do testify that the Father sent the Son to be the Saviour *of the World'!* And again, '*All* [persons] that the Father giveth me **shall come to me**; and him that cometh to me I will in no wise cast out.' And, lastly, again, 'And I, if I be lifted up from the earth, will draw *all* [ALL!] *men* unto Me'!

Love, Itself, has unequivocally told us He, personally, will draw ALL men unto Himself! He has told us, also, that 'no man *can* come unto Me, except it were given unto him of my Father.' This effectively means the Father has given unto the Son for His possession, ALL MEN, else Life could not have said 'I WILL draw ALL men unto Myself'!

I
AM
He That Liveth

Life's Victory – The Redemption Of All – *Secured!* – *Con.*

<u>Do</u> <u>you</u> <u>begin</u> <u>to</u> <u>see</u> <u>now</u>? And as the word, 'men', is a generic term, it literally means: All people – all males, females, children, infants, newborns, of all countries, cultures, creeds, and, oh yes! Even ALL religions! **No one is exempt from the Father's edict!** No one is excluded from Life's Great Love! All will be redeemed! All will come to know the Truth! And all will, by the miraculous, irresistibly-transforming Power of Love, Itself – of *Life, Himself,* willingly, without coercion, accept the Grace of Life, the Lord of Life, as their <u>personal</u> Redeemer, and that of the *entire* World!

This is why we have cause for rejoicing, *now!* **The Victor**, Life *<u>Himself</u>*, lives today! We can turn to Him with any personal

I
AM
Alive *For Ever*
More

Life's Victory – The Redemption Of All – *Secured!* – Con.

failing, difficulty, trial, struggle, perplexity, anguish, heartache, or loneliness, and be granted the strength we need to carry on, receive **Peace** in the midst of the storms of human life, and obtain a 'cleansing' of our minds and a 'purification' of our hearts, known as 'forgiveness'. And, thereby, experience an ongoing communion with Him, literally *feel* His Presence, actually receive **His compassionate Love** <u>*streaming*</u> into our Hearts! We need only seek Him in prayer and sincerely ask!

Precisely how **the Great Restoration** is to come about, and *when*, we are not told. Ill-consequences will be experienced by many, some quite severe, as **the Justice of Life** is administered, and the injustices of Life are brought into balance.

I AM
He Who
Searches
The Hearts

Life's Victory – The Redemption Of All – *Secured!* – *Con.*

> We are *assured*, however, such 'reapings' are **remedial** in nature, **purging** in effect, and **cleansing** in outcome!

Life will have it no other way, and for that, too, we can rejoice! All are in **the Great School of Life** on earth. There are many lessons to be learned. The most important lessons are often 'hard-won' and require *tremendous* effort, as was the Victory secured in our behalf! But, it will all be worth it! Life, Himself deemed it all 'worth it'! Can you do any less?

Faith
Is
The Gift
Of God

Essay V

The **Faith** of Jesus *Given* You!

Power!

I AM The Bright And Morning Star

Power – The Faith *of* Jesus **Given** Unto You

What, beloved friend, *IS* the Power that will prevail in your life? What **Power** will enable you to cast out doubt and uncertainty? To banish fear and worry, and its distracting anxiety? Allow you to turn your burdens over to **the Lord of Life** and sleep restfully and peacefully, and to wake up refreshed and renewed? – In spite of trying and normally unsettling circumstances?

There is only ONE Power, and that is the Power of Faith! But, **whose** Faith? For so few sincere Christians experience this Power! *Why?* Friend, it is primarily because they are attempting to exercise their *own imperfect*, prone-to-waver, faith. Listen carefully, then, to the Apostle Paul, and discover the secret *he* knew regarding Faith's Power.

I
AM
God Almighty

Power – The Faith *of* Jesus **Given** Unto You – *Con.*

'I am crucified with Christ: nevertheless I live; *yet not I*, but <u>**Christ**</u> **liveth in me**: and the life which I now live in the flesh I live by – **the faith *of* the Son of God** – who loved me, and gave Himself for me.'

And, therein, lies the long sought, elusive, **master key**, if only we have the spiritual wisdom to see it! In fact, herein resides **the Secret** to the 'Holy Grail' of the Christian life. Note well, now, the following excerpted words:

Christ liveth in me:

The Life I <u>*now*</u> live, I live by

The Faith <u>*of*</u> the Son of God

I
AM
The Lord
Your
God

Power – The Faith *of* Jesus **Given** Unto You – *Con.*

It was not Paul's faith, not his *personal* belief, that empowered him to preach the Glorious News with boldness. He did ***not*** say,

'I live by my faith IN the Son of God', But rather, 'I live by **THE** Faith ***OF*** the Son of God.'

In other words, Jesus' own *personal* Faith empowered him! There is a world of difference!

Most are unaware that to live a life of **Victory** and experience ongoing **Peace** and quiet **Confidence** in our lives, we must consciously receive a measure of Christ's Faith, *which never doubted!* **Allowing** Him

I AM Thy Salvation

Power – The Faith *of* Jesus **Given** Unto You – *Con.*

to exercise **His** Faith *through* us, we reap the rewards of Faith and Trust in God – A life of Inner *Freedom* and *Joy!* Ask for this, daily, and receive!

The Effectual Fervent Prayer of a Righteous Man Availeth Much

Essay VI

To

Open the Heart *to* Life and Love!

Prayer!

I
AM
That
I
Am

Prayer – To *Open* the Heart to Life and Love

Shortly before the author commenced writing, and well before he had any idea that he would, he penned a brief prayer. He asked, among other things, that the Creator's purpose for his life 'will have been fulfilled' by the close of his earthly sojourn. He asked, too, that the 'joyful streams of living water', promised to those who earnestly seek Him, might be made 'to flow out from within' him – 'to refresh, bless, and inspire mankind,' Little did the author know that within a remarkably brief period of time, his prayer request would begin to be granted.

> *His writings, apparently, were to become that designated 'channel' Ordained by God through which 'Living Water' is intended to abundantly and vigorously flow!*

I
AM
The
Rose
Of Sharon

Prayer – To _Open_ the Heart to Life and Love – *Con.*

This prayer, actually, has been in the author's heart for a lifetime. But, he now adds one further request: That his writings may admirably serve the purpose for which they have been brought into existence, to bless the reader as much, and even more, as they have blessed him!

I AM The Lord Thy Saviour

The Christ Follower Prayer

Oh! I pray to become more worthy of
Thy Astonishing Love!
My Blessed Lord and Redeemer – *this* day!
And that I may gladly give my Life to You,
In eager and prayerful service,
Without reservation, *this* day!
And that You might cause Joyful Streams
Of Living Water to flow out
From within me – to refresh, bless, and
Inspire Mankind, as did Jesus – *this* day!
And that You may grant unto me
The True Riches of Life – Genuine Faith,
Bright-Shining Hope, and Christ-like
Love and Consecration to Thy Will –*this* day!
And that by the close of my earthly sojourn,
Your purpose for my life will have been
fulfilled,
That I become One with Thy Presence,
To do Thy bidding, now perfectly
Surrendered, *Forevermore*

Love Ye One Another

Essay VII

The Sole Message Given *by* God – to Mankind!

The Divine Message!

I AM Thy Redeemer

The Divine Message – The *Sole* Message Given by God to Mankind!

The Divine Message of our God is both profound and simple at the same time. In fact, it is due to Its *utter simplicity* that so many people cannot bring themselves to believe It constitutes the **sole** requirement of God to mankind! Surely, they reason, our Creator must require much more! – 'There have to be multiple rules to be followed, numerous commandments to be obeyed, untold directives to be adhered to!' Or so they think! But, this is all untrue. Spiritually mature people do not need *anything other* than the Rule of Love to govern their lives, and direct their paths. And what IS Love but **placing the welfare of others *first*, and having their best interests at heart, *always!*** Listen to what the Apostle of Love, John, had to say in I John 1:5 on this matter:

I
AM
He That
Comforteth
You

The Divine Message – The *Sole* Message Given by God to Mankind!
– *Con.*

> <u>*THIS*</u>, *then, is THE Message we have heard of Him, and declare unto you, that God is Light [The Light of Love], and in Him – is no darkness – at all*

The definite grammatical article 'THE' highlights the fact of the centrality and singularly paramount significance of this teaching. It is not 'a' Message *among* equally important messages, but really the SOLE communication our Creator wishes to impart! Listen, now, again, to John and begin to see this recurring theme throughout his inspired writings:

I
AM
For
You

The Divine Message – The *Sole* Message Given by God to Mankind!
– *Con.*

> *For <u>THIS</u> is THE Message that ye heard from the Beginning [of the ministry of The Master], that we should Love One Another (I John 3:11)*

Note, there is no mention of any kind of religious acts or practices, whether ritualistic, or ceremonial, or group fellowship, or corporate worship. The **One Law** of Love overshadows all other considerations, and supersedes them. These other activities may be beneficially participated in should one so choose, but they are not a necessity mandated by God.

I
AM
Thy
Shield

The Divine Message – The _Sole_ Message Given by God to Mankind!
– *Con.*

> *That which we had from the beginning, that we Love One Another, And <u>THIS</u> is Love that we walk after… THE Commandment… heard from the Beginning (II John 1:5-6)*

And lastly, hear God's Supreme Messenger of Love, Jesus of Nazareth, affirm this Truth – firsthand:

> *<u>THIS</u> is MY [<u>Sole</u>] Commandment, That Ye Love One Another, <u>as</u> <u>I</u> <u>have</u> <u>loved</u> <u>you</u> (John 15:12)*

I
AM
Thy Exceeding Great Reward

The Divine Message – The *Sole* Message Given by God to Mankind!
– *Con.*

The 'as **I** have loved you' is where the DARING comes in! Beloved, could anything be more clear? It is childlike simplicity. Its observance creates Oneness, Unity, Profound Belongingness, Joyous Fulfillment! **Love Ye One Another!** God speed the Day mankind enshrines – these four Divine words – in their hearts!

Love Is the Fulfilling Of the Law

The Divine Message – The _Sole_ Message Given by God to Mankind! – *Con.*

The <u>Heart</u> *of* The Divine Message

Implicit within the All-Solicitous admonition to 'Love Ye One Another' lies a mighty Truth. He Who made this timeless statement intriguingly qualified it with the words '<u>*AS*</u> I have loved you.' And precisely <u>*how*</u> did He love His disciples over the course of His ministry? – He loved them with selflessness, courage, and DARING! For it is only in **Daring to Love** that we, as individuals, grow spiritually, emotionally, and psychologically. Futher, <u>that</u> Daring **must** begin by loving *ourselves!* This, surprisingly, is a wholly unselfish act that allows us to begin to Love as we are meant

Love Is the Fruit of The Spirit

The Divine Message – The _Sole_ Message Given by God to Mankind! – *Con.*

to – and as never before! So embrace The Divine Message! Enshrine It in your heart through the **living of It** every day! Once you do so, you will **become** the Divine Messenger *YOU* are meant to be, and a whole new world of Purpose, Power, and Fulfillment will unfold _**before**_ your very eyes, and from _**within**_ your very heart! No longer a fearful, hesitant, doubting, or confused person, you will have become, at long last – FREE!

Blessings! And Godspeed you to your **assured** Destiny!

Jesus Of Nazareth, A *Man* Approved Of God

Essay VIII

A Human Face *on* The Divine Power!

A Mirror Reflecting Life's Heart!

God
Is
Love

A Mirror Reflecting Life's Heart –
A *Human* Face on the Divine Power!

Beloved friend, there is something you simply have to know, must know, about the Heart of Life, if you are to be set free to live and to love as you have never done before. The Power that formed all things in the universe, that conceived you in the secret realm of thought, you must know is a Power seemingly beyond your comprehension. When you, my sister, think on the earth, its majesty, its grandeur, or my brother, on its almost inconceivable complexity and interrelatedness in all of its workings, then do you not marvel at it all, and have your breath taken away in such a moment? In such a moment, or moments, when you behold a glorious ocean spray from billowing waves, or vistas of mother earth's bosom, her mountains, a riot with flowers in

By Love Serve One Another

A Mirror Reflecting Life's Heart –
A _Human_ Face on the Divine Power!
– *Con.*

Spring. Or, what of the Power manifest, so evident, in a thunderstorm with its great clashes of electrical energy, its electrifying displays. Such Power! Such Energy! Such a demonstration of stored-up forces that bespeak of ordered, natural Law, being outpictured on the grandest scale before your eyes.

Yet, for all this beauty, the wonder elicited from this *Power*, this _Something_, commanding Nature to move, and dance, and to be in motion, in an active state of change – and becoming, for all of this – there is a distance, not in spatial terms or a dimensional interrelating, but in emotional terms, in feeling terms, in heart terms! Yes,

Be Rooted And Grounded In Love

A Mirror Reflecting Life's Heart –
A *Human* Face on the Divine Power!
– *Con.*

a distance! And it would seem to be as wide as you and the furthermost star! Wherein two orders of being, if you will, remain separate and apart from each, the other! One is too high, too lofty! The other, is too low, too condescending. One is too grand and glorious, the other, too small and undistinguished. One is too incomprehensible, the other, easily known.

Yes, no doubt, it is true this great Power does 'speak' to us, and move us, and even humble us, while witnessing the workings of Itself. But, still, those of us who are most sensitive to such things, we find ourselves in a kind of despair because we cannot *relate* to *a Power*, as we do to *a Person* – a fellow human being! No matter how grand, or

Speak
The Truth
In Love

A Mirror Reflecting Life's Heart –
A *Human* Face on the Divine Power!
– *Con.*

glorious, or spectacular that Power may be! For all intents and purposes, at least in the minds of those persons who have pondered this deeply, such a Power, too, *even a Power that created us*, could not fathom the depths of our hearts – the depths of our humanity! Could not really identify with us! Could not truly understand us! *Even though that Power be the Maker of us all!*

Does this make sense to you, my friend? For to truly be able to do that, such a Power would have to 'know' what it is like to cry, and to sigh, and to yearn, and to long for, and to ache for, and to dream, and to feel for, and to be vulnerable, and to be afraid. Such a Power would have to come down to 'our level' and view the world from our

Walk
In
Love

A Mirror Reflecting Life's Heart –
A *Human* Face on the Divine Power!
– *Con.*

perspective. And these 'attendants' to human life, that which makes us human, that which literally constitutes our very humanity, ***cannot*** be known – apart from an *'experiential identification'* with the states of mind and body of the human creature itself!

Oh, don't let those words intimidate you! They simply mean that for such a Power to **know** mankind through and through. To be able to **understand** from the *inside out* what it means to be human. To be able to **share** in the 'beingness' of man. To be able to truly **love** men and women, and **bear** a profound sense of **'kinship'** with even children and babes. This Power could only do one thing to achieve this capability! And only one

Love
In
The Spirit

A Mirror Reflecting Life's Heart –
A *Human* Face on the Divine Power!
– *Con.*

thing! Else, It, no matter how transcendent or knowing or 'caring' It could be, – Its very transcendent nature, itself, would serve to forever come between Itself and Its created ones.

There are many who have tried to worship such a Power as this through the millennia. And they have striven to do so with great ardor and intensity of effort. They so greatly desired to come into a 'relationship', if you will, with so great a Power. But, their efforts, though valiant, did not, and my friend I tell you now, could not, take them where they so longed to go! This Power, as conceived and understood, by ancient, and modern man, could not, and CANNOT –

Abound In Love One Toward Another

A Mirror Reflecting Life's Heart –
A *Human* Face on the Divine Power!
– *Con.*

<u>'satisfy the hungry heart of man'</u>! And no wonder! It has been said that 'like attracts like', but in this instance, more to the point, it is only 'like that <u>can</u> understand like'. We can only understand those things that we are like, or what is like us – or what has *become* us. Only 'like can understand like'! 'Unlike cannot understand like.' To understand a person, you must first find out those ways in which you are not only similar, but identical, the same, at least at the most basic level. Then, my friend, you will come to understand that person – but, not and never until!

So, the question I ask you, my friend, is 'Will mans' heart forever remain 'unsatisfied' and 'hungry'?' A very wise man

Let Brotherly Love Continue

A Mirror Reflecting Life's Heart –
A *Human* Face on the Divine Power!
– Con.

once said, 'Only *God* can fully satisfy the hungry heart of man!' Yet, this true statement begs a question! Yet, the question remains, 'What **_kind_** of a God'? A Force, though infinitely intelligent, that is *aloof* to man, *unaware* of man's heartache and Soul-ache? Uncomprehending of man's greatest needs, wants, yearnings, and desires? Would this Force truly be a God, a Creator God, man could worship 'with all his mind, *all his heart*, all his soul, and all his spirit'? – In any truly meaningful way? How could he do so, how could YOU do so, my friend, if what you had to give to this Force, *It was incapable of receiving?* And, make no mistake about it, my searching, hoping friend, a Force, however exalted – without the 'experiential identification' or to put it in

Love Covers *All* Sins

A Mirror Reflecting Life's Heart –
A *Human* Face on the Divine Power!
– Con.

plainer words, 'experience of being human' could not be said to truly **know**, **understand**, **share**, and **bear kinship** to, could then most assuredly <u>not</u> LOVE man! – As man needs, and longs, and hopes for – to be loved! And as man will always yearn to be loved!

Now, however, **Glory Be!** The *wondrous* good news is that the Power, the Heart of Life, that formed the world has, or has taken on, *a human face!* A more intriguing, yet more accurate thought still, is that man is discovered to have a countenance mirroring the face of this Power! For man is made 'in the Image (or likeness) of God', *not* the other way around, as in 'God is made in the Image (or likeness) of man'! And it is THIS Wonder that makes – all the difference!

Love
Is Strong
As Death

Essay IX

The Eternal Verity *of* Life!

With All Certainty – All Is Well!

I Have Loved Thee With An Everlasting Love

With All Certainty – All Is Well

Perhaps you have heard it said, my friend, that 'All Is Well'. This is an expression that has come down to us from poets and philosophers, theologians and thinkers, alike. Such a short phrase, it is. But, oh, *how inviting* it is! How we would *like* to believe it! How we *long* to believe it, about so many things! Yet, we cannot. Though, strange as it may sound, should you take the time to just 'be' with this phrase, to just 'let it rest' in your mind, to simply let it occupy a place in your thoughts, for a time, something – yes, *something*, about these three words, seems to transcend these three words, and would leave you wondering what that something might be! – 'All Is Well!' Have you ever recited these three words and felt their bold message strike a responsive cord in your heart? Is there any real truth to it – after all?

Great Peace Have They Which Love Thy Law

With All Certainty–All Is Well – *Con.*

In order to answer this question satisfactorily, convincingly, and honestly, and in order for it to have a positive impact upon your life, you must understand the following distinction: To say that 'All Is Well' is *not* the same thing as saying 'All Is Well – Right *Here* and Right *Now*'! The latter phrase speaks only to the immediate, narrowly-focused view of the moment, whether that moment be truly only a moment, or many years of moments. While, the former phrase speaks to a much grander, higher, far-reaching perspective, one that takes in 'the whole', not the partial! And it is from that perspective that the phrase 'All Is Well' takes on the Clarion Call of Truth, and presents to those who believe that this is so, an assurance, a quiet certainly, that becomes an absolute knowing that 'this simply has to

They Shall Prosper That Love Thee

With All Certainty–All Is Well – *Con.*

be, must be, and indeed, IS for me – the Truth!

Now, there are really only two questions that this phrase addresses: How can you say, 'All Is Well' in the world, the global arena at large, and how can you say, 'All Is Well' in your neighbor's 'localized', individualized, personal world of her or his private affairs? How can you say this when you know full well the world is in a terrible state of affairs, with the threat of wars and hardship for so many, and your neighbor is, perhaps, suffering from severe financial difficulties or unrelenting marital discord?

But, more than this! How can you say 'to *yourself*' that 'All Is Well' when you know

The Lord Preserveth All Them That Love Him

With All Certainty–All Is Well – *Con.*

that your health is steadily deteriorating, perhaps from an as-yet-unidentified ailment that is robbing you of all your strength and joy in living? With no physician able to explain your malady! Is it possible to know, then, my friend, that 'All', yes, 'ALL' is well? – in your world? The world that is nearest to you? The question, itself, would seem absurd, except for the fact that the phrase, that little three-word arrangement, that all-inclusive proposition, continues to turn up in the human psyche as evidenced in humanity's literature, music, theater, art, and history. Its staying power alone suggest that it harbors a powerful truth. A truth that transcends any truth of the moment!

He Will Love Them And Bless Them

With All Certainty–All Is Well – *Con.*

But, it goes further than even that! This little phrase, 'All Is Well', embodies and proclaims, at the heart of its meaning, a glorious truth that, as the title of this essay declares, 'With All Certainty', cannot be compared to any other truth! So Grand is it! So Wonderful is it! So *personally* meaningful and All-Important is it to you, yes, you! My friend! Listen, only one thing, and one thing *alone*, can make this phrase mean what the intuition of so many tell us it must mean! And that one thing is – *the Ultimate Intention of Life – toward you!* And every other 'you' that ever existed, does exist, or will exist after you are gone!

Does that sound too far-fetched? It is not! The deepest need of every human being is to

What Shall Separate Us From The Love of Christ?

With All Certainty–All Is Well – *Con.*

know that it is *so* loved, and means *so* much to someone, actually, to the 'Great Someone', that Their commitment to them, even though they be frail, weak, morally imperfect, and prone to evil – is Absolute, Steadfast, and Unalterable! A Love *so great* that It would *never*, under *any* circumstances, 'give up' on *any* human being no matter how far they may have strayed from, as what the psalmist of old called, the 'paths of righteousness'!

You see, friend, you can know, with all certainty, that All *IS* Well, only if you know that All *Will Be* Well with you, personally, and every other 'you' to whom these words were meant to give comfort! If there is a destiny that you are assured of reaching beyond this life, a destiny that will find you

[*No*] Creature Shall Be Able To Separate Us From the Love Of God

With All Certainty–All Is Well – *Con.*

liberated from the trials and tribulations that beset you now, then, in anticipation of what IS to be, while holding the 'Outcome' in view, you can say to yourself confidently, and truthfully, 'All Is Well!'

So, seek to make the best of any trying times. But, remember these words, too, for complete assurance! 'And, I, if I be lifted up from the earth, will *draw* ALL men unto Me.' No one was ever 'drawn' against their will! And when you come to fully understand this, you, too, will reassuringly say, first to yourself, and then to others, 'All Is Well! With All Certainty! I know that All Is Well!' And one day, you will know it, too!

His Love Is Perfected In Us

Essay X

The **Wellspring** of *Thrilling* Life!

The Magnificent Obsession!

Glory Shall Be Revealed

The Magnificent Obsession

You, my friend, are Heir to a great, wondrous, *Magnificent Obsession!* Yes, you! It was bequeathed to you, and it only awaits your Awareness of its existence, and subsequent implementation! Even as it is true that a child cannot and will not be granted his or her Legacy until such time as he comes into maturity, into adulthood. Even so, men and women are not granted knowledge of their priceless Inheritance, certainly not in its fullness, until they become 'mature' in their understanding of Life, and particularly Its meaning. And when they do, whether they be 18 years of age, or 78 years of age, *The Magnificent Obsession* becomes an absolute Reality to them, embracing them, possessing them, filling them with a Power and a Purpose such as they have never known!

Behold What Manner Of Love!

The Magnificent Obsession
– *Con.*

Whereas before, a person may have simply drifted through Life, with no definite aim or purpose. Whereas earlier, a person may have struggled daily in their interactions with others, apparently not able to establish any truly satisfying relationships. Whereas formerly, a person was either dissatisfied with Life, or even totally empty of any Joy in living. Now, NOW, they come to a startling and thrilling revelation! Usually, after having found their old ways of interacting with and reacting to people, situations, circumstances, and Life, as a whole, ineffectual and often hurtful, it is THEN, most often that *The Magnificent Obsession* makes Its appearance! For, you see, my friend, the person – and perhaps I am speaking about you here, is now ready to

Love
Thy Neighbor
As
Thyself

The Magnificent Obsession
– *Con.*

mentally entertain something unfamiliar, altogether different, even dramatically apart from anything even thought of before! The result? A transformed Life forever! *The Magnificent Obsession* becomes the Whole of one's existence! It occupies every waking moment of your mental life, frequently consciously, always subconsciously. And whenever you need help, particularly *immediate* help, in your interactions with others, It springs, literally *leaps* into your conscious awareness, providing you with the Wisdom, Knowledge, and priceless Guidance, meeting the precise need of the moment! So Great is the Power of Its All-Enveloping purpose, and Its nature to extend and expand out to all people within your reach, and then even beyond!

Love Ye The Stranger

The Magnificent Obsession
– *Con.*

Now, normally, you would think that an 'obsession' is something to be avoided at all costs. And you would be correct. For to be obsessed is to be preoccupied in an intensely abnormal way, to be irrationally, emotionally attached to some concept or endeavor. But, further, to be obsessed with something, anything, is to lose one's self-determination, to forfeit one's objectivity, to surrender your personal freedom, often in a detrimental and harmful way. *The Magnificent Obsession,* however, is altogether different! And that is why It is called <u>Magnificent</u>! There is nothing negative or hurtful or harmful about It! Its very nature is to extend authentic freedom to the individual, to enable them to begin to live a life sublime, wholly fulfilling, won-

Love The Lord Thy God With All Thy Heart

The Magnificent Obsession
– *Con.*

drous, even miraculous! It liberates the individual from the tyranny of their 'little self'.

Are you, my friend, ready for *The Magnificent obsession* to enter your life? Do you want It to? It can, you know. And It will do everything for you as I have cited above. It has no favorites. You It will possess, when you are ready for It to! And It will permanently set you free! You should know, however, at the outset, that your embracing of *The Magnificent Obsession* does pose some risk. And once It embraces you, you will, at times, be misinterpreted, held in suspicion, envied, and by the few, even 'hated'. One such Individual, gave Himself over to It so wholeheartedly, so completely, so perfectly, that false charges

Love Your Enemies

The Magnificent Obsession
– *Con.*

were brought against Him. He was tried, convicted, and then sentenced to death. But, even here, *The Magnificent Obsession* did not desert Him, or prove to be His undoing! His utter commitment to It, and to the One Who gave It to Him, was honored beyond anything anyone of His detractors could imagine! You know the outcome, don't you? Every sunrise service is a celebration of His *Magnificent* Victory!

But, His was a Unique Mission in demonstrating and planting *The Magnificent Obsession* on the earth. So, fear not that anything as drastic as His Life's unfoldment should occur in yours! Nonetheless, you should be prepared for opposition, at times, and expect it. For remember! *The Magnif-*

Let Them Also That Love Thy Name Be Joyful in Thee

The Magnificent Obsession
– Con.

icent Obsession serves as a shield to those who give their life to It, and It will so insulate your mind and heart from the few detractors you will encounter, that any negativity sent your way will be stripped, made devoid, of all power to harm you! Such is the promise of the One Who knew and lived *The Magnificent Obsession* as none ever had before, or since!

Now, my friend, what is *The Magnificent Obsession?* Is It not the mature Awareness that *your* life – <u>has</u> <u>no</u> <u>life</u> – apart from your giving of yourself away – to others! Seeking other's happiness! Other's welfare! Other's best interest! And in the process, YOU become supremely happy! So, now, you tell me, my friend, What could be more Magnificent, *than that?*

My Love
Be With You All
In Christ Jesus

Essay XI

The Answer to All *Life's* Questions!

The One Sole Explanation of All!

The Creation Awaits the Manifestation of the *Sons* of God

The One Sole Explanation Of All

Is the meaning of the world, and the myriad forms of life, and the universe obscure and bewildering to you? Can the presence of such marvels and mysteries of existence as science beholds 'out there' and seeks to identify, classify, and categorize be explained and understood at the most fundamental level, as to their *purpose*, I mean? *Why* they are? Yes, the Great *Why* of their Being! Some people feel such questions are nonsensical to ask or even ponder, since who can know such things? For to pre-suppose a 'why', implies or postulates a 'One' to entertain the 'why'; in fact, to actually formulate the why in the first place, to precede the 'what', or substance, of Creation! Meaning, then,

The One Sole Explanation
Of All – *Con.*

would be the special purpose for which 'the All' was created! But, if there is a *special* purpose, an *intended* reason for being, *what could it possibly be?*

I'm going to share with you, now, a concept that I sincerely wish you will entertain. And that grand idea is this: *IF* you knew the meaning of 'the All', why the Universe is, you would know the meaning of YOU. That makes sense, doesn't it? Because you, naturally, are a part of the All. But what many do not realize, is that, conversely, to know the meaning of you, *IS – to know the meaning of 'the All'!* Of *All* life, of *All* worlds, of *All* universes! For, as you will one day come to see, the Universe is

The One Sole Explanation
Of All – *Con.*

founded upon YOU! You are the one who gives it meaning! You are the one for which It exists! Are these arrogant and vain words? Fool-hardy or insane words? Come and see!
Natural Science and 'Revealed' Religion, alike, both recognize the existence of the *Macro*cosm (the gargantuan universe, or totality of all – matter, energy, light, life-forms, etc.) and the *Micro*cosm (or, the miniature universe – as an atom or cell, or even a human body). The Ancients believed and taught the concept that 'the Above' was reflected in 'the Below', and 'the Below' was *a reflection of* 'the Above'. Worded another way, 'the Without' (whether interstellar space, or a distant galaxy) is *contained in* 'the Within' (such as a grain of sand, or a wildflower, or the body of a

The One Sole Explanation
Of All – *Con.*

woman, or man), while 'the Within', and note these words, is a *replica of* 'the Without'! Interesting play on words, you might say, but what does it actually mean? Is there any practical significance to it relative to the matter of 'the One Sole Explanation Of All'? Most assuredly, I tell you – there is!

Listen, now, to these *scientifically* accurate statements: 'For the earnest expectation of the CREATION [*literal* Greek translation – the Whole Creation, or physical Universe!] *waits for* the MANIFESTATION of the Sons of God. For the CREATION [or, Universe] was made subject to vanity [*decay*], not willingly, but by reason of Him Who has subjected the same in Hope,

The One Sole Explanation
Of All – *Con.*

because the CREATION [Universe] itself also shall be delivered from the bondage of corruption into the glorious liberty of the Children of God. For we know that <u>*the whole CREATION* [The **Macro**-Cosmic Universe] *'groans*</u> and travails' in pain together until now. And not only *they* ['they' not in original Greek], but *ourselves also. . ,* even we ourselves [*The **Micro**Cosmic Universe*] *groan* within ourselves, waiting for the adoption, to wit, the redemption of our body.' Here, we have, 'As [it is] Above, So [it is] Below'! One reflects the other!

The reason for the Universe, or the Creation, IS, or is yet to be, *to serve man!* It was created *for* man's enjoyment, *for* man's wonderment, *for* man's being entranced,

The One Sole Explanation
Of All – *Con.*

fascinated, and delighted by its awesome beauty and immense grandeur! But, this beauty could not even be perceived if it were not already *within* man! Indeed, there is no 'Beatific Vision' associated with it apart from man's conscious contemplation of it! It is man's consciousness that imparts beauty to the Universe! As Below [in man], so Above [in the Universe]! The ancient maxim, 'Man is the measure of All Things' is as true now as it was when this statement was uttered! And this is so because Man is 'in the Image', bears the likeness, or reflection of, the Great Imaginer – otherwise known as God!

So, you see, my friend, the explanation of YOU, the fact of your existence, the miracle

The One Sole Explanation
Of All – *Con.*

of your personal, individual consciousness, your awareness, is the only explanation needed to explain the existence of *everything else!* And WHY is it that YOU are here? What is your meaning? Your purpose? Is not that explanation contained in the statement, 'I AM come that YOU might have Life, and that YOU might have it more ABUNDANTLY'! Think about this for a moment, and then see whether or not you agree!

'To have Life More Abundant'! And there is *no* restriction placed upon the word, 'Abundant'! What could this mean but to live a life that is Radiant, Joyful, Thrilling, Victorious, Exalted, Life-Glorifying, and

The One Sole Explanation Of All – *Con.*

<u>LOVE</u>-FILLED! Free from all restraints or limitations, that would diminish life, or confine it! This is YOUR purpose for being – and destiny! And it is a purpose that you will one day MANIFEST for all CREATION to see!

Essay XII

A Wish The World *Will* Make!

The Ultimate Request!

Ask
And It Shall
Be
Given You

A Wish the World Will Make

My friend, a great Visionary of our time personified the conscience of individual man and woman, or child, as a seemingly insignificant, lowly, cricket. This tiny creature was wont to spend his time – with of all things – a wooden boy, symbolic of mankind. Like his counterpart in the 'real' world, who can be relied upon to incessantly chirp or sing, this tiny cricket never ceased to admonish, instruct, and to guide the wooden boy in the ways of Wisdom, Honor, and Truth – that would surely lead to him becoming a REAL boy. He is best remembered by the song that became his theme – *When You Wish Upon A Star*. I can remember him once having said with great sorrow in his eyes and deep sadness in his

A Wish the World Will Make – *Con.*

heart, 'You know, not many people *believe* that anymore.'

Now, no truer words were ever spoken, but thankfully, the few who do wholeheartedly believe it are growing in numbers. Their hearts are incapable of denying the validity of these *inspired* words of this *inspired* Message given to mankind! For unknown to most, this very short song is a philosophy and *a prophecy*, and speaks to the most fundamental aspects of REALITY! The hidden meaning of this song, I will now unveil, as it was given unto me to know.

When you wish upon a star, Makes no difference who you are, Anything your heart desires will come to you

A Wish the World Will Make – *Con.*

This first stanza plainly tells us that *anyone*, regardless of his station in life can 'make a wish' – and have it come true. Just for the asking. Just by making a request. On the surface this appears to be contrary to human experience, but there are conditions. One, the wish must be 'upon a star', and two, the wish must be a desire of the 'heart' – a 'heart's desire'. Having met these two conditions, *your* wish, request, dream – call it what you will – WILL come to pass! According to this precise formula.

But, to 'wish upon a star', you have to turn your eyes heavenward – to 'lift up your eyes', to fix your gaze upon a focal point of illumination, or *wisdom*; radiant warmth, or *love*; and energy, or *power*. Moreover, stars, or suns, throughout history have been

A Wish the World Will Make – *Con.*

symbolic of exalted, benevolent beings – either the Supreme Being, or Beings who have become ONE with God. Also, a 'heart's desire' is *always* a 'Soul's Sincere Desire'. It is a desire belonging to the highest aspirations of man. It is, in fact, a heartfelt prayer involving the best intentions towards others and yourself. It is a desire that is totally pure, wholesome, honorable, and Godly.

A Soul's Sincere Desire is, additionally, a desire *planted within you* by your Creator. It is a part of the Divine Plan for you as an individual. Actually, it is much more than a mere desire, it is an expression of God's very WILL! And God's Will CANNOT and WILL NOT be thwarted. It stands supreme

A Wish the World Will Make – *Con.*

and Will be Victorious over All things – *in the end!*

If your heart is in your dream, No Request is too extreme, When you wish upon a star as dreamers do

Your heart, my friend, <u>must</u> be in your dream – your *whole* heart. It can't be a half-hearted desire. It has to be something you long for, yearn for, even *ache* for – something that you feel belongs to you – that you have a right to claim. Anything less will prove to be ineffectual. Notice carefully, too, the second verse – a strange and marvelous statement: '*No request* is too extreme'. What could be more wonderful than that! – A veritable Aladdin's lamp! Yet, the Great Teacher said that exact same thing

A Wish the World Will Make – *Con.*

only in different words centuries before: '*Whatsoever* you shall ask in my name, *that will I do* [for *you*]'.

Lastly, don't overlook that you have to wish upon a star '*as dreamers do*'. Now, how do dreamers wish upon a star? A true, authentic, dreamer uses the leans of his or her divine imagination or INNER VISION to visualize what it is he wishes to come to pass. In other words, he holds it there in his consciousness, though all circumstances be to the contrary, *until* it becomes a reality in the external world. This has been called the science of the Immaculate conception; it is an essential ingredient. Now, we come to the heart of the song.

A Wish the World Will Make – *Con.*

***Fate is kind. She brings to those who love,
The sweet fulfillment of their secret
longing***

Who, or what, my friend, is this 'Fate'? Fate, or 'the Fates', in Greek and Roman mythology signifies *the feminine aspect of Deity*. She IS God. Her very nature is kindness. She is sympathetic, gentle, tenderhearted, generous, and ever-so-loving! Her chief interest is in those who love – for She IS Love! She is God THE MOTHER – divine counterpart of God THE FATHER! Eternally co-existing with Him in indivisible unity, She is the complementary aspect of the One God. And what is Her principal endeavor, purpose, or mission? It is to *bring fulfillment* to human beings. Which human

A Wish the World Will Make – *Con.*

beings?–Those who love!– Unconditionally! It is to bring fulfillment to those human beings who have learned how to give their love as flowers freely breathe their fragrance into space – never withholding from anyone at any time. Such a person does not love 'to *be* loved', but rather, loves '*to* love'! And, what kind of fulfillment is being discussed here? – And fulfillment of what? *Sweet fulfillment* of their *secret* longing. It is their innermost longing from the depths of their being – their *heart's center*.

Another point, you need to understand, friend, is that you don't have to strive, struggle, or strain to achieve your heart's desires. Your heart's desires will COME to you – actually be BROUGHT to you! This is

A Wish the World Will Make – *Con.*

not to say, however, that you are to do nothing. Oh, you have your part, but you must not fret or worry. This is always fruitless. You should rest in faith, trust, confidence, and reliance in the Supreme One Who WILL answer your petition in 'Her' own time, and in 'Her' own way! It appears, however, at this point, that this philosophy blatantly ignores the hard, cold, 'realities' of physical life – sickness, disease, tragedy, and heartache. But does it – *really?* Listen!

Like a bolt out of the blue, Fate steps in and sees you through, When you wish upon a star, your dreams come true

The key thought, here, is that God WILL see you through! But through *what? – Through*

A Wish the World Will Make – *Con.*

sickness, disease, suffering, misfortune, calamity, and even that which man calls 'death'. We will experience these things for a time, to be sure, but eventually we will have the VICTORY over them – nevermore to experience them again – to have them banished forever from our experience!

So, it comes down to this question: What is the GREATEST REQUEST that man could ask of God? It could only be to be like God forevermore. To be *free* from the limiting conditions mentioned above – indeed, to be ONE with God. THIS is the Ultimate – the 'extreme' request – to which this song alludes. It is to partake of, and manifest, 'Her' every attribute, totally, in 'Her' fullness!

A Wish the World Will Make – *Con.*

This is man's destiny, my friend. This is YOUR destiny! It is CERTAIN. For notice: It is not a question of *'IF'* man will wish upon a star – only *'When'*. All men, without exception, will one day wish upon a star – the DayStar on High – and all men will attain the highest pinnacle of being – which is God MADE MANIFEST, *in themselves!* This divine celestial song affirms uncompromisingly and without reservation that FULFILLMENT awaits man. This is its keynote message. It has never been denied man – and never will. It has been said before by others, notably, 'ALL men will come unto Me in due time (their appointed time), but theirs is the agony of awaiting'. And again, 'And I, if I, be lifted up from earth, will *draw* ALL men unto Me' – *through the*

A Wish the World Will Make – *Con.*

magnetic, ALL-conquering, EVERY –heart-transforming, power, of Everlasting Love!

God speed the day when that time of awaiting shall be over, and when this, YOUR promised time, of fulfillment of *your* Dreams, and of *Life's* Dream, for you, *will have come true!*

Essay XIII

The **Hush** That Fell O'er *The* Earth!

A Silence Untold!

And Laid [Jesus] in His Own New Tomb

The Hush That Fell O'er The Earth

Early one morning, long ago now, a mighty hush fell upon the earth. It descended from who knows where. A silence – *so* still, *so* quiet, it was deafening. It fell upon the tropical rain forests of Guatemala. It lighted upon the plains of the Sahara desert. It made its appearance in the high mountains of the Sierra. And it permeated the mists arising up from the Pacific Ocean. It was found to be everywhere. Wherever man was residing, or traveling, or wandering, the intense silence was there. A stillness unlike any other any person then living could recall. It was unprecedented. And it was frightening.

At the arrival of a particular time, on this early morning, prior to dawn, an eerie sensation seemed to fill the very air men

The Hush That Fell O'er The Earth
– *Con.*

breathed. In fact, there was virtually no stir in the air, at all. The usual sounds of night – the insects, the birds, the rustling of the leaves of the trees ceased their activity. And all was still. It was as though the earth, the planet itself, was holding its breath. As if it were anticipating something to happen, bracing itself for its arrival, hoping that it would come, but wondering whether it would, praying that it would, fearful that it wouldn't! But, its knowledge was limited, and our beloved planet Earth, was bewildered, and apprehensive, as was man!

Some entertained a thought, but just as quick did they attempt to banish it! It brought no comfort, only a deep disquieting and

The Hush That Fell O'er The Earth
– Con.

troubling of spirit. So men tried to force it from their consciousness, but it would not leave. It had made its entrance into their minds, and having done so, refused to depart. The weight of it was so heavy that men, and women, felt a coldness begin to grip them, encircle their being, envelop their human form. The thought was unthinkable, yet they were compelled to think it! And that was that the earth, the planet, and all therein – including the world of men, was somehow in dire jeopardy of an imminent danger. A calamity of unprecedented proportions about to strike within minutes, even seconds! But, from what or how or from where – was unknown! What had precipitated this event? – Whatever it was. *Why* was the globe, the

The Hush That Fell O'er The Earth
– *Con.*

entirety of the planet Earth, and mankind upon it, in this state with these feelings at this particular time? What did it all mean?

To answer this question, you must go back in time some 72 hours. For it was then that the inception of this drama began. At that precise time, a man, whom had been tried and convicted as a threat to the State, had closed his eyes for the last time as a human being. He breathed his last breath as the son of a human mother. He felt the last stab of pain to wrack his beaten, bleeding human body. He ceased to live, as a man, and became as one who never was! His body was taken to an above-ground 'cave', and laid upon a cold, hard slab. His body was

The Hush That Fell O'er The Earth
– *Con.*

prepared with spices and linens in the custom and manner of his people. He was entombed behind a huge boulder, effectively sealing the burial chamber – *forever!*

Now, *within minutes* of 72 hours having elapsed from when his head was bowed for the last time, the Earth lay still, and strangely quiet. Somehow, Mother Earth must have sensed, as did man, that 'time of fulfillment' was about to occur. And that depending upon the outcome, man, and the oceans, and the continents, and all creatures native to the Earth, would either *perish, cease to be* – or the Earth, and all therein, would be set free, in some wholly mysterious way, from ultimate destruction and eternal oblivion!

The Hush That Fell O'er The Earth
– *Con.*

As the minutes ticked down, the stillness grew moreso! Finally, the last minute of the 72-hour period was ticking away! Sixty seconds! Forty-five! Twenty-five! Ten! Nine! Eight! Four! Three! The final second was at the door! What would 'be' on the other side? Two! No time to think now! No time to do anything! – *ONE!* Then, IT happened! Then, IT occurred! The heavens fairly shouted it out!

GLORIOUS MORNING! JESUS IS RISEN! NO TOMB COULD HOLD HIM! NO STONE COULD SEAL! GLORIOUS MORNING! THE WORLD, THE PLANET, AND ALL THEREIN, HAVE A SAVIOUR! JESUS, THE LAMB OF GOD, THE KING OF THE WORLD!

The Hush That Fell O'er The Earth
– *Con.*

My friend! No one knows what would have happened to our beloved planet had this man not risen from the grave! Some have conjectured that the very Earth, itself, would have ceased to be, at that very instant, had He not come forth from the tomb in precisely 72 hours as He said He would. This was so, some believe, because without the Lord of Life's Presence in the World, permeating the planet, all the atoms making it up, would have disintegrated from loss of His sustaining power – and who knows? Perhaps even 'bereavement' regarding what would have been His permanent absence! Seventy-two hours was the limit!

Now, whether or not the Earth experienced the stillness I described in this discourse, for

The Hush That Fell O'er The Earth
– *Con.*

dramatic emphasis, in order to stimulate thought, actually happened – I cannot say. I suspect it may very well have. I have presented it, here, as a distinct possibility to ponder. Because, you may recall, during the time of this Man's dying, a great darkness had descended upon, we are told, 'the whole land', and actual historical records from around the world confirm this was so! It extended throughout the Earth! Though, traditional historians are at a loss to explain it to this day!

If such an occurrence as this preceded and attended this Man's 'departure', does it not make sense that perhaps some phenomena preceded His 'arrival' back to the world – in *Life Triumphant?* Whatever the case, men's

The Hush That Fell O'er The Earth
– *Con.*

hearts *did* grow still, and reflective, if not numb and paralyzed out of shock, disappointment, and fear! These were the men, and women, who lived and worked side by side with Him in His very active ministry, yet *they* were still now! Their Master was gone!

But, the 'Hush That Fell O'er The Earth' – whether on the actual Earth 'plane', or within the hearts of men, did not last long! It was *shattered* by the resounding shout of Triumph by the One whose 'Coming back' *redeemed* an entire World! An entire Planet! The Entire Earth! Rest assured, my friend! Such a 'Hush' will never be – *again!*

Eye Hath Not Seen, Nor Ear Heard

Essay XIV

A Visionary View *To* Embrace!

– An Overview of God and Man!

A Visionary View to Embrace

The following ideas, my friend, are more than mere ideas. They are more than mere concepts or beliefs. Some of these 'viewpoints' you will, no doubt, immediately recognize as the Truth. That is to say, corresponding to Reality. Others, you may have faint glimmerings of understanding and acceptance, but you still hold out reservations and hesitations regarding their acceptance. No matter. Truth will make Itself known to all people in Its own time, and in Its own Way. Curious though! – *how* most believe that it is *they* who determine the time and place and manner of acquiring Truth – when *they* feel *they* are ready to do so! But, this too, is a mere mistaken belief that will be discarded over the course of time, by those who presently subscribe to it.

A Visionary View to Embrace – *Con.*

Do not feel, my friend, that you must accept, or agree with, or even understand what I am about to present to you for your review and evaluation. For what you **know** to be true, you will find re-affirmation here. For what life-view presented here you **wonder about** – relative to its accuracy, or completeness, or truthfulness, simply let it be, and remain in your consciousness neither judged nor pre-judged till such time as your life experiences shed greater light upon its validity one way or the other. And for any particular view you **feel strongly against** – as being in error, a falsity, or distortion of The Truth, feel free to affirm the Truth as *you* see It – as *you* know It! For *if* you are in error regarding your assessment, that is only

A Visionary View to Embrace – *Con.*

so *for now*. Tomorrow brings new understanding, and more complete knowledge! – *Should* correction of your present view be in order! So! Proceed with gladness!

- Fear is the only darkness, and ultimately there is nothing to fear! You have only yourself to overcome! You are here to manifest balance – which is beauty, harmony, order, cooperation, and goodwill!
- You have a unique Life Purpose, which you can discover, and uncompromisingly live! To serve your fellow-woman and -man is the overarching reason for which you

A Visionary View to Embrace – *Con.*

were born! Human life is always short, whether lived three days or 100 years, but your Divine Life is continuous, and uninterrupted! You are an Heir to Immortality, and human life is only a foretaste to the Great Life to come! You are never alone, though you be in utter solitude! You are never uncared-for, though you feel bereft or lost! You are a child of God – beloved, honored, reverenced, and adored, and whatever you *do* or <u>not</u> *do* never changes that status, nor alters that evaluation by your Creator!

- You are an actual Extension, a literal Manifestation of Immortal Mind, when you freely choose to align your

A Visionary View to Embrace – *Con.*

will with Its Own! Because of what the Universe has already done for you, in your behalf, you are **now** in an unchangeable state of Salvation!

- All *actions* in nature call forth their predictable *re*-actions, as do all *deeds* in the human realm call forth inevitable con-*sequences*. – But, however dire such 'outcomes' may be, as a tornado hurtling down through an ancient, forested meadow; or the so-called 'punishments' said to be administered by Deity Itself – their purpose and *assured objective*, is to *purge* one's Soul and *restore* a 'lost' or misguided one to sanity (reason), wholeness (health), and true love

A Visionary View to Embrace – *Con.*

(harmony)! The human race, therefore, is destined to be saved as a 'totality', as a 'whole'. Humanity is a 'corporate body', and the loss of any one single, solitary soul would diminish the Whole, leaving it fractured and incomplete. Therefore, every created member is vital to its 'completeness' – and *Ultimate Perfection!*

- You and your fellow man are ONE, though you, now, for a time, appear to be separate and apart! And what your sister feels, you will one day feel! The world is presently in its spiritual infancy, and is barely at the cock crow of the early dawn! Disharmony

A Visionary View to Embrace – *Con.*

of any kind: Dislike, hatred, envy, jealousy, ill-will, selfishness, etc., all – are the telltale signs of spiritual immaturity; the exclusion of others, the ignoring of others, the disdain of others, all – are actually earmarks of self-hatred and self-loathing! You and every other human being who has ever lived or will live will be redeemed! This is a foregone conclusion!

- Free Will will never be a detriment to the above occurring, since Free Will, as man understands it, does not exist! When every individual man makes the supreme discovery that his or her *deepest* longings are in complete

A Visionary View to Embrace – *Con.*

accord with those of the Creator, your Creator, then they, and you, will know there is only ONE WILL, and ONE DESIRE, and ONE MIND operative in the Universe! No opposing Will – *ever!* Only agreement and identification with God's Will! At long last manifest through you – and from you – and all others!

- Life ***does not*** demand strict, rigid adherence to codified beliefs (which are only limited articulations of Great Mysteries), but Life ***does*** require the *observance* of the Inviolate Principle (Divine Law) of Love and Good-Will in the affairs of women and men! As well as the forfeiture of 'self', the

A Visionary View to Embrace – *Con.*

    casting off of arrogance, and the elimination of disdain for others, and a feeling of superiority over others! Love will one day rule the world, and will dethrone every form of human tyranny now present in the human heart, mind, and soul, which enslaves, binds, and deceives man into manifesting that which he was never meant to give expression to! The so-called 'Golden Rule' will one day be recognized for what It truly IS: Divine, Inviolate, Universal Law, governing the affairs of men – and nations, alike!

- Mankind's departure from the living of the Great Law of Life, Love, and

A Visionary View to Embrace – *Con.*

Liberty necessitates that such blatant and subtle 'breaches' be addressed and remedied. The causes, and consequences, alike, must be undone if that which man calls Redemption is to take place. The reversal of all that was not meant to be – nor meant to continue – must be effected. All contributing factors would have to be dealt with in a permanent and unchallengeable way. And only an Action of a Representative from the Greater Realm can accomplish this – in behalf of all others entrapped and now helpless to extricate themselves from their present estate. And such an Action would be *costly*. – And such a

A Visionary View to Embrace – *Con.*

One who was qualified to reverse mans' present state could *only* be, *appropriately* and *correctly* be, referred to by the use of *one* word, and one word, *alone!* And that word, my friend, is – *SAVIOUR!* As much as this word, at the present state of mans' unfoldment, is held in disdain and disrepute! It will prove to be the key to the Renewal, and ReBirth, and Transformation of the World!

- Love heals all wounds! Peace of Mind comes to those who extend Peace, denying it to no one! Happiness is a natural result of creating something worthwhile and beautiful with the intent to give expression to Self!

A Visionary View to Embrace – *Con.*

Though not mans' greatest need, *Self-*expression is mans' primary need! Trust in Life and the forsaking of worry can and must be learned! No one can diminish your worth, nor injure your heart apart from your permission! You don't have to change your fellowman to be happy! You only need change your ideas about him! All people are deserving of Love (meaning respect and decent treatment) always! Solitude is your friend, and she will confide secrets of the Universe to you while in her presence! You can and must learn not to take offense at any provocation! Obstacles can always be used for your

A Visionary View to Embrace – *Con.*

> highest good! Prayer truly does change things – namely, YOU!
- Answers to all questions pertaining to your life exist, but you must diligently seek them out! The learning of the Great Lessons of Life usually takes a lifetime, and is hard-won. Winning their possession, however, is worth every effort you expend to make them yours! Every day is a precious gift to be lived and offered gratitude for! And you must seek your Creator, daily, if you are to live a Joyous, Worthwhile, Triumphant Life! To yield is to be strong, and to prevail! You are not living, but only existing, until you give expression to Love!

A Visionary View to Embrace – *Con.*

You reside in a Living, Nurturing, Teaching Universe, and you, my friend, are Its prized Pupil!

Behold, I Stand At the Door And Knock

Essay XV

A Tale Most Beautifully *Told!*

The UnHidden, Secret Truth!

He That Hath An Ear, Let Him Hear

A Tale Most Beautifully Told

It is said that a wonderful stranger is seeking entrance into the habitation of the heart of each and every individual, and He stands *outside* of 'the door' of the heart. There He waits with, we are told, astonishing patience. And though He earnestly desires to come in and bestow His wondrous gifts, he continually knocks hoping that He will be heard. He continually speaks, knowing and calling every individual by name, hoping that His kind tone will entreat the person inside to open the door and behold Him face to face.

Yet, He is forever barred, apart from the occupant letting Him *enter*. Therefore as this account is related, the person within

A Tale Most Beautifully Told
– *Con.*

this domicile, the person behind this door, enclosed within a locked dwelling, if he should *not* pay heed to the persistent knocking and ignore the stranger, he will *one day* find this stranger no longer at his or her door, but gone forevermore, leaving the person within the house, departing from the person, *leaving them to a certain fearful, and irrevocable fate!* Their time to consider and open the door, and invite the stranger in as a permanent guest – generous and liberal as it was, is now gone forever – irretrievably gone, or so the story is told. And it is this story, my friend, as it is told, that is **not** beautiful (or that is U̲nbeautiful, to coin a word) though we are assured that it is!

A Tale Most Beautifully Told
– *Con.*

Is this story the Truth? Is the admonition actually saying this, or saying *something else*, something so wonderful that most have not even dared entertain the thought? Is the re-telling of this brief narrative in the manner in which it is told, and has been told, for countless centuries, so full as it is of such deep significance and eternal import – Is the recounting of it *accurate?* For *if* it is true, what does this interpretation actually *say* about the strange male visitor, Himself? Does it not say, *if* this interpretation were true, that the One who is said to have Infinite Patience – is *lacking in* patience? Would it not say that the One who has declared that He would '*never* leave *nor*

A Tale Most Beautifully Told
– *Con.*

forsake' – *never* abandon – His children, is indeed – *not* true to His own word? Would it not say, *if* it were true, that the One Who professes undying Love and everlasting Concern for humankind, that this One harbors a Love that does indeed *have its limits*, and would indeed *'die'* toward one, should that one not invite Him into their home? My brother, it would say all of these! *If* – it were true – *as told!*

Now, the story IS true, I assure you, BUT it is *not* true as it is conveyed! Notice carefully now, and see for yourself precisely what this little wondrous vignette, this miniature story, has to say –

A Tale Most Beautifully Told
– *Con.*

and what it doesn't say! And take careful note of the ASSUMPTION that revolves around this story. Carefully now *analyze* the words: 'Behold, I stand **_at_** the door, and knock: if any man hear My voice, and open the door, I will **_come in_** to him, and will sup with him, and he with me . . . *He that hath an ear, let him hear.'* The great assumption here, that colors the entire interpretation of this story, is that which so few have ever bothered to question. It never occurred to them that they could be viewing this whole episode from the wrong perspective. And what is that wrong perspective? Can you not guess, my friend? It is really quite obvious, but for some enigmatic reason,

A Tale Most Beautifully Told
– *Con.*

it has eluded the brightest of theologians – and thinkers, and the average woman and man whose intelligence is quite sufficient to uncover the error!

Are you familiar with a door? It is used as a means of **entrance to** a room, or a house. It is affixed to **hinges**, that **inward** swing, that serve a vital purpose if the door is to fulfill its designated function. It allows, from one locality or space, **passage into** another, locality or space. But, where have you been, my friend? Haven't you seen or observed? Did you not know? Such a door also serves – **as an *exit*** – where the door ***outward*** swings, allowing departure *from*

A Tale Most Beautifully Told
– *Con.*

<u>within</u> an inside room – to an *outside* area. Now, what does this diversion into functionality have to do with our understanding of this story? It has everything to do with it! In fact, it is the ALL of it!

My friend, the wonderful stranger is not standing OUTSIDE of the door, OUTSIDE of the house, OUTSIDE of the heart! No! Read carefully! <u>The story nowhere says this</u>! For this story to make sense, to be a glorious story commending the Visitor in this story to any and all, making this Stranger, and His Message, so irresistibly attractive and compelling, only one explanation is possible! Only

A Tale Most Beautifully Told
– *Con.*

one interpretation upholds His Character attributes, such as **Infinite Patience** (wherein He waits till <u>WE</u> are ready), **Total *Unwavering* Commitment** (where abandonment is <u>never</u> an option), and **Undying Love** (that is wholly <u>Un</u>conditional, promised <u>never</u> to be withdrawn!).

So, one last time I ask. What is the Answer here? What is the *correct* interpretation? It is this: The Stranger is standing INSIDE of the door! INSIDE of the house! – *INSIDE of your HEART!* He is seeking to go forth from the *Inner* Chamber of your heart, to the *outer* enclosure of your heart! He is seeking to

A Tale Most Beautifully Told
– *Con.*

go from the *Inner* Shrine of Beauty – where Salvation resides, and carry it to the *outer* court of your heart – where doubts and fears, dislike and disquieting exists! He seeks to bring healing to your OUTER intentions and motives – where it is wholly needed! Yes! And residing WITHIN, He *can* never (is unable to) depart – and never will! **Till** – we open the door from WITHOUT to allow Him to 'come into' *our outer restless hearts – and troubled surface minds!*

This is *why*, my friend, the qualifying statement is added, *'He that hath an ear to hear'!* It is to alert us to the fact that there is more to this story than would be

A Tale Most Beautifully Told
– *Con.*

popularly understood and told. The stranger WITHIN is destined to COME OUT! And come out He will! – At the appointed time! And His COMING OUT, *by each person's welcoming and grateful hand,* will transform the inhabitant of the 'outer court' of the heart into an ever-humble servant of the Stranger who so loves him! Now **that** Tale *IS* understandable! Now **that** Tale *IS* logical! Now **that** tale *IS* worth rejoicing over! For it brings Honor to the Creator, showing Him to be the Supreme and All-Powerful Redeemer, *through* His Beloved Stranger Within! – Making the Tale the Most Beautiful – *as it was meant to be told* – all along!

Essay XVI

The **Whispered** Words *Of* Wonder!

Revealed *to All!*

Words Whispered Through The *Ages*

The Whispered Words of Wonder

All down throughout recorded history, men and women have been graced by 'hearing', coming to know intimately, apprehending, four simple words. These four words have strengthened man far more than any other composed by the most brilliant poet, playwright, lyricist, or author. These four words have caused men and women to dare to do, to dare to be, to dare to overcome any obstacle which might have obstructed their path. No more wonderful words have ever been heard, or penned, or recorded for posterity! They are so important, so necessary to life, so essential, that had mankind not been allowed to hear them, or better still, experience them, mankind would not, with virtual certainty, be here

The Whispered Words of Wonder
– *Con.*

today! What, then are these four cherished, treasured, even reverenced words?

I will begin to tell you. They are words that express a vital, unbreakable connection between men and the Greatest Reality. They are words that declare for all time that this connection is something that man need never fear severing, because man has nothing to do with sustaining it. They are words that implicitly, yet clearly, show, that man is of incalculable value to the Greater One, and such value transcends anything man at present is even capable of conceiving! They are words that assure mankind he is

The Whispered Words of Wonder
– *Con.*

not alone, that there is a communion of being of which he is only dimly aware of. They are words that put to rest for all time the notion that man is merely a cosmic happenstance, an accident of the universe! They are words that declare relationship between beings of a 'like order', though not exact order. They are words that declare the transcendent nature of the Great Someone, which brings rejoicing to man's heart! Have you guessed what these words might be? Do you realize what these words **must** be?

Consider, now. The language in which they are spoken is of no consequence.

The Whispered Words of Wonder
– *Con.*

English, Spanish, Portuguese, French, Latin, or Greek. No matter, they still mean the same. Their meaning is not lost. Could you but know it, words actually are not all that important, because words essentially are tools that create mental and emotional images and conceptions. And it is, again, the meaning that constitutes the message! The four words are not, strictly speaking, the message. The meaning is the message! And the meaning is always the same, always that which is most needed, always that which is a Mighty Truth among Truths. Do you know what these words, these *symbols*, say to us? If you saw these words, *would you recognize them?*

The Whispered Words of Wonder
– *Con.*

You have been patient long enough! But, it was necessary for you to begin to apprehend the full meaning of them. Sometimes telling people truths outright leaves them staring into space and blinking their eyes unintelligibly, uncomprehendingly, without adequate preparation. And these four words, more than any other, require *preparation* – if they are to be understood. I, therefore, ask this question one last time: What are these four wondrous words? They are: 'I AM with You.' There they are! And there they stand before you for your consideration. Perhaps no more important words have ever been spoken in the history of the world. They are

The Whispered Words of Wonder
– *Con.*

words infused with life themselves! Powerful! Awe-Inspiring! These words have literally enabled, yes, actually ensured, the survival of the human race! Had they never been uttered, even if man still lived, his existence would be hollow and reduced to pointlessness. How grateful we should be that they were given to us that we may live! Interesting, too, these words, though said to have been literally voiced on several momentous occasions during the course of human history, these same words have been, and are being 'spoken' to modern man, as they were spoken to medieval man, or the Renaissance man. Yes, to countless thousands of people in every

The Whispered Words of Wonder
– *Con.*

country, of every race, of every philosophy and creed. Yet, in the vast majority of the time, these words are spoken in a hushed, whispered tone. Don't you find that intriguing? There has to be significance to this fact! And that is something you can know, because it is important that you do know!

Words that are spoken softly, calmly, clearly, with a quiet power, are words that reflect the speaker and His attributes. Even His intent and motives! When such words are communicated in this fashion, we can know they are words of concern, and care. Words of humility and security. Words of assurance and good-will! So,

The Whispered Words of Wonder
– *Con.*

hear them once again, and begin to see the Majesty and Beauty and transforming Power they possess, 'I AM with you'. You see, my friend, a loud voice would only serve to detract from the message. An overwhelming, demonstrably authoritative voice would only serve to distance the speaker from the hearer, in fact, interfere with the hearing! It was, and is, all said, the way it is said, for the best reason possible. And that reason is to let man know forevermore that the 'I Am' Who is with him, loves him *beyond* belief! And the 'I Am' *still* whispers these words of wonder, to all, *today!*

Essay XVII

Concluding Poem

A Cosmic Wave Overtaking *The* World!

God's Dream!

A Cosmic Wave *Overtaking* the World!
– God's Dream

Upon the crests of Cosmic Waves

Heaven *bursting* through Earth's seams,

Flowers *blazing* with radiant, deathless Love

Rides a glorious Vision – ***Christ's Dream!***

Each day a little closer comes

This reach of Reality's hold, Heart-held By the **Saviour's** Inner, Glorious sight

A Cosmic Wave *Overtaking* the World! – *Con.*

– God's Dream

– A **Vision** So Grand, and Eternal, too
Destined to embrace – the **All** *of you!*

Stirrings in your ***Soul*** of Souls **Heart-yearnings** growing ever *more* keen, Thoughts exalted above one's clay-fashioned Abode – Spirit *drawn* to realms unseen!

A Cosmic Wave _Overtaking_ the World! – *Con.*
– God's Dream

Mystical longings more potent
do grow
Deeper the depths from which
feelings arise
Inner senses _awakening_ – to
heights of the skies!

Oh! How glorious! And Joyously
True!
The Heart of Life – ***Wed to You!***
Transcendent, Exalted,
Liberated, so Free!
A _Joining_ taking place within,
Oneness revealing **a Unity
Supreme**

A Cosmic Wave *Overtaking* the World! – *Con.*
– God's Dream

The Aim, the Goal – *of Resurrection's Dream!*

Racing O'er the Earths It goes
From the deepest wells to the swiftest streams
To the highest mountain peaks – and climes!

The **Universe** *awakened!* All Beauty beheld!
Swirling round, the new-born procession proceeds,
All who had been without, are

A Cosmic Wave <u>*Overtaking*</u> the World! – *Con.*
– God's Dream

now entered Within
– ***God's Rapturous Being!***

As miracles spring about the feet of the Redeemed!
<u>*Immersed*</u> in the Glory of Life Supreme!
All Life awakened – to God's Dream!

All things possible have come to pass, And **all** disbelief is discarded, *at last,*

A Cosmic Wave *Overtaking* the World! – *Con.* – God's Dream

The All-Redeeming Love has Won
Every Soul back – ***to Life's Radiant Son!***

Lo, I AM With You – *<u>Always!</u>*

Jesus, The Christ

The Final Disclosure

Dear, *Gentle* Heart, This You MUST Know, <u>Deception</u> Was CONQUERED in the <u>Far</u>, Long Ago! Possessing <u>*No*</u> Power O'er Your Destiny or Fate, To Be Banished Forever – <u>*at* a *Future Date!*</u>

Beloved, for *far too long* has it been taught that untold numbers of God's children will lose their salvation *because* they were **deceived** by malevolent forces (fallen angels), false teachers (sincere, or otherwise), or their own 'corrupt' heart. This teaching has produced more fear, anxiety, mental instability, anguish, etc., than perhaps any other doctrine. People have been taught that there is **a stupendous battle** underway for their souls (which outcome is uncertain), and that *if* people are not **constantly diligent**, even <u>obsessively</u> so, they will be deceived and end up as 'castaways'. **This, however, (praise be to God) is all untrue!**

The Final Disclosure
– Con.

Jesus, the Saviour, has appointed a time when ALL deception will cease, and **The Truth** will stand, _wholly_ understood, desired, and welcomed. And He has decreed that:

> _No_ false belief, adhered to in good faith, or even _obstinately, stubbornly clung to_ – in _ill will_, at _any_ time, **can disqualify any person from ultimately obtaining God's Promise of Salvation.**

The Atonement of our Lord made upon the Cross at Calvary provides us **bedrock Assurity** of this unalterable God-determined, **God-Willed outcome!** Yet, most devote students of the Word are oblivious to this FACT, due to faulty teaching and tradition.

But, if YOU would like **the Ultimate Assurance** that you _never_ need fear deception again, and **the Scriptural references to prove it**, please email the

The Final Disclosure
– Con.

author who will gladly provide you with **an eye-opening** and **rare research paper** at no cost to you. Fear of deception, beloved, has been altogether defeated in Christ, <u>*BY*</u> Christ! God's **Ultimate Revelation** (that of *The Mystery*) was given us that we might **KNOW** this is so! (Romans 16:25, Ephesians 1:10) This TRUTH will have then set you free! As you STAND FAST in the **Liberty** of this priceless and precious Knowledge (Galations 5:1) – **Godspeed!**

Wisdom Words of Blessing – and *Farewell!*

Within you resides the Arbiter of Truth (I Cor. 2:10, **The Holy Spirit**) – the Sole and Final Authority for <u>*your*</u> life. Accept ideas from <u>*no one*</u>, no matter how learned, or credentialed, or lauded by society – or seemingly wise or humble or unrecognized as yet – <u>*unless*</u> such ideas **Ring True** to your Inner Being, <u>*unless*</u> those ideas register an **Inner Validation** in your soul, <u>*unless*</u> you can say with absolute and firm conviction, 'This **<u>I KNOW</u>** – *to be True*'!

> # **Wisdom Words
> of Blessing – and *Farewell!*
> – *Con.***

If this confirmation does not occur, and you are uncertain as to any idea's validity, simply 'suspend' or *defer* judgment – *until* such time as **Life** **sees fit** to disclose the full Truth to you. This way, you remain safe, genuine, and open to recognizing Truth when it comes. And you may rest assured, the Truth ***will*** come *when* – you are meant to know it – and are prepared to understand it.

> # Wisdom Words
> of Blessing – and *Farewell!*
> – *Con.*

So, bearing this fundamental concept prominently in your mind, view this book for precisely what it *IS*: a sincere attempt to point to '**THE Way**', offer Insights, and suggest Guidance; as you move toward a Life of Greater Fulfillment and Personal Victory over self and the world – which Victory YOU **will** find, as *you* turn more and more often – to *your* **Source of Truth** – and *your* **Saviour** and **Redeemer**, the Great, Ever-Faithful and Unfailing –Christ of God–*Within!*(Col. 1:27)

About The Author

A devotee of Jesus and student of scripture since childhood, Mack seeks to teach others about *'the Deep Things of God.'* Writing with poetic majesty, yet with elegant simplicity, he **'paints'** *word-pictures* that captivate the heart, and awaken the soul. His mission is to reveal aspects of **the Fullness of the Gospel of Christ** *few* know of, with special emphasis on the Lord's singularly unique Life-Purpose and the **All-Redeeming Nature** of His Love. Mack has authored numerous books, facilitated classes on spirituality, and gives talks on living a Radiant Life. He has been called to unveil to others – *nothing less* – than the uttermost **'Depths –** *of **The Heart** of **Love!'*** He presently resides in Central Virginia, and graciously welcomes comments.

__Catalog of
Author's Books__

(Page 1 of 3)

**The Untold Truths of
   The Forgotten Cross!**
       (Its *Hidden* Mysteries – Unveiled!)

When Love Rose *Victorious!*
       (The Cosmic *Reach* of the
          Resurrection – Proclaimed!)

A Saviour Beyond!
       (Your *Fondest* Dreams!)

The Unknown Lord of Life!
       (His *Seldom* Taught Truths!)

Those Wondrous Words!
       (The *Most* Wonderful *Ever* Spoken!)

A Healing Mercy Rose!
       (Love's *Beauty* Come to *Restore!*)

Catalog of
Author's Books – *Con.*
(Page 2 of 3)

A Poet's Revelations!
   (On God's <u>*Undreamt*</u> of Love!)

An Eternal Christmas
   (A Hidden Dream of Love's Birth!)

Until True Love Comes!
   (To Set Free Your Heart!)

Take Heart Beloved!
   (Hope to Give Courage and Heal!)

The Ultimate of Visions!
   (A World Given Back to Love!)

The Blessings of Wealth!
   (God's Will For Your Prosperity!)

Catalog of Author's Books – *Con.*
(Page 3 of 3)

In Jesus' Presence!
(A Peace to Calm <u>All</u> Hearts!)

Oh! Saving Sentiments!
(Thoughts to Exalt and *Free!*)

Oh! Sacred Rhymes!
(*To* Strengthen a <u>Devote</u> Heart!)

The Truth At Last!
(<u>What</u> to Fear *About* God!)

Look to a Brighter Tomorrow!
(The Way to Victorious Living!)

When Love Comes for You!
(The Empowering Gifts of God!)

An
Out-Reach of

Mercy Rose Ministries

Proclaiming

The
Depths
of

The **Heart *Of*** **Love!**

For More Information:

Go to

Authentic Life Publications

through

www.themercyrose.com

or

Facebook page:

Teachings of The Mercy Rose

or contact directly

mackethridge@hotmail.com

FURTHER RESOURCES

The Christian Universalist Association
http://www.christianuniversalist.org/about/beliefs/universal-salvation/

Tentmaker
http://www.tentmaker.org/books/Bibleproofs2.html

Merciful Truth
http://www.mercifultruth.com/

Universal Salvation University
http://richardwaynegarganta.com/universalsalvation.htm

Associates for Scriptural Knowledge
http://askelm.com/doctrine/d100801.pdf

LAST PARTING THOUGHTS

You, Dear Heart, you who have suffered from Obsessive-Compulsive Disorder for *so long*, your days of being tormented with terrible soul-chilling thoughts of grave punishment, and even everlasting torture, by a God who is either a merciless cruel tyrant or a nightmarish deity who does not possess the Divine **Power**, or the determined **WILL** to SAVE His own children, to CAUSE them to be redeemed *without violating their free will*, you now KNOW to be only a figment of **fallen mans' *darkened* imagination**! Any and ALL Scriptures which seem to say our Creator is *this* kind of being are either misunderstood, or grossly **mistranslated**. You have now been told God's Absolute TRUTH! **Hold fast to It**, and you will never fear God again! Leaving OCD worries to dissolve – and completely – *vanish away!*

In God's Astonishing Love! **The Author**

Printed in Great Britain
by Amazon